All in the Family

All in the Family

The Private Roots of American Public Policy

Patricia Strach

STANFORD UNIVERSITY PRESS

STANFORD, CALIFORNIA 2007

Stanford University Press
Stanford, California
©2007 by the Board of Trustees of the
Leland Stanford Junior University. All rights reserved.

Printed in the United States of America on acid-free,
archival-quality paper

Library of Congress Cataloging-in-Publication Data

Strach, Patricia.
 All in the family : the private roots of American public policy / Patricia Strach.
   p. cm.
 Includes bibliographical references and index.
 ISBN 978-0-8047-5608-2 (cloth : alk. paper) — ISBN 978-0-8047-5609-9
(pbk. : alk. paper)
  1. Family policy—United States. 2. Family—United States. 3. United States—
Social policy. I. Title.

HQ536.S7693 2007
306.850973—dc22

                                    2007000015

Typeset by Thompson Type in 10/12 Sabon

In memory of
Mathea and her brothers

Contents

List of Illustrations

List of Tables

Acknowledgments

I owe a special debt of gratitude to those people who poked, prodded, and pushed me to improve this book with helpful comments in presentations and written drafts: at the University of Wisconsin, Karen Bogenschneider, David Canon, Rudy Espino, Mike Franz, Jess Gilbert, Dave Parker, Travis Ridout, Kendra Smith, Joe Soss, Kathy Cramer Walsh, Graham Wilson, and John Witte; my colleagues at the University at Albany, Scott Barclay, Cheng Chen, Peter Breiner, Sally Friedman, and Bruce Miroff. I am grateful for comments I have received from a host of scholars, especially Kathleen Sullivan, Priscilla Yamin, and Gwynn Thomas and to the reviewers of this manuscript for their thoroughness. I have been fortunate to work with a very professional editorial staff at Stanford University Press, in particular Amanda Moran and Jared Smith. There are three people who have made especially noteworthy contributions to this project: Alisa Rosenthal, who told me my original idea was "boring" and encouraged me to write this book instead; Paul Manna, my "shadow advisor," for spending many early mornings sketching out this project; and most especially John Coleman, for absolutely everything.

I am appreciative of financial assistance and research support I have received along the way. This book was made possible with funding from the Dirksen Center for Congressional Research, the University of Wisconsin Dissertator Fellowship, and with assistance from the Institute for Legal Studies at the University of Wisconsin and the APSA Centennial Center. For seemingly thankless research assistance, I thank Bob Comis and Wes Nishyama for their hard work.

Finally, though all of the above individuals (and many more) contributed to my growth as a scholar, I wish to thank my family and friends for their support over the past six years. This book is dedicated to the memory of my grandmother, Mathea, and my great uncles, who never saw the book's completion but would have raised quite a toast if they had.

All in the Family

Family and American Public Policy

On September 10, 1996, Congress passed the historic Defense of Marriage Act (DOMA) in response to a Hawaiian Supreme Court ruling that potentially could have paved the way for same-sex marriage.[1] DOMA set out, for the first time, a federal definition of marriage that was inclusive only of one man and one woman. While proponents of the Act claimed a victory, and opponents feared a setback to the cause for gay rights, a more subtle question loomed large. If marriage, adoption, and divorce are determined by each of the fifty states, what impact would a *federal* definition of marriage have?

Although it is easy to dismiss congressional action as purely symbolic, activists on both sides of the issue had good reasons to justify a national response. Members of Congress may not be charged with creating laws that define family, but they are charged with creating scores of policies that incorporate family to achieve various goals. Then-Senate Majority Leader Trent Lott (R-MS) summed up the far-reaching effects a new definition would have when he noted that same-sex marriage in any single state "could also affect the operations of the Federal Government. It could have an impact upon programs like Medicare, Medicaid, veterans' pensions, and the Civil Service Retirement System."[2] The imposition of a new definition would ripple through policies from taxation to Social Security to military affairs because family connection is an important component of these and many other federal programs.

As Lott clearly points out there are real policy implications associated with changing the definition of marriage at either the state or federal level because marriage—and family more generally—are part and parcel of a host of federal policies. However, it is not so clear what exactly family does in federal policy. In other words, what role does family play in seemingly nonfamily federal policies like Medicaid and veteran's benefits? In searching for answers to this question, I found that the existing theoretical frameworks for evaluating family in politics do not begin to scratch the surface. Political scholars generally treat family as an institution firmly embedded in the private realm, or they equate family and public policy with so-called family policies designed to protect, promote, or define American family life, such as state-level marriage and adoption laws or federal welfare and family-leave programs. Neither one of these frameworks can illuminate why Senator Lott and his colleagues would be concerned about a range of policies from Medicare to the Civil Service Retirement System, let alone analyze how family operates in these policies.

Federal policymakers have an unmistakable interest in family, but political scientists do not have a framework for understanding how family is employed in the policy process and with what effect. The goal of this book is to clarify the relationship between seemingly private family life and federal public policies. The book asks two important questions. First and foremost, *how do policymakers employ family in the policy process?* I provide a somewhat different framework for thinking about the relationship between family and public policy. I look at how family is a *means* used throughout the policy process to achieve a wide variety of policy goals. As a means in the policy process, family does not fall on the "private" side of the public/private divide but it is an important component of day-to-day policymaking at the federal level. Further as a means, family's import lies not in so-called family policies, like welfare, but in a broad cross section of federal policy from tax to national defense.

Looking carefully at the ways in which family is employed to achieve a host of "nonfamily" goals, I show that policy actors rely on family in the policy process in three key ways. First, family acts as a criterion of eligibility to determine who qualifies for goods and services. For many public policies, qualifying individuals include a specified individual and his or her family, such as Social Security pensions for retired workers and their non-wage-earning spouses. Activists voiced a concern in the DOMA debates about redefining marriage because it would also mean extending eligibility for a host of federal programs and services from immigration visa preferences to federal health-care benefits.[3] Second, family acts as an administrator that distributes goods and services to its members. Though scholars usually associate bureaucrats with public employees, family members are expected to act in ways prescribed by the legislature and overseen by executive agencies. Housing vouchers and education tax incentives, for example, require parents, guardians, or adult children to implement policy on behalf of their kin, just as traditional state or federal workers might. Third, family acts as a normative ideal that helps policy actors garner and maintain support for a policy position. Every day one can hear rhetoric about the needs of American families as the rationale to lower or raise tax rates or continue agriculture subsidies to support "family farms." Policy actors justify their policy positions on grounds that are personal and above reproach, an appeal to American families. As a criterion, administrator, or normative ideal, family is an important part of American policymaking.

Second, this book asks *what are the consequences of employing family broadly in public policy?* Family is rooted throughout the policy process and in a wide array of public policies. Yet, embedding family in public policy can be problematic. When policymakers incorporate family as a criterion, administrator, or normative ideal they include very specific assumptions about what constitutes a family or what roles its members should play. These assumptions may be controversial or exclusive of particular family arrangements, such as early-twentieth-century immigration provisions that looked for evidence that marriages were "love matches" rather than arranged. As a result, Japanese immigrants were subject to intense scrutiny and, at times, forced to marry their alleged spouse once they reached an American port because their marriages did not resemble the American notion of a "love match."[4] Assumptions, like those about what it means to be married, are part and parcel of American public policy and can have a real effect on social practices. Yet, even if particular assumptions are entirely fair or accurate when policy is created, social practices change over time. The Earned Income Tax Credit (EITC), for example, spelled out in painstaking detail a four-pronged test (relationship, residency, age, and ability to prove one's identity) to determine if a minor could be considered a taxpayer's "child." In the past three decades, the growing number of children living in homes with a parent or guardian who is not biologically related to them has created problems for stepparents, foster parents, and informal guardians (aunts, grandparents, or neighbors) who try to take advantage of this federal tax program.

A close look at family as an important means of policymaking shows that underlying any objective policy goals are the particular means that policymakers use to get the job done. At the heart of this project is an analysis of the proverbial black box in public policy, its structure. By structure, I mean more than statutory rules, requirements, or procedures. I am concerned with values—abstract principles—and assumptions—historically contingent presumptions—that underlie how policies accomplish their goals. Values and assumptions are important components of public policies, and they have long-lasting effects. When the ways that Americans live their lives deviates from the expectations policies use to accomplish their goals, it creates a disjuncture, or what I call a policy gap. These gaps affect individual Americans like self-supporting college students from middle-class families who are ineligible for federal aid because formulas base eligibility on the income of their parents. Gaps also have an effect on the policy process. They are sites of political contestation. Connecting what is in policy to politics more broadly shows that policy gaps open windows of opportunity, motivating problem definition, creating bridging policy communities (interested in the means rather than just the ends), and allowing diverse coalitions to form. Essentially, by unpacking public policy's black box, I show how a policy's form influences the politics that surrounds it. I look at how policies that rely on family adapt to changing family practices in Chapter 3 and in the case studies on immigration (Chapter 4), tax (Chapter 5), and agriculture (Chapter 6). In the conclusion (Chapter 7), I discuss the real-world impact policy gaps have for American citizens and residents.

The focus on family and its relationship to federal public policy makes two important contributions. Notably, it reincorporates family into the study of politics by providing a theoretical framework to evaluate the often hidden or subterranean work that the American family is expected to perform. I show that family is not outside the study of mainstream politics but part and parcel of how American policymaking functions at the federal level. My research suggests that the ability of policymakers to accomplish their goals is intimately tied to the strength and organization of American families. To state it bluntly, the capacity of the American state rests on the capabilities of this so-called private organization.[5] Second, this research adds to Theodore Lowi's call to examine public policies in depth to understand how policies determine politics. By looking at the values and assumptions that underlie public policy—and not merely the objective goals policies are supposed to accomplish—I show how the roots of change may lie in the gap between how policies expect Americans to act and the ways in which Americans actually do act. Ultimately, as American political development scholars have shown, change is not an extraordinary event. Indeed, it is a necessary and built-in component of public policy.

REEVALUATING FAMILY IN POLITICAL SCIENCE

Though a full definition and discussion of family as it is used in this volume is provided in Chapter 2, a few words about the object under study are appropriate here. Family has many different definitions, from the particular individuals who compose it (i.e., mom, dad, and biological children) to the significance it has in social life (i.e., the foundation of American life).[6] Defining family based on any particular relationship (biological, legal, or social) or by its significance is bound to exclude particular groups based on the researcher's not the policymaker's definition. For example, the U.S.

Census defines family as "two people or more (one of whom is the house-holder) related by birth, marriage, or adoption and residing together."[7] The census definition excludes those individuals without a legal relationship and those who do not live together, both categories of individuals considered family in other policy areas.

To get around the problem of excluding too many families, I define family quite generally as a kin relationship. I leave it to policy actors to decide whether these relationships are determined by blood (i.e., biological parents and their children, siblings), law (marriage, adoption), or affection ("uncles" or "grandparents" with no biological or legal standing). By looking only at kin-relationships, I exclude individuals who are not considered related but I leave a great deal of leeway to capture the variation in who may be considered kin in any policy. The reader will see in the chapters that follow that how policymakers conceive of family differs between policy areas as well as within components of each of these policies. Indeed, immigration and tax policy have very different definitions of "child," and until 2004, there were five separate definitions of "child" *within* the tax code.

Theoretical Underpinnings

Family plays a significant role in the speeches given by politicians, in campaign slogans of the major political parties, and most importantly, in the creation and implementation of law and policy. Yet, it is surprisingly absent from mainstream research in American politics. One of the goals of this project is to reevaluate the place of family in political research. As it stands now, family is rarely included in political research outside of the private sphere or "family policy" even though family is used in politics extensively outside of these areas.[8]

First and foremost, family is treated as a private institution that prepares one for political participation but plays a minor role once one is already involved in politics. A rush of behavioral work in the 1960s and 1970s examined the role of families as agents of political socialization. The general results of this body of literature showed that family matters in political socialization, but a lot less than conventional wisdom might have led one to believe.[9] More recent research in this vein has not addressed family as systematically as the earlier literature but it continues to place family firmly in the private realm, either encouraging or discouraging political behavior of individuals once they enter the public realm of politics.[10] Family is also addressed in relation to so-called family policy, or those policies designed to protect and promote family life such as welfare, child support, and family leave.[11] Scholars in these fields directly address family because it is the object of the policies that they study. There is very little outside of these policy areas that also looks at family.

Though individual pieces on family have been very influential, the net result of the broad spectrum of political science scholarship has been to associate family with the private sphere or "family policy." Scholarship that falls outside of these areas—on the executive or legislative branches or on a wide variety of public policies—is then free to disregard family as an analytic category of little importance. Political science is generally silent on the many ways that family is used by political actors to achieve political goals.

Thinking of family as divorced from politics misses the way it is employed daily in law and policy. Feminist scholars have called into question the relationship between family, politics, and gender. They have challenged the public/private divide, arguing that the very lines between "politics" and "family" are themselves malleable.[12] Research in this tradition has shown how family, home, and the private sphere have been intimately tied to gender and, in particular, women's identity.[13] At times, women have been able to marshal their claims on the private sphere and as keepers of the family to successfully enact social change where male reformers have failed.[14] But more often, women's connection to the private sphere has been used to justify their marginalization in the public.[15] Feminist scholarship has also started to break the association between family and "family policy," narrowly defined. New research in this tradition suggests that family is the basis of American citizenship. In everything from past and current immigration law to the Reconstruction-era Freedmen's Bureau, who may marry and who may conceive are essential for defining who is an American.[16]

Like feminist scholarship, this book challenges the division between a private sphere of domestic life and the public realm of politics. But the aim is slightly different. I do not examine in depth the relationship between gendered actors and family in politics, though this certainly plays a part in the analysis here. Rather, I put family at the center of my analysis. In conjunction with existing feminist scholarship, my research suggests far-reaching implications for women's equality. Feminists see the family as a source of power relations, especially in regard to gender.[17] Women's inequality in the family leads to inequality in society and politics.[18] The extensive use of family across policy areas suggests that these implications may be far more extensive than previously thought. With a primary focus on family, this book demonstrates that kin relationships are employed across policy areas and throughout the policy process. Family is not a separate sphere that prepares one for political action, it is not the exclusive domain of welfare and family leave, and it is not the feminine counterpart to a masculine world of politics. Family is an integral part of the detailed criterion, administration, and justification in the American policy process. Quite simply, the "private" realm of family life makes possible American "public" policy.

To be clear, the ability of policymakers to achieve their goals and the capacity of the state to carry out its duties depends on the capability of American families. This view is different than the more common conception of family best summed up by President Jimmy Carter: "if we want less government, we must have stronger families, for government steps in by necessity when families have failed."[19] Carter's statement lends strong support for examining so-called family policy. The state provides child care, basic goods, and counseling to aid families in need. But looking at family as an important means in the policy process shows that the state does not step in only when families fail, but rather continually depends on the capabilities of family to determine eligibility, implement programs, and justify action.

As a criterion of eligibility, the state relies on family to both extend and limit the number of individuals who may claim benefits. Scholars have puzzled over the exceptional nature of welfare provision in the United States, especially the lack of universal health care.[20] Rather than universal programs, major social services in the United States are distributed based on many different criteria, such as merit (Social Security, private health care) or need (Medicaid). I argue that these criteria work in conjunction with family connection. By using family as a criterion of eligibility, more individuals may receive benefits. Yet, expanding provision to politically popular groups limits the drive for larger and more encompassing programs.[21] Alice Kessler-Harris explains the profound effect the 1939 amendments to the Social Security Act had on the titled program: "Congress added dependent wives and aged widows in order to shore up the legitimacy of a system in trouble. It did this by making the benefits of already-covered (mostly white) males more adequate by granting extra benefits to those who had aged wives to support and extra insurance to those with young children who survived them."[22] Adding family extended the benefits to nonwage earners, but it also extended support for continuing an exclusive pension system for the elderly.

As an administrator, family becomes an important determinant of what kinds of policies the state will be able to implement. The state has long had the ability to marshal resources of nongovernmental actors to administer federal policy, from private companies who contract with the state (especially in the area of defense) to nonprofits that receive grants to provide services.[23] Increasingly, political scientists write of the "hidden," "subterranean," and "shadow" state, which differs from advanced industrial (largely European) states not in *what* it provides but *how* it provides it.[24] The American state relies much more heavily on indirect provision, especially tax incentives. Yet, in pointing out tax incentives as a component of American welfare provision, we often fail to analyze who does the work to carry out these incentives. State capacity, most often associated with the ability of federal bureaucracies to carry out policy prescriptions, may better be defined by the resources the state is able to marshal.[25]

Finally, state actors are able to draw on the symbol and rhetoric of family to support their policy positions. According to political scientist Paul Manna, federal policymakers are able to extend their reach when they have the capacity to carry out programs in a particular area as well as the license, or "the strength of the arguments available to justify government action."[26] Somewhat ironically, even though family is seen as a private institution, policymakers invoke it for public ends. Talking about family builds license for policymakers to act in a host of policy areas.

A state's capacity lies not merely in the ability of formal institutions to provide direct services, but in "the state's ability to coerce, induce, or persuade actors to behave in ways that mitigate the need for state services or that provide goods and services in an alternative form."[27] Thus, the American state has been able to provide more than the sum of services by federal agencies. Indeed, much of American public policy inside and outside of welfare provision relies on other institutions: corporations, nonprofits, organized religion, and family.

Why Family?

Family, then, is an important means in the policy process. It increases the license and capacity of federal policymakers and the state that they work to shape. Chapter 2 chronicles the extensive use of family as a criterion, administrator, and normative ideal throughout the policy process and across policy areas. Though it is beyond the scope of this project to answer in the depth it deserves, nevertheless, the question remains: why family? In part, family is like any other organizational arrangement. This project draws on public administration and political development scholarship that questions the traditional boundaries of state provision. Indeed, the literature on new governance shifts the focus from the dots, or traditional government agencies, to the lines that connect those dots, the networks between the state and other actors. Shifting the focus from government to governance puts public objectives and the tools used to carry out these objectives at the center of analysis, leaving flexibility in the particular actors that work on behalf of public ends. Though new governance scholars are concerned most with traditional actors—corporations, public-private partnerships, nonprofits, and charity organizations—their framework leaves open the possibility to think also in terms of the hallmark of "private" institutions, family. The state relies on nonstate structures to carry out a great deal of public business. Academics work within frameworks that generally leave family out of this equation, but it should not be surprising that policy-makers are not so encumbered. They utilize the full range of community, religious, and social institutions to achieve their goals.

Thus, in part, family is an organization like any other that policymakers draw upon. But, in part, family has particular characteristics that distin-guish it from other institutional arrangements. Americans think about family differently than other institutions, and they desire family relations for themselves. Family is generally considered to be "natural" and pre-political, existing before the state. The state reinforces in public policy and court decisions that it does *not* act to create families but merely to support what is already there.[28] The idea that families are natural and pre-political dates back as far as Aristotle who wrote that families are an important forerunner to the city-state, but no thinker reinforced the naturalness of the family in liberal thought as much as John Locke.[29] In Locke's hypothetical state of nature, what the world looked like before politics, individuals form and live in families.[30] Indeed, some scholars to-day still hold the view that "the family is a universal human institution."[31] The naturalness of family means that policymakers tiptoe around the idea that they might harm families or put them at any sort of disadvantage. Including family members in benefits merely reinforces a structure they are there to protect or at the very least not cause any harm. Americans also live in families. Though there may be a very large discrepancy in actual family practices—families can be large or small, composed of individu-als related by biology or the bonds of affection—most Americans desire family life for themselves.[32] Indeed, nearly three-quarters of all American households are composed of kin relations. Unlike work, which is not considered "natural" by Americans, or organized religion, which many Americans may not experience personally, family is an institution most Americans desire and experience (for better or for worse). Family ap-proaches near universality.

Policy actors capitalize on the normative power and social organiza-tion of families. Though the Constitution speaks in terms of rights and individuals, in practice much of American policy and law is governed by family status. As Kathleen S. Sullivan shows, the domestic relations of the common law—which provide the rights and responsibilities of fathers, mothers, children, and servants—carry through to this day.[33] Married couples, for example, are still considered one person in the eyes of the law for a host of financial responsibilities. Policymakers operate within a legal setting where family members are given status, and they must base new policies on the legal standing already in place.

Family and the Discipline of Political Science

The potential payoff for including family in the study of public policy in particular, and American politics more broadly, is quite high. However, the hurdles to doing so are equally elevated. Political scientists have a near aversion to family. A simple search for "family" in the title words of articles in the top 28 political science journals since 1907 shows that the discipline has a paltry 72 articles. The modest attention devoted to family by political scientists becomes even more striking when compared to other social science disciplines: history 702 articles (44 journals); sociology 2,734 articles (29 journals); and economics 276 articles (27 journals).[34] Other social science disciplines routinely incorporate family into their analyses in many ways and, as a result, have increased the explanatory power of their models. For example, economists have learned that individual preferences are shaped by family situations. Incorporating family in their models has allowed economists to better predict shifts in labor markets and consumption patterns.[35] Family is no less important in political analysis. Politicians of all stripes actively claim to be pro-family. Republicans routinely invoke "family values," while Democrats up the ante by claiming to represent "working families." Legislators frequently employ family on the floor of Congress and in the legislation they create across the broad spectrum of political issues, from national defense to domestic agriculture production. Far from being confined to one particular party, one part of the legislative process, or one policy issue, family is pervasive in American politics.

The extensive use of family in politics and the limited study of family in political science means that political science research tends to focus on a limited part of the complex relationship between American families and the state, or it ignores that relationship altogether. This is problematic in two regards. First, this limited focus imposes a preconceived definition of what constitutes politics. Rather than let the empirical statements and actions of our subjects determine what is appropriate for analysis, assumptions about what constitutes politics predetermine which topics are properly the domain of political science. Second, a lack of attention to family means that research about family is dominated by other social science disciplines. Relying on other disciplines to study family cannot substitute for the incorporation of family into political science research and analysis. As one might expect, these other disciplines treat family in relation to their own analytical, theoretical, and methodological concepts and questions rather than politics. Other social science disciplines, for the most part, are silent on the important political questions about the way that the state and families interact, such as: Are appeals to family an effective tactic by political candidates and parties? Are they effective in justifying a policy position?

Rethinking the place of family in political science scholarship requires two steps: first, breaking down long-held associations about the appropriate place of family in political analysis (private sphere and "family policy"), and second, putting the family-state relationship at the center of analysis. Just like the relationship between governmental branches or among members of a policy community, family plays a fundamental role in maintaining the American state. Political scientists need not study family relations the way economists, historians, or sociologists might, but they can study the ways that family is used by political actors and the state to achieve specific political ends. In other words, it is the family-state relationship that is of paramount importance to political scientists, rather than individual families.

KEY CONCEPTS AND THE THEORETICAL ARGUMENT

This project offers a theoretical framework in which family is evaluated as the means in rather than the ends of the policy process. But looking at family as a means opens up a can of worms about how policies accomplish their goals more generally. Surprisingly, very little scholarly attention is devoted to systematically explaining what actually lies within policy rather than what ought to be there.

Scholars have done an impressive amount of research on the actors, institutions, and ideas in the policy process,[36] but we still know very little about what goes into policy and what effect this has on politics more generally. Despite Schattschneider's now famous claim that new policies create new politics and Lowi's typology of government coerciveness developed to advance the proposition that policies determine politics, political scientists have devoted comparatively little attention to how policies achieve their goals.[37] Public administration scholars have been more vigilant in this quest, developing a number of classificatory frameworks to compare the multiple ways a particular policy goal may be achieved.[38] By grouping large numbers of policy instruments—such as direct government, vouchers, and tax incentives—into a smaller number of categories, scholars hope to "make sense of what seems at first sight to be the bewildering complexity of modern government's operations" and to understand what governments "can do in any given case."[39] They have worked hard to show which tools are most effective for achieving policy goals.[40]

As helpful as these analyses of policy tools are for understanding particular options policymakers have when they create public programs, they risk oversimplifying complex public policies. Policies are often taken as a reflection of their goals and tools. Recent attention to public policies' unintended consequences shows that policies have an impact far greater than an analysis of goals and tools might suggest.[41] Joe Soss and Suzanne Mettler argue that what goes into policy and how it is implemented can affect the very ways that citizens participate in politics. By comparing two direct government programs set up to aid citizens who are unable to work (Aid to Families with Dependent Children [AFDC] and Social Security and Disability Insurance), Soss demonstrates that even with a similar goals and tools, participation in AFDC reduces political efficacy.[42] Likewise, Suzanne Mettler shows that there are unintended consequences even with a program as generous and well-regarded as the GI Bill. For women, "marginalization from generous social rights can hinder, for decades, their capacity and inclination to participate as active citizens."[43] Simply looking at the goals a policy seeks to achieve and the tools used to achieve them leaves out much of what goes in public policy and its long-lasting effects.

To better understand how policies accomplish their goals, I developed a number of concepts that break down the inner workings within public policy and lay out what I call a policy structure, both what goes into policy and where it is located. *Policy structure* as I use it includes both substance (values and assumptions) and organization (core and periphery). Policies are more than the goals they seek to accomplish; they include the means to accomplish those goals as well. The substance of policies, in Giandomenico Majone's description, consists of "values, assumptions, methods, goals and programs."[44] Of these, for the purposes of this project, values and assumptions are the most important. *Values* are broadly shared and relatively uncontroversial principles like liberty, equality, merit, and family. They provide continuity and agreement in policymaking. *Assumptions* are predispositions and biases that translate values into practice, such as what liberty entails, who is entitled to equality, and what particular individuals constitute a family. Assumptions are more specific, more controversial, and more likely to deviate from social practice. Over time, policies reflect American commitment to values like individual merit even though what is considered meritorious and who deserves the rewards of merit has changed significantly. Social Security pensions, for example, are designed around the core principle of individual merit. Yet, Social Security as it was originally planned excluded large segments of the American workforce, and even today individuals who have not engaged in the paid labor force are eligible for it.[45] Public policies reflect both the kinds of values legislators say *ought* to be included and the assumptions that actually *do* get included.

In addition to substance, policies also have an organization made up of two parts: the core and the periphery. The *core* holds the central tenets of policy. Core values and assumptions are pivotal to the policy itself, providing stability and remaining relatively constant over time. In the case of Social Security, the core is made up of the value of individual merit and assumptions that translate individual merit into a contributory structure so that the more one puts into the system, the more one gets out of it. The *periphery*, however, is made up of the more mundane values and assumptions built around the core that are readily adaptable.[46] Social Security's peripheral values include family, expanding eligibility to non-wage-earning spouses, and the more commonplace assumptions that create the formulas to determine how much each recipient will get based on what they have paid into the system. The distinction between core and periphery is fundamental for explaining the impact of change on public policies because not every component of a policy is equally important. The contributory structure of Social Security is far more important to continuing the program than any particular formula in any particular year.

Values and assumptions embedded in the core and periphery may be unfair or inaccurate from the very first day policy is created. However, they also become outdated if social practices change over time. If social practice diverges from the structure of policy, it creates a *policy gap*.[47] An ever-widening gap destabilizes support for the policy and opens up what John Kingdon describes as a "window of opportunity" for policy entrepreneurs to exploit, potentially triggering sizable restructuring.[48] Policy gaps are important in public policy because they are identifiable places where political contestation is likely to occur. Further, knowing where gaps form in the core or periphery indicates the size of change if they are successfully closed. Gaps in the core result in dramatic policy change, whereas changes in the periphery account for incremental adjustments.

Following in Lowi's footsteps, I argue that policy structure shapes politics. However, structure alone does not explain why and how policies change. The mere presence of a policy gap does not automatically entail its elimination.[49] An analysis of policy structure aids in understanding how policies adapt to changing social practice by identifying those components of public policy that are likely to be contested and the potential obstacles to reform depending on where policy gaps are located (core or periphery). It broadens the lens with which scholars may view theories of policy change and places traditional theories of policy change between micropolicy structure and macrosocial practice. Whether the gap makes it on the agenda depends on Kingdon's three streams—problem definition, policy solutions, and politics—coming together. Ultimately, policy change is most likely when diverse coalitions form around the means and ends of policy, when policy expands to new constituencies (rather than taking away from entrenched interests), and when the change is relative minor.

Family, Policy, and Policy Change

Putting together both the discussion of family and the analysis of the inner workings of policy structure shows that when policymakers create policy—across a broad spectrum of areas—they embed family in the structure in three ways: as a criterion of eligibility, as an administrator, and as a normative ideal. Family becomes an important value in the core and periphery of policies that, on their face, do not seem to be particularly family oriented. Immigration policy, for example, is now based largely around the principle of family unification, but "family" is only widely agreed upon in the abstract. In practice, policymakers create legislation underwritten by very specific and historically contingent assumptions about family, such as what constitutes a family and what role family members ought to play. The original definition of "child" in the 1952 Immigration and Naturalization Act, the foundation of current immigration policy, included only biological and "legitimate" children of United States citizens and legal permanent residents. Since 1952 American families have changed in a number of ways. Compared to sixty years ago, young adults are marrying later and having fewer children. Divorce and remarriage are more common, as are the number of children living in homes with single parents or nonbiological parents. Whether the original definition of "child" in immigration policy reflected social practice in 1952, it certainly does not reflect the social practice of American families almost six decades later.

When social practice deviates from the values and assumptions in public policy, it opens up a policy gap where political contestation is likely to occur. Policy gaps alter the politics of the policy process: providing opportunities for problem definition, creating policy communities interested in the means, and providing the political will for creating coalitions between the two types of policy communities: those fighting for particular ends (expanding the EITC) and those concerned with the means (family). In all three policy areas evaluated in this book, gaps arose and were contested. They were not, however, all successfully closed.

An analysis of policy gaps, ultimately, shows that the policy process is not fundamentally stable, rather the potential for contestation and change is part and parcel of the policies themselves. Like much political development research, which "exposes sources of disorder, introduces incongruity and fragmentation into depictions of the political norm, and pushes to the foreground an essentially dynamic view of the polity as a whole," I look at the inherent instability in American politics.[50] Contestation, in this account, is a potential and regular part of each and every public policy.

Although current classifications within political science, and public policy literature in particular, place little emphasis on family outside of political socialization or explicit family-related policies, I find that family plays a far more significant role, affecting the politics surrounding public policies. Though thinking about family and the means of public policy—across policy process and policy areas—may seem to be a bit unorthodox to political scientists, it is not foreign to political actors. In reference to DOMA, Senator Trent Lott hinted at the true magnitude that family change could have on public policies when he asked members of Congress to think about what would happen across the broad range of public policies if family were redefined: "Imagine the financial and social consequences of taking such a step."[51] Certainly, they would be extensive.

OVERVIEW OF METHODOLOGY AND CHAPTERS

The central questions that guide my research are: *How do policymakers employ family in the policy process? What are the consequences?* To answer these questions, I have developed a theoretical framework and a detailed analysis of the ways in which policies accomplish their goals. The goal of this book is to evaluate how well this theoretical framework and conceptual analysis of policy holds up and adds to what we already know about the politics of policymaking. In this book, I focus specifically on twentieth-century federal policy, defined as "the sum of government activities, whether acting directly or through agents," specifically related to the legislative policy process.[52] The chapters that follow expand on the concepts discussed in this chapter and apply them to three policy areas.

Chapter 2 lays out the theoretical framework for thinking about family in politics and then tests the framework by evaluating where family occurs in the policy process. In this chapter, I analyze the content of three important components of the policy process: public speech and debate (the *Congressional Record*), statutory law (the *U.S. Code*), and administrative rules and regulations (the *Federal Register*). I find strong support for the framework: family is used in each stage of the policy process and further it is used broadly across policy areas from veteran's benefits to congressional pay. Family plays an important part in the policy process, as the framework suggests, rather than just in family-oriented policies.

Chapter 3 looks at the consequences of this widespread use of family, specifically looking at how policies adapt to changing family practices. It elaborates on the concepts and theoretical arguments presented here about policy structure and politics more generally. It ties structural elements of public policy to actors and institutions in the policy process to broader social practices in which Americans engage.

Chapters 4 through 6, the heart of this research project, look at four individual qualitative case studies in three policy areas designed to show the importance of the theoretical framework and of understanding policy structure more generally. Cases were selected based on theoretical and practical criteria. First, rather than look in depth at any one policy area, this book was designed to look at multiple areas. This is not a study of any one policy but how family operates throughout the policy process. Thus, I selected the maximum number of areas (three) that could reasonably be examined in depth in a book this size. Second, in selecting policy areas, I first eliminated any that might be associated with "family policy," including health, education, and welfare. Scholars have done an admirable job examining policies designed to protect and promote American families, especially in regard to welfare. Because I argue that family is used extensively *outside* family policy, I removed those areas most closely associated with family from consideration. Next, I used the *U.S. Code* chapters as a proxy for policy areas and ranked the relative importance of family as measured by the percentage of family words in the *U.S. Code* (Appendix B). I broke the list down into three tiers: high family importance, medium family importance, and low family importance. From each of those tiers, I chose a policy area that served different constituencies and had different goals. That is, the policies are not clustered around any particular focus (i.e., social services or foreign affairs) and, further, they serve overlapping but not identical populations (i.e., rural and urban, wealthy and poor). Ultimately, the policy areas—immigration, taxation, and agriculture—reflect a great deal of diversity.

Though the general policy areas were chosen to be diverse, the individual cases within these three areas were chosen to be comparable with one another. Because this book asks how policies adapt to changing family practices, I chose cases with the potential for policy gaps in values and assumptions but variation in the outcome. Gaps were contested in the four case studies but only closed successfully twice. The individual cases include:

Immigration Policy. The 1975 amendments to the Immigration and Naturalization Act (INA) to allow single people to adopt abroad and the 1995 (unsuccessful) attempt to amend the INA to eliminate visa preferences for adult brothers and sisters.

Tax policy. The 2001 reduction/elimination of the marriage tax penalty in the Earned Income Tax Credit.

Agriculture policy. The 1996 elimination of "temporary" New Deal agriculture subsidies and their subsequent reinstatement.

Though family functions to some degree as a criterion of eligibility, administrator, or normative ideal *within* each case, I highlight one particular function for each case. Chapter 4 focuses on family as the criterion of eligibility in immigration policy; Chapter 5 concentrates on family as an administrator in tax policy; and Chapter 6 focuses on family as a normative ideal in agriculture policy. All three draw evidence from archival resources (including extensive government documents), policy histories, in-person interviews, and large public datasets.

The conclusion, Chapter 7, draws out the larger implications of this research and addresses how assumptions about family in public policy not only affect politics, but also American citizens and residents.

CHAPTER TWO

Family in the Policy Process

Family plays a central role in American politics, though that role is often overlooked by scholars who rely on traditional categories of analysis for politics and public policy. At the most basic level, the very subject of politics (public life) is often defined in opposition to family (private life).[1] American political scientist Robert Dahl sums up the dichotomy when he explains the difference between the domain of politics, gaining and maintaining control over policies, and the domain of civic and private life including family. He makes abundantly clear: "*Homo civicus* is not, by nature, a political animal."[2] When family is addressed in relation to public policy, scholars often equate family and public policy with "family policy," or those programs designed to protect, promote, or define family such as the federal Defense of Marriage Act (DOMA) and public welfare provisions or state-level adoption and divorce laws. Thus, family is considered only in relation to particular public policies like Family and Medical Leave or Women, Infants, and Children. This project challenges the categories of analysis that define politics in opposition to family and disregard the study of family outside of so-called family policies. Instead, I argue that family is part and parcel of the American policy process. It is an important *means* to achieve a wide variety of policy ends. By shifting the analysis from ends to means, one can shed light on a key question that has previously been obscured: *how do policymakers employ family in the policy process?*

This chapter answers the question by proposing a new way of thinking about the role of family in the policy process. Policymakers use family as a means to achieve a host of policy goals in seeming "nonfamily" policies from national defense to agriculture. In this chapter, I propose three ways that family is employed: as a criterion of eligibility that determines who qualifies for goods and services; as an administrator that distributes goods and services to dependents; and as a normative ideal that garners and maintains support for policy positions. The bulk of the chapter is devoted to empirically testing the theoretical framework by looking at the language policymakers employ (in the *Congressional Record*), the laws they write (in the *U.S. Code*), and the administrative rules they use for implementation (in the *Federal Register*). I find that contrary to the traditional categories of analysis, which consider family as "private" or only part of so-called family policy, family is part and parcel of the policy process across a host of policy areas. First, however, I provide a definition of family and further elaboration on the theoretical framework.

FAMILY DEFINED

At the outset, the working definition of family I employ throughout this book is a kin relationship between two or more people defined by blood, law, or affection. This description is left intentionally vague to capture the variation in groupings of individuals considered family in any particular policy. For example, family in immigration law is defined strictly through blood, marriage, and adoption. It includes nuclear family members and grandparents. Family in tax policy, however, is defined through blood, marriage, and adoption *as well as* financial dependence. It includes cousins that are financially dependent upon a taxpayer but not adult children who are self-supporting. Because I wish to see how policymakers and the policies they create talk about and define families, I use kinship as a proxy for family but I do not start with a preconceived idea about which particular individuals qualify as kin. In the empirical research for this book, I have cast as wide a net as possible when looking for indicators of family relationships. Appendix A lists the forty-one terms from *spouse* to *offspring* used to determine where family relationships are included in public policy. I leave it to policymakers to determine whether one is considered a spouse or offspring based on blood ties, legal procedures (marriage or adoption), or affection.

With this general starting point, the reader should take note that there are two important distinctions used throughout this book when discussing family. The first is between "family" (singular), an abstract reference to the idea of a family, and "families" (plural), the actual social practices of Americans. In the singular, the American family may be lauded as the bedrock of American society or as a shortcut for determining who may receive benefits. At the same time, the social practices of American families may be very different. The distinction between "family" in the abstract and "families" in practice underlies discussions of how family is used in politics as compared to social practice that lies at the heart of the analysis in Chapter 3. The second key distinction is between family as the means and the ends of the policy process and is the basis of the theoretical framework and empirical analysis presented in this chapter.

THE THEORETICAL FRAMEWORK

Family, like taxes, is often equated with the ends or outputs of the policy process. Therefore, when scholars address "family policy" they focus on those programs that seek to protect and promote American families the same way that scholars who address "tax policy" examine legislation to raise or lower taxes. Increasingly, however, scholarly research is shifting from a focus on program outputs, like welfare or the individual income tax, to the means used to accomplish them, such as block grants for states to create aid programs for the needy and tax expenditures to encourage individual retirement savings. Public administration scholars look to policy instruments and tools, from contracting to vouchers to tax incentives, as the primary unit of analysis in thinking about and analyzing public policy.[3] In a similar vein, political scientists and policy experts could benefit from rethinking the place of family in the policy process. Like taxes, family is a category of public policy but it also more widely used as an instrument or tool to achieve other policy goals. DOMA, which defined marriage for federal policies as a union between one man and one woman, illustrates the value of distinguishing between means and ends. As an end of the policy process, DOMA is truly exceptional because even though federal policymakers debate family issues and federal courts have ruled on family matters, the fifty states determine who may marry, divorce, or adopt.[4] Though Congress is not charged with defining family law, it relies heavily on family in many of the federal policies it *is* charged with creating. In the case of DOMA, members of Congress were acutely aware that eligibility for scores of federal benefits and services is determined by family status.

Understanding the important role that family plays as a means in the policy process will shed light on essential political questions such as, How does an ideologically diverse assortment of political actors form a coalition to support or oppose a public policy? Why do particular components of "nonfamily" policy become vulnerable to criticism when demographic practices change? How do symbols and rhetoric work to support continued (and increased) spending for policies with shrinking constituencies? The theoretical framework of this project helps to uncover answers to these questions. I propose three ways in which family is employed as a means in the policy process: as a criterion of eligibility, as an administrator, and as a normative ideal.

Criterion of Eligibility

At the most basic level, family determines who is eligible to receive benefits and services. Though state programs are set up to benefit particular individuals for their actions, such as veterans who receive education benefits or retirees who receive Social Security, a significant component of government spending is providing benefits to an individual's family. Thus, survivor benefits are an important part of military and domestic protection spending. The Department of Veteran's Affairs provides education benefits, home loan guarantees, dependency and indemnity compensation, medical care, pensions, and burial costs to specified family members of disabled or deceased veterans.[5] For the families of American servicepersons killed in the line of duty, the benefits are significant. A Marine captain's widow and two children receive a first-year annual payment of $58,920. With insurance and education, the total lifetime benefits could reach $3.6 million. Similarly, a Naval petty officer's widower and three children could receive lifetime benefits of $2.5 million, and an Army corporal's widow (no children) would qualify for lifetime benefits of nearly $2 million.[6] In 2002, 2.4 million disabled veterans and 308,000 surviving spouses and family members received $22 billion in disability compensation and survivor benefits alone.[7]

Like the Department of Veteran's Affairs, the Social Security Administration accommodates non-wage-earning spouses, giving them benefits. Data from the Social Security Administration show that nearly 40 percent of Social Security pension, survivor, and disability beneficiaries are spouses (and children) of wage earners; this includes 19 percent of Social Security recipients, 100 percent of survivor beneficiaries, and 38 percent of disability recipients.[8] Even spouses who have worked during their lifetime may receive benefits based on the paid-employment of their husband or wife.

The Department of Veteran's Affairs and the Social Security Administration are just a couple of the federal agencies that administer policies that rely on family to determine who receives goods and services. Many other policies, from immigration preference categories to college savings accounts to federal health-care programs, also rely on family as a criterion of eligibility. Far from promoting the ideal of individualism, the state determines who receives "what, when, how" not by merit alone but by family relationship as well.

Administrator

Family also acts as an administrator that provides services and distributes benefits to its members. Though public policy literature traditionally paints bureaucrats as workers in state and federal agencies, new scholarly work increasingly questions traditional ideas of governance.[9] Administrators, those individuals and organizations that implement public policy, are not only civil servants but also employees in public-private partnerships, nonprofits, and private firms. From teachers in charter schools to private companies that contract to process Medicare paperwork, the essential functions of government are being carried out by nongovernment employees. In the words of political scientist Paul Light these alternative bureaucrats have become a "shadow government," carrying out necessary public duties beyond the purview of civil service regulations.[10]

Families, too, act as shadow bureaucrats when they implement public policies governed by the nation's tax code. Policymakers provide a host of tax incentives to encourage particular types of behavior: buying fuel-efficient cars, saving for retirement, and investing in distressed urban areas. When incentives in the tax code encourage or require taxpayers to provide goods and services for someone else, that taxpayer essentially acts as an administrator carrying out laws made by Congress and rules specified by the Internal Revenue Service (IRS) on another's behalf. Individual taxpayers—parents, grandparents, siblings, and adult children—must learn about and apply complex education, housing, and welfare provisions in the Internal Revenue Code (IRC). They are held accountable for doing so correctly.

Even though it may seem entirely natural and normal for parents to act on behalf of their children, for example by saving for a college education, policymakers do not give incentives for *any* taxpayer to give to *any* college student in *any* way. Rather, the qualifying taxpayer, relationship with the student, and savings method are specified at length. Family members must act under strictly prescribed criteria, the same way that financial aid officers must in making decisions about who receives federal Pell Grant funds. Policymakers assume that bonds of affection and conventional legal practices will be a sufficient means to ensure that the tax code is an efficient way of subsidizing policies from education to child welfare. For policymakers, the "natural" caregiving associated with familial relationships can be capitalized on for policy goals.[11] Relying on family members to administer public policy takes the burden of administration away from government and places it squarely on "private" individuals. In this way, the state's capacity to accomplish a number of policy goals increases.

Normative Ideal

Finally, family acts as a normative ideal that helps to garner and maintain support for a particular policy. In the words of Robert Rector, of the Heritage Foundation, family is the "rhetorical ketchup in any dish.

It's like being in favor of children." Similar to apple pie issues, framing a policy debate as "pro-family" makes it harder to attack a particular position.[12] Deborah Stone explains that "political actors *deliberately portray* them [conditions, difficulties, issues] in ways calculated to gain support for their side."[13]

To some observers of American politics it may seem as though rhetoric and symbols, like family, are nothing more than "rhetorical ketchup"— serving no real purpose and having no lasting effect. However, as Murray Edelman demonstrates, symbols are not superfluous to politics, symbols are at the heart of politics. He explains: "it is not 'reality' in any testable or observable sense that matters in shaping political consciousness and behavior, but rather the beliefs that language help evoke about the causes and discontents and satisfactions, about policies that will bring about a future closer to the heart's desire, and about other unobservables."[14] The language of family is more than a way to make particular policies more palatable; family defines what citizens think politics is and what policies ought to accomplish. By invoking family, a policy actor turns his or her position into one that appeals to common values—values that are above politics. Policymakers since World War II have invoked the family farm as an American cultural icon, one that resonates with urban and suburban Americans to justify both district-benefiting agriculture programs and the more general elimination of the estate tax. For many Americans, family farms define agriculture policy.

The theoretical framework proposes that family acts as an important means in the policy process to achieve a wide variety of policy ends. Policy actors may rely on family to determine who qualifies for public programs, how those benefits are distributed, and what language will be used to justify policy positions. I argue that family's importance is not only in debates over "family values," but rather in the day-to-day workings of the policy process.

FAMILY IN THE POLICY PROCESS

To evaluate the strength of this theoretical framework, I searched for words that express a kin relationship (see Appendix A) in three key parts of the policy process: public speech and debate, statutory law, and administrative regulation. Specifically, this search is designed to test two aspects of the theoretical framework. First, the search is designed to evaluate around which policies and debates family words cluster. If family is the object or ends of policy, as the discipline conventionally thinks of it, then I would expect to find family words in these three sources clustered around policies and politics designed to protect, promote, or help American families, such as family leave or welfare. However, if the theoretical framework that I have laid out is correct and family is a means in the policy process, then I would expect to find family dispersed across a wide variety of policy areas from national defense to agriculture.

Second, in addition to testing the particular policies in which family is embedded, this search is also designed to test at what stage in the policy process family is used. Even a casual observer of American politics would be able to point to numerous examples of the ways that policymakers rely on family to frame political issues and shape the debate that follows, such as Republican "family values" and Democratic "working families" rhetoric. If family is a rhetorical device alone, I would expect to find the search words concentrated only in the *Congressional Record*. However, if family is truly used as a means in the policy process as I have a described (a criterion of eligibility, administrator, and normative ideal) then I would expect to find family words across the three parts of the policy process under examination and not limited to political rhetoric.

To test these expectations, I have analyzed ten years of the *Congressional Record*, the transcript of floor debates, proclamations, and remarks; the *U.S. Code* (as of 2002), which is the official record of all general and permanent laws enacted by Congress; and ten years of the *Federal Register*, the public record of federal regulations' public notices.[15] These three sources provide a bird's-eye view of the overall policy process and line up well with its three major parts: public debate and discussion, statutory law, and administrative rules and regulations. In addition to the bird's-eye view, I selected a week at random (July 13–19, 1997) to add necessary context. When family words are employed, *how* are they used by policymakers and for what ends? By evaluating the policy process as a whole and the context within debates, this section shows that far from being confined to the traditional categories of analysis, family is used across policy areas in all three parts of the policy process. In other words, family is an important means to achieving policy ends generally.

Public Speech and Debate

The starting point for my analysis is congressional debate and discussion. Public speech and debate, a forum very different from either statutory law or proposed administrative changes, provides legislators with a stage on which to make the most convincing arguments they can muster.[16] To study public speech and debate, I used the *Congressional Record*, which includes the transcripts of floor debates by both houses of Congress as well as the extension of remarks—House tributes, statements, and other supplemental remarks—and a daily digest—a summary of the day's events. The unit of analysis used to look at the *Congressional Record* is an entry.

Entries in the *Congressional Record* vary considerably in length. They can be anything from a short sentence or paragraph to hours of debate on the floor. In determining the importance of family, two categories may be employed: volume, the number of family words used in an entry; and breadth, the number of entries that contain family words as a percentage of all entries in a chapter. High volume and narrow breadth indicate that family is the object of discussion and most likely policy, such as one finds in discrete legislative debates on welfare (Temporary Assistance to Needy Families) or family leave (Family and Medical Leave Act). In contrast, a significant breadth, regardless of volume, suggests that family is at work in the policy process for a range of policy goals, and family is used in ways consistent with the theoretical framework developed above. Although using entries as the unit of analysis can seriously undercount the volume—or the number of times family words are used—using entries does provide a stable measure of the breadth.

From January 1992 through October 2002, there are 271,430 entries in the *Congressional Record*, and 87,016 of them include family words. To put this in perspective, in a typical week, legislators invoke family words and images an average of 218 times, or in nearly one-third of all speeches, tributes, statements, and daily business of the *Congressional Record*.

Figure 2.1 shows the number of entries, limited to weeks when Congress is in session.[17] Figure 2.1 shows peaks and valleys, but overall there is a relatively constant number of entries per week, just above 200. Figure 2.2 shows the percent of entries in the *Congressional Record* that includes family words when Congress is in session. It points to a remarkable feature of family assumptions: they are ubiquitous. Over the span of ten years, or 571 weeks, family words crop up in every single week when Congress is in session except two.[18] Figures 2.1 and 2.2 point to an often underappreciated fact about Congress: the business of Congress is conducted in the language of family.

Looking more closely at the week selected at random for further contextual analysis shows in this period 156 entries contained family words. One might expect family words to appear frequently in commendations paying tribute to couples' anniversaries or even justifications legislators provide for being absent from Congress. However, family words also materialize in the top legislative issues for the week. The *Congressional Quarterly Weekly Report* lists "major legislative action" for the week of July 13 ranging from Defense Appropriation to Vocational Education. Family words occur in *Congressional Record* entries for each of the nine pieces of major legislation listed.[19]

In this particular week, family words overwhelmingly occurred in a contentious issue facing reconciliation by the House and Senate—the fu-

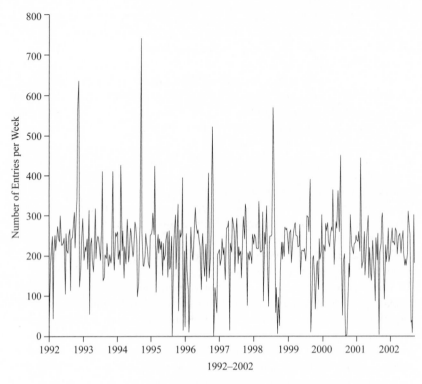

FIGURE 2-1
Number of Family Words in the *Congressional Record*
SOURCE: Author's analysis of the *Congressional Record*

ture of the budget, and taxation in particular.[20] The heart of the matter of taxation dividing the House and Senate, Democrats and Republicans, is not "merely" ideological differences about the size of government or even giving Americans a few extra dollars to invest in the economy, rather, in the words of Representative Kenny Hulshof (R-MO), "It is about freedom to make choices in raising a family." To prove his point, he talks about Debra, a divorced mother of three children. "Keeping more of her money means being able to help her three children reach their dreams. The dream of Debra's college-bound daughter is to attend college and become a doctor. For Debra's middle daughter, she aspires to be a teacher. And although Debra is determined to help bring her daughters' dreams to fulfillment, it is not going to be an easy task" (143 Cong. Rec. H 5386).

Legislators do not shy away from personalizing public policy; in fact, they regularly make points in reference to their own families, families they

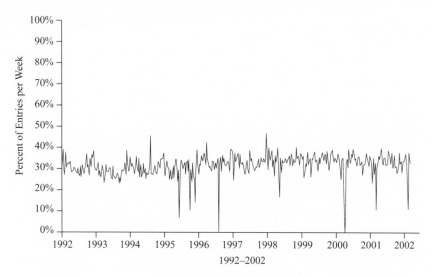

FIGURE 2-2
Percent Family Words in the *Congressional Record*, 1992–2002
SOURCE: Author's analysis of the *Congressional Record*

know, or American families more generally. Family words, in taxation as well as many other issues, are an appeal to shared values. Values that not so subtly reinforce the importance of family at the same time that they bolster support for a particular policy position. By appealing to an important institution, one that is seemingly above political wrangling, policymakers are able to register legitimate support or opposition to programs that may have—on their face—nothing to do with American families.

Foreign affairs, a policy area that brings to mind diplomats and foreign countries, nonetheless is talked about at times in Congress specifically in family terms. A case in point is the discussion in the Senate on Foreign Operations Appropriations on July 17. In this one debate, families are mentioned in reference to U.S. policy positions in Cuba, China, Libya, and Egypt. Senator Barbara Mikulksi (D-MD) explains why she supports an amendment to cut foreign aid to countries that violate U.S. sanctions against Libya.

The families of those murdered on Pan Am 103 need no reminder of why we have sanctions on Libya. They live with this tragedy every day of their lives . . . They [the victims] were so young. They were college students, a young Army lieutenant, a businessman and a lawyer. They were sons, daughters, and fathers. We swore that we would never forget them. We would improve airline safety, we would fight terrorism and most importantly, we would seek justice (143 Cong. Rec. S 7623).

In addition to Cuba, China, Lybia, and Egypt, in this one week arguments that invoke family images were used to support or oppose U.S. foreign policy positions on Cyprus, Haiti, and Guam. Policymakers appeal to family across policy areas because it personalizes policy: using family words and images puts a concrete name (Debra) and face (college student son or daughter) on issues. It also allows policymakers to express their position in terms that are almost above reproach. Although one might disagree with the policy position, it is difficult to attack the justification.

In tying their policy positions to shared values, legislators are able to appeal to a broader constituency and shield themselves from potential criticism of their actual vote. Politicians, who are blame avoiders as much as they are credit claimers, seek many ways to hide their actions from public view or at the very least make them more palatable.[21] The family, in particular, is effective because in addition to being a shared value, it is one that is experienced concretely and personally. Unlike abstract values of equality or liberty, references to family loss and pain, as Mikulski describes, strike an immediate chord.

Perhaps no policy position is more politically unpopular for a politician than voting to increase his own salary. Conventional wisdom has it that one should approach this issue quietly—or, like the strategy in the House for 1997, without public debate of any kind. Senator Ted Stevens (R-AK), however, made a very public appeal for a raise, not for himself or any other Senator, but for the very hope that in the future the Senate will be a place that includes "family people."

What I am trying to make people in the Senate think about is, what will be the decision made by young people who are thinking about coming here when they look at the cost of living in Washington, DC, which is the highest now in our Nation the cost of property here, the cost of renting a home or a condominium. I am talking about family people. When we came down here, we came down here with five children and had to have a home that five children could live in. There is no way a person can come here now at the salary level we have now and buy a home for that, where five children can live with their mother and father, unless they are extremely wealthy. . . . [A]s a practical matter, the judgments made by future generations will be: We, as a family member, cannot take that job [of Senator] (143 Cong. Rec. S 7652).

By appealing to the family, Stevens tries to take a politically unpopular position and give it a strong justification.[22] Stevens puts a pay raise almost above politics and political wrangling—who would possibly want a Senate without family men and women? In so doing, he reinforces family values and structural assumptions in public policy. Because it is commonly appealed to on the floor, it is not questioned that families are important to Americans in all aspects of their lives; this view seeps into the creation of public policy in committee and closed-door sessions.

Do policymakers in Congress talk about the family equally? In other words, family may be merely a popular Republican buzzword, one that goes along with their shift in 1994 to conservative family values in the Contract with America. Or, family might be associated with gender, so that women in Congress are more likely to talk about family concerns. That is, family may be nothing more than a particular approach to politics. Looking carefully at the July 1997 week selected at random, I coded all statements in the *Congressional Record* by party and gender. The results show that family is not the stronghold of either party or gender.

Though the push for family values is tied closely with the Republican Party, during this week House Democrats talked more about family than their conservative counterparts. Of the 218 statements made about family that week, Democrats were responsible for 125 (57 percent). Republicans, on the other hand, made ninety-three statements, only 42 percent. In other words, 33 percent of Democrats made statements about the family whereas only 24 percent of Republicans did. The Senate tells a much more balanced story for the same week. Of the forty-five statements made about family in the *Congressional Record* by Senators, 51 percent are by Democrats and 49 percent by Republicans. Overall, 33 percent of Democratic Senators invoked the family in that one week whereas 31 percent of Republicans did.[23]

The results of gender analysis must be taken with the caveat that there are many fewer women serving in Congress in July of 1997 (fifty-three in the House and nine in the Senate).[24] In the House, for this one week, men talked less about family than women did. Twenty-six percent of men and 43 percent of women used family in their public speech. The Senate shows a much more balanced view. Thirty-two percent of Senate men and 33 percent of Senate women used family in that week. In both chambers together, 27 percent of men and 42 percent of women talked about family.

As a normative ideal, specific family assumptions are reinforced in everyday speech and debate. The rhetorical use of family is not limited to conservative discourse, however; it is used extensively by members of both parties and genders in both chambers. Though family does not structure public policy the way it might if it determined eligibility or acted as an administrator, it does reinforce the family as a value and relatively unquestioned structural assumption.

Statutory Law

Public debate provides a forum to tie particular policies across a wide spectrum of policy areas to family. As the results demonstrate, policymakers often take the opportunity to justify their policy positions in terms of family. But it requires less commitment for policymakers to speak about family than it does to do anything about it. To put it simply, because policymakers *talk* about family values does not necessarily mean that they *do* anything with them.

To evaluate where family occurs in public policy, I look at both statutory law (*U.S. Code*) in this section and proposed administrative rules and regulations (*Federal Register*) in the next. As was the case for rhetoric in the *Congressional Record,* family is used across policy areas. Using the week selected at random shows that family operates in these two sources in two primary ways: determining eligibility and administering policy.

The *U.S. Code,* or statutory laws of the United States, is comprised of forty-eight titles (listed in Appendix B). Of these forty-eight titles, only one stands out as particularly family oriented—Title 42, Public Health and Welfare. Because the government provides assistance to low-income families for food, housing, and shelter, it would not be surprising to find that there are a large number of family-related (or kin) words in this title. The names of many programs such as "Women Infants and Children" or even chapters like "Family Violence Prevention and Services" have the family search words built into them. In absolute terms, it is true that Title 42 has the highest volume (7,979) of family words. In fact, Public Health and Welfare dwarfs all of the other titles. Thirty-four percent of all entries that include family words are in Public Health and Welfare. But what is particularly noteworthy for the argument presented here is not so much how many times these words occurred in this one title, but how often they occur *outside* of it. Nearly 66 percent of all family words appear in *other* titles. Family words crop up across forty-four of the forty-eight titles.[25]

The absolute number of family words in a title presents only the volume of words used and not their breadth. For the purposes of evaluating the framework, the absolute number matters less than their relative use; family words will always be used in greater volume when family is the object of policy rather than a means used to broader ends. As in the case for public debate, a better measure in public law is breadth. How many chapters employ family words?

Table 2.1 presents the results of a chapter-level analysis.[26] Though Title 42, Public Health and Welfare, has the greatest absolute number of chapters that include family words, it falls substantially when controlling for the total number of chapters in the title. Setting aside the titles with fewer than fifteen total chapters, which may overstate the findings, leaves the top five titles. Among these five, Public Health and Welfare sinks to number four behind Veteran's Benefits (74 percent), the IRC (52 percent), and Indians (52 percent) and is only 5 percent above Title 5, Government Organization and Employees (43 percent).

TABLE 2-1

Percent of Chapters That Use Family Words per Title of the *U.S. Code*

Title	Name	Chapters with Family Words (N)	Percent Chapters with Family Words
38	Veteran's Benefits	(31)	74
3	*The President*	*(3)*	60
11	*Bankruptcy*	*(5)*	56
26	Internal Revenue Code	(33)	52
25	Indians	(23)	52
14	*Coast Guard*	*(7)*	50
32	*National Guard*	*(2)*	50
42	Public Health and Welfare	(70)	48
12	*Banks and Banking*	*(7)*	47
5	Government Organization and Employees	(20)	43

SOURCE: Author's analysis of the *U.S. Code*

NOTE: Italicized entries have fewer than 15 chapters.

At first, these results may seem surprising—as a percentage of total chapters, family words occur more often in the titles that do not seem to have a direct family connection. These results will remain a mystery as long as family is associated with the ends of public policy rather than the means by which policy goals are accomplished. Policymakers regularly make assumptions about families, and these assumptions are embedded in structure of policy. Although the top two categories, Veteran's Benefits and the IRC, are not about family per se, they depend on family assumptions to determine beneficiaries and administer benefits. A closer examination of each shows how family assumptions structure policy.

Title 38, Veteran's Benefits, tops the list with 74 percent of its chapters containing family words. One glance at the content of the chapter reveals why it is so high: much of the law surrounding benefits is concerned with who gets them. And with military servicepersons, many of whom have been disabled or killed in service, governmental provision, by necessity, often must extend beyond the service member to those who have lost emotionally and financially. Policymakers' assumptions about the dependent relationship of military personnel to their families mean that family is the natural criterion to determine eligibility. For example, section 1916 of the *U.S. Code* covers National Service life insurance and specifies very clearly that family alone may claim benefits. The insurance "shall be payable only to a widow, widower, child, parent, brother or sister of the insured." In specifying who is eligible, policymakers have shown an assumption that family takes priority in the distribution of benefits. In short, family status determines eligibility for this and thousands of other programs. But it is not merely an abstract commitment to the ideal of family. Instead, policymakers have concrete images, or assumptions, in mind when they specify not merely "kin" or "next of kin" but exactly which family members count. The law goes on to specify that upon death of the beneficiary, the remaining payments are to be distributed according to a particular order:

1. To the widow or widower of the insured, if living.
2. If no widow or widower, to the child or children of the insured, if living, in equal shares.
3. If no widow, widower, or child, to the parent or parents of the insured who last bore that relationship, if living, in equal shares.
4. If no widow, widower, child, or parent, to the brothers and sisters of the insured, if living, in equal shares. (38 USCS § 1916)

The traditional nuclear family is predominant. Widows and children come first, followed by parents and then siblings. In part, this order is determined by legal precedent and in part by cultural norms. Looking closely at Veteran's Benefits shows not only that family is an important part of the means of the policy, but also that particular family assumptions become embedded in policy.

Title 26, the IRC, also has a broad distribution of family words. Like Veteran's Benefits, one can see the importance of family structures in this area of policy as well. Family assumptions drive both the eligibility and the means by which benefits are provided. The IRC does more than list the benefits that any individual is qualified to receive, as was the case in the previous example; it provides incentives for individuals to act in ways that policymakers feel desirable. Because the tax code requires individuals to fill out *personal* income tax assessments based on *household* size, income, and expenses, the code is a likely place to find family assumptions determining eligibility and as a vehicle to administer policy. In the eyes of much of the IRC, individual taxpayers are members of families.

As an example, section 72 of the IRC provides credits for individuals for "qualified educational expenses." The IRC defines not only what qualifies as educational expenses but *who* qualifies as well:

(i) the taxpayer,
(ii) the taxpayer's spouse, or
(iii) any child (as defined in section 151(c)(3)) or grandchild of the taxpayer or the taxpayer's spouse, at an eligible educational institution (as defined in section 529(e)(5)).

In this instance, the IRC provides a benefit to the individual taxpayer should he or she choose to seek additional education. But it also provides a benefit to spouses, children, or grandchildren *through* the taxpayer. In a relatively efficient and cost-effective manner, the state is able to provide educational aid to individuals by giving incentives to relatives.

Administrative Implementation

Once policy has been debated and codified by legislators, the daunting task of implementation is left to executive agencies. Federal departments, agencies, and offices publicize in the *Federal Register* any rules and regulations they wish to enact as well as notices of changes to their policies. The *Federal Register* is the official daily publication of executive agency rules, proposed rules, administrative notices, and presidential documents. The unit of analysis for the *Federal Register,* as for the *Congressional Record* and the *U.S. Code,* is an individual entry. The entries in the *Federal Register* are neither as passionate and engaging as those in the *Congressional Record* nor as comprehensive in scope as in the *U.S. Code.* Instead, they reflect the particular needs of policy implementers to put statutory law into practice. Yet even in the *Federal Register*, family words appear each and every week between 1992 and 2002.

Family words in administrative implementation occur far less frequently than they do in public speech and debate. Indeed, in the ten years between 1992 and 2002, family words appeared in 31,172 out of 717,778 total entries. To put this in perspective, family words occurred in approximately fifty-five entries per week, accounting for 9 percent of all entries. Figure 2.3 depicts the total number of entries per week that include family words in the *Federal Register* and Figure 2.4 the percent. Though family words are not used as often as in the *Congressional Record*, they too, have remarkable consistency.

Significantly, family words are not confined solely to departments whose domain is family health and well-being. Once again, looking more carefully at the second week of July 1997 illustrates the range of departments and agencies that rely on families to aid in administering policy. Of the sixty-three entries in the *Federal Register* with family words for this week, forty-nine of them refer to kin relationships. The Department of Health and Human Services, with eleven entries, by far has the greatest number. Together with the Departments of Housing and Urban Development and Education, these family-oriented organizations account for roughly a third of all entries in the week. Yet, outside of these three are many agencies not traditionally associated with promoting or protecting family welfare that use family words: the Department of Justice, the Department of Transportation, the Department

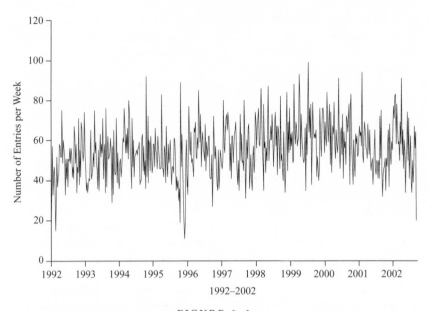

FIGURE 2-3

Number of Family Words in the *Federal Register*, 1992-2002

SOURCE: Author's analysis of the *Federal Register*

of the Interior, the Department of Agriculture, the Department of Defense, the Federal Emergency Management Agency, and the Environmental Protection Agency.[27]

Family is a part of a wide variety of public policies across the policy process. Family works as a normative ideal in political rhetoric and as a criterion of eligibility and administrator in statutory law and administrative regulation. Yet as the more detailed analysis of the week of July 13–19 demonstrates, family is not vague and abstract but contains very concrete assumptions about what constitutes a family, what roles family members are expected to carry out, and what duties a family may be expected to perform. Oftentimes, these assumptions reflect gendered norms about dependency and the proper roles for family members.[28] The strict preferences providing for family members throughout Veterans' Benefits reflect assumptions about the financial and other dependence of families, especially spouses and children, on veterans. When veterans die or are disabled in service, their beneficiaries are given financial compensation to help with the loss. The size of the benefit and the choice of beneficiaries are determined by place in the family: immediate nuclear family first, then parents, siblings, and at times it extends well beyond this.

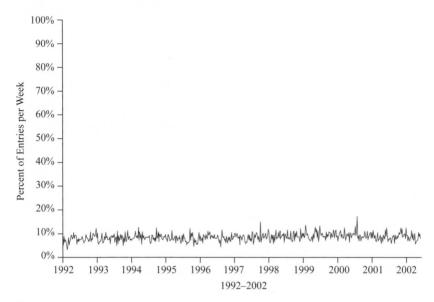

FIGURE 2-4
Percent Family Words in the *Federal Register*, 1992-2002
SOURCE: Author's analysis of the *Federal Register*

These assumptions may not be unusual or unreasonable. In fact, they often seem perfectly natural and normal: Who deserves benefits more than a spouse? Who is needier than a child to receive financial compensation? Scholars who study gender, race, sexuality, and religion know that family is often intimately tied with each of these. Including specific assumptions about family across a host of policies has potential consequences for long-term stability and change. It also has consequences for American citizens and residents who find particular family norms reinforced in American public policy—norms that may discriminate against alternative family arrangements.

FAMILY PRACTICE IN AMERICA

As the previous section has shown, policymakers often embed very specific assumptions about the behavior and organization of American families. Even if these assumptions are entirely accurate when the policy is made, over time social practice may deviate from the assumptions embedded in policy. Public policy may remain static, but American families have changed in a number of key ways.

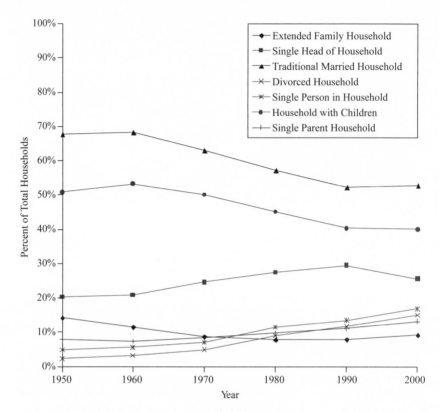

FIGURE 2-5
U.S. Household Demographics 1950–2000
SOURCE: Author's analysis of census data provided by Ruggles et al. "Integrated Public Use Microdata Series: Version 3.0." (Minneapolis: Historical Census Projections, University of Minnesota, 2003.)

American family life has undergone a large transformation in just the past fifty years. Since 1950, American households have been less likely to follow an idyllic "Leave it to Beaver" family model. Figure 2.5 charts the makeup of American households from 1950 to 2000. Using a data-set drawn from the U.S. Census for the past five decades, the lines track changes in American family life. The downward slope of the lines associated with traditional families along with the upward slope of lines associated with nontraditional families suggest the traditional nuclear family has lost ground to alternative family arrangements. A close look at Figure 2.5 shows that households with married partners, households where children reside, and households composed of extended family members have decreased over time. In place of more stable and larger familial arrangements,

Americans are increasingly divorced, living as single parents, or living as single persons (delaying or forgoing marriage and childbearing). Though most households (59 million) are comprised of children biologically related to a parent, a significant number of householders have stepchildren (3.3 million) or adopted children (1.6 million).[29]

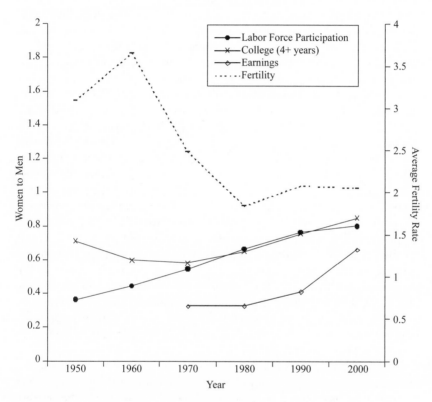

FIGURE 2-6

U.S. Employment, Education, Fertility 1950–2000

SOURCE: Data 1950–1990 from Susan B. Carter et al. *Historical Statistics of the United States: Earliest Times to the Present.* (Cambridge: Cambridge University Press, 2006) and for 2000 from *Statistical Abstract of the United States: 2006* (Washington, D.C.: U.S. Census Bureau, 2005) and 2000 annual income from U.S. Census Bureau, "Educational Attainment in the United States" (Table 8) http://www.census.gov/population/www/socdemo/education/ppl-157.html

NOTE: Labor force participation (percent of women in the labor force/percent of men in the labor force), college 4+ years (percent of women completing four or more years of college/percent of men completing four or more years), and earnings (mean income for women year-round employment/mean income for men year-round employment) are given as the percent of women to men and are read on the left axis. Fertility rate is the number of births women would have if they experienced birthrates occurring in a given year. Fertility rates are generally expressed as the births per 1,000 women, here they are given per individual woman and can be read on the right axis.

American households look different than they did just fifty years ago. Part and parcel of Americans' changing family practices, are Americans' changing work practices. The most striking aspect of work and family has been the influx of women—especially middle-class wives and mothers—into the paid labor force. Figure 2.6 illustrates that women's labor force participation, education, and earnings are converging with men's. Using women's achievement as a percent of men's achievement as the basis of comparison, the figure shows that for labor force participation, years of schooling, and income women are approaching "1" or equal rates with men. Women have substantially increased their labor force participation, their schooling, and their income. Indeed, white women especially have made inroads into white-collar employment.

Women have made advances in all three areas, but it is important to note with regard to labor force participation that *both* men's and women's participation have changed dramatically in the past five decades. By 2000, women made up nearly half of the labor force. This is due to two complementary processes. First, a growing number of women are working in the paid labor force. Though in 1950 only 30 percent of women were in the labor force, by 2000 that number doubled to 60 percent. Second, older men (fifty-five and above) have significantly decreased their participation. In 1950, 87 percent of men fifty-five to sixty-four, and 46 percent of men sixty-five and above participated in the labor force. But by 2000, only 67 percent of men aged fifty-five to sixty-four and 18 percent of men sixty-five and over did.[30] In similar fashion, married men are decreasing their labor force participation while married women are increasing theirs. Between 1970 and 2004, married men's labor participation rate dropped 9 points (from 86 percent to 77 percent). Women's labor participation rate in the same period grew 20 points (from 40.5 percent to 60.5 percent).[31]

Changing work practices has also had consequences for family demographics. One consequence of American women's increased labor force participation has been lower birth rates. Figure 2.6 shows the fertility rate—which can be read on the right axis—for women in the past fifty years.[32] Over the past five decades, the average woman has had fewer children, 3.7 in 1960 but just over two in 2000 when American women barely met the replacement rate of 2.1 children. After World War II, the "baby boom" ushered some of the highest birthrates in the twentieth century. The number of live births per one thousand women soared to 26.6 in 1946 but has declined ever since. By 2003, there were approximately 14.1 births per one thousand women.[33] Fewer births means that family size, by 2004, has dwindled. Forty-five percent of all families are two persons, 44 percent are three or four persons. Only 5 percent are six or more persons.[34]

These fewer children have very different life expectancies. In 1950, the life expectancy for men was 65.6 years, for women 71.1. In 2005, life expectancy was projected to be 74.9 for men and 80.7 for women.[35]

Beyond the concerns of family advocates who lament the decline in traditional family practices, the Census data point to problems that might arise in American public policy. Social practices may impact public policy with respect to policy gaps in three forms: gaps could form with respect to values, with respect to assumptions, or not all. First, if family is embedded in a wide range of public policies, as was demonstrated in this chapter, social practices that suggest family is no longer important or valuable to Americans could potentially be devastating. When family is firmly embedded as a core value in public policy, to remove or eliminate that value would mean dismantling the policy. Because a policy like immigration is heavily dependent on families to determine eligibility, removing family would mean essentially rewriting federal immigration laws. Do the changing social practices indicate that Americans do not value family?

To date even though American families have undergone significant transformations, the value of family has not diminished. Arland Thorton in a meta-analysis of public opinion about family issues concludes that "while most people are now more accepting of a diversity of behavior, they still value and desire marriage, parenthood, and family life for themselves."[36] Even as the composition of families is changing and single-person households are increasing, the vast majority of Americans live with at least one other family member.[37] Seventy-three percent of all American households consist of some combination of family members.

Rather than throw family out altogether, Americans have chosen to adapt the value to their changing lifestyles. Chris Labonte, of the Human Rights Campaign, illustrates perfectly how Americans can hold family as a value even when the assumptions about family in federal and most state laws do not recognize their own families when he said, "whenever I hear anti-gay legislation, I think they are not talking about *my* family."[38] Gay rights organizations, like the Human Rights Campaign, chose in the late 1990s and early 2000 not to fight against family—to take it out of federal law and policy. Rather they chose to fight to be included in the definition of family already there. In the past fifty years, specific conflicts over family issues like marriage, divorce, and parental responsibility have not translated into widespread dissatisfaction with family in the abstract, but have remained focused on particular aspects or assumptions about family.

Second, policy gaps may form with respect to more specific assumptions about family. After World War II when policymakers sat down to create

American public policy, they did so with specific assumptions about family as illustrated in the analysis of the *U.S. Code* above. These assumptions often have diverged from American social practice, as measured by U.S. Census data. With respect to the three policy areas I examine in this book, gaps have occurred in the family assumptions in all three. Social practices that deviate from the assumptions embedded in policy have created windows of opportunity for change.[39] Large-scale changes in American families, at least since World War II, have challenged many of the assumptions embedded in public policies at that time. Evaluating the politics behind gaps is an important part of this book.

Third, and finally, even though social practice changes, gaps may not occur in public policy. It does not follow that merely because (1) families have changed and (2) a particular public policy uses family there necessarily will be a disjuncture between policy and practice. Policy gaps form only when the social practice is at odds with values or assumptions in public policy. This means that Americans no longer value family, and thus policies built around family (such as immigration, which uses family as a criterion of eligibility, or tax, which relies on family households for determining income, tax rates, deductions, and credits) are no longer valid. Or Americans' particular social practice deviates from particular assumptions about family embedded in policy. For example, the fertility rates of women outside the United States is likely to have a greater impact on immigration policy—which relies on assumptions about how families enter the country—than in agriculture policy, which relies on images of a traditional family farm.

CONCLUSION

Far from being confined to "family-oriented" policies like welfare or family leave, family plays a role throughout public policy and the policy process. The extensive use of family words in the policy process supports the theoretical framework developed in this chapter. The inclusion of family into a host of nonfamily policies begs the question, what happens to public policies that rely on family when family practices in America change? Even though policymakers may find embedding family in public policy to be efficient or politically popular, the difficulty is in the details of policy. Family is not only an abstract concept. Instead, policymakers hold and incorporate into policy very real and concrete assumptions about what constitutes a family, what roles members of families may be expected to perform, and what families can expect from the state. For members of American families, particular roles are reinforced by the very foundation of public policies set up to serve them. As this chapter demonstrated, family practices have changed quite dramatically in post–World War II America. What has happened to American public policy as a result? Chapter 3 discusses how disjunctures between policy and practice open windows of opportunity for political contestation, though policy change does not always result.

CHAPTER THREE

Changing Social Practices, Changing Policy

Policy actors rely on family in the day-to-day business of policymaking to determine recipients, distribute benefits, and justify policy positions in scores of "nonfamily" policies. As Chapter 2 demonstrates, many public policies rest on a foundation that includes very specific notions about who is considered a family and what may be expected of members, like veterans' benefits that spell out the order of beneficiaries (widow, children, parents, siblings) and education tax credits that detail the acceptable familial relationships to distribute tax benefits (parental and grandparental). Even if these assumptions are an accurate depiction of family life at the time they are created, over time social practices in America have changed dramatically. The family policymakers had in mind during large expansions of state capacity and public policy from the Progressive Era through World War II may little resemble contemporary American family life. This observation leads to the second important question addressed in this book: *how do policies that incorporate family adapt to changing social practices?*

On the one hand, this question simply asks about how and why policies change. Political scientists are developing a growing body of literature that explains the role of actors and institutions in the policy process for inhibiting or facilitating change. They find that change results from powerful political actors, interest groups, and even ideas.[1] On the other hand, this question is more nuanced. It focuses attention on one aspect of policy change: how policy goals are achieved. In other words, how actors, interests, and ideas coalesce around the *means* to achieve policy goals rather than just the ends. Though Baumgartner and Jones demonstrate how media and public opinion surrounding nuclear power changed nuclear energy regulation and John Kingdon shows how fights over waterways changed the transportation policy agenda, here I am looking not at how family affects so-called family policy but how it affects those policies that seem to have little to do with family relations: immigration, tax, and agriculture.[2] This approach is akin to asking how Americans' taxpaying practices affect education or transportation policy carried out through tax expenditures.

The focus on how policies accomplish their goals means that this investigation differs from traditional theories of policy change in the emphasis I place on the proverbial black box of public policy—how policies accomplish their goals. For this project, how policies accomplish their goals is more than the rules, regulations, and procedures in law. Instead, I offer an original analysis of the internal structure of public policy made up of values and assumptions, which are the building blocks of public policy, and the core and periphery, the location within policy where values and assumptions fall. In particular, I examine the relationship between these structural elements of public policy and the public more generally. I pay special attention to what I call policy gaps, or the disjuncture between the values and assumptions in public policy and the broader social practices of Americans. These gaps offer the opportunity to enact change.

This analysis acts as a complement to existing theories of change, taking the developed literature on policy change and widening the lens with which one views it. Rather than seeing only the actors and institutions of the policy process or even expanding to the role of ideas and media, I situate the literature on the policy process between the structure of public policies on one side and to the broader practices of the American public on the other. The actors and institutions of the policy process remain the causal mechanism for change, but the shifting costs of maintaining the status quo or the mounting attractiveness of alternative options are the result of a growing policy gap. The focus of this chapter and the book as a whole is to understand the elements within public policy that facilitate its operation but also contain "within itself the seeds of change."[3]

THEORIES OF POLICY CHANGE

Theories of policy change start with the important political actors that make change happen. The Constitution vests all legislative powers in Congress, and much policy research is situated around this key body. Researchers disagree, however, on how far and wide the net should be cast beyond congressional policy actors. At the most parsimonious side of the spectrum are congressional theories of policy change that focus on institutional rules, such as Keith Krehbiel's emphasis on coalitions where policy change results when the status quo "lies outside the gridlock interval."[4] Other scholars examine organizations within Congress, such as committees or parties, as the enabling vehicles for change to occur.[5] Moving beyond Congress, but staying within the bounds of government, some researchers expand their focus to include the other branches—executive, judicial, and administrative—although the de facto comparison is almost always with the legislature.[6] Policy change may also extend beyond the bounds of elected officials. Change may be the product of resourceful entrepreneurs, inside and outside of formal governmental roles, who seize political opportunity to bring about their own policy goals.[7] Likewise, change may come from the efforts of extragovernmental actors, such as interest groups, who work tirelessly on behalf of a particular cause.[8]

The focus on actors and institutions in the policy process may lead one to believe that policy change works within a very specialized and closed system. Yet ideas in the social realm can and do influence public policy.[9] Research on policy stories and framing, which delves into how issues rise or fall on the national agenda, includes both elements of the policy process and social ideas that influence policy stability and change. Kingdon's analysis of agenda setting, Baumgartner and Jones's research on policy monopolies, and Deborah Stone's work on policy stories show that how people think (influenced by the media among other things) has lasting effects on policy.[10] Some scholars have even put ideas—rather than the policy process—at the center of their theories of change.[11]

Whether staying entirely within the policy process or venturing into the social realm to examine ideas, current theories of policy change give little heed to policy. By studying actors, institutions, and ideas scholars neglect the complexity of actual policies and treat the components of policy as if they were equally important. Although these observers of American politics may know that policies are as complex as the processes that create them, their theories of change often refer to policies in one-dimensional terms. Policies are categorized as part of broad policy areas such as housing, transportation, or the environment. These policies may be further broken down into Lowi's fourfold classification: distributive, regulatory, redistributive, or constituent.[12] However, the characterizations of policy as "redistributive housing" or "regulatory transportation" provide only a very broad description and leave the inner workings of the policy as a black box. It is often taken as a given that policy is a reflection (albeit imperfect) of its intended goals.[13]

Historical institutionalists, who have written about the "unintended consequences" of policy, vividly illustrate that what policies are intended to do and they actually do may be very different. Policy feedback, or "the ways in which previous policy choices influence present political processes," suggests that decisions early in the design of policy can have long-term policy consequences.[14] These (unintended) policy consequences can be very different from the goals that policymakers originally had in mind. In part, unintended consequences occur because policymakers do not adequately assess the needs of their constituents or there are insurmountable hurdles to implementation. Unintended consequences can also be attributed to structural elements of public policy. Although the goal of redistributive housing policy may be to provide housing for Americans, underlying this objective end are normative values and historically grounded assumptions. Research that does not dig beneath the surface to find what is actually embedded in policy—and not merely what is supposed to be there—misses an important answer to the question of *why* policies change. Though the goals of redistributive housing programs may remain laudable, outdated assumptions about the needs and expectations of potential recipients may make the programs expensive, ineffective, underutilized, and politically unpopular. Without breaking open the black box, the structure of policy is ignored in favor of process attributes. Thus, scholars are able to point to the pivotal member of Congress in any particular roll call vote, but they cannot equally point to a pivotal part of policy.[15] They can show the importance of interest groups but not necessarily to what those groups are responding.

Theories of policy change that do not unpack the structure of policy also do not differentiate between central tenets of the policy and more extraneous details. A cursory glance over any public policy shows that equality among the component parts of a policy is entirely fictional. Some parts are clearly more necessary for the continued operation of the policy than others. The distinction between central tenets and peripheral details helps explain *how* policies change. Though current theories of policy change tell us that the magnitude of change varies—it may be large and dramatic as the result of exogenous shocks such as transportation security after the September 11, 2001 attacks on the World Trade Center and the Pentagon, or small and steady as is the case with scores of adjustments to the tax code—the relationship between process and outcome is unclear.[16] That is, the same process can lead to very different policy outcomes: incremental policymaking may result in dramatic policy outcomes just as an exogenous shock may result in incremental adjustments to policy.[17] The answer to how policies change lies not only in the process, I argue, but in the structure of the policy. Whether change is large and significant or small and incremental depends upon what is being amended but also where in the policy it falls. That is, amendments to the core of policy, such as how immigration to the country is determined (by birth, regional quotas, work skills) will have a more dramatic impact than amendments to the periphery, such as the number of immigrants admitted in any particular year. When policymakers challenge core values or assumptions in public policy the change will be large and dramatic, but contesting peripheral assumptions will result in change that is both smaller and more common.

Scholars of American public policy may acknowledge that policies have a structure, but they rarely tie the structure to the policy process or theories of change. Theodore Lowi and Giandomenico Majone are exceptions. Lowi's oft-cited typology stems from his proposition that policy content is intimately tied to political processes while Majone briefly notes that certain "values, assumptions, methods, goals, and programs" are pivotal to the policy itself and ultimately give the policy stability while other values, assumptions, methods, goals, and programs are adaptable and easily replaced by new ones.[18] Like Lowi, this book starts with the understanding that what is in public policy is important for determining the politics surrounding it. And like Majone, this book builds off the idea that policies are composed of building blocks of values and assumptions that are essential (the core) and those that are more extraneous (the periphery). Developing an understanding of the structure of public policy will aid scholars in their thinking about why policies change and also how extensive policy change is likely to be.

Scholarly contributions to theories of policy change have done a great deal to explain the complexities of the policy process and necessary actors for policy change. The analysis presented in more detail in the next section does not replace these theories. In fact, it often draws extensively on the collected body of work these scholars have created in explaining how the policy process works. The aim of this book is not to challenge political science scholars on their models but to situate the policy process within the structure of policy on the one hand and social practice on the other. Ultimately, this approach offers a more nuanced understanding of change that takes into account actors, institutions, and ideas *as well as* the structural features of public policy around which they coalesce. Before policy entrepreneurs act, before reforms are passed by Congress—or implemented by the bureaucracy—policies in place or under consideration have a particular structure. Understanding that there is a structure to policy and that it plays a role in the life course of the policy helps to connect microscopic *policy structure* to actors and institutions in the *policy process* that push for policy change to broader macroscopic *social practices*.

POLICY STRUCTURE, POLICY CHANGE

What is policy structure and where can one find it? At a purely descriptive level, policies may be broken down into statutory elements or rules, procedures, and requirements. However, such basic description provides little ground for political analysis. Scholars have devised a number of more sophisticated ways to categorize and compare public policy in the hopes of better understanding how it works, such as classification based on the coerciveness of policy or the resources on which policymakers draw.[19] These schema have proved helpful for making sense of one aspect of policy design in particular—the vast array of potential instruments, from vouchers to tax expenditures, used to accomplish a particular goal. However, I take a somewhat different approach. In asking *how* policies accomplish their goals, this book looks beyond the particular policy instrument or tool employed and instead takes into account policy structure, the values and assumptions embedded throughout policy about Americans' social practices as well as what government should be doing, how to do it, and with what affect.

Policy structure, composed of both substance of public policy (values and assumptions) and location (core and periphery), is essential for understanding the broader context in which policy change occurs. I argue that even if values and assumptions are entirely accurate when enacted, they have the potential to become outdated. If social practices are fundamentally at odds with the values and assumptions embedded in policy, a policy gap opens up, providing a window of opportunity for policy change. Whether change is small and incremental or large and significant depends on whether the gap is in the core or the periphery.

Values and Assumptions

In a discipline like political science that emphasizes empirical research, studying exactly those parts of public policy that are most difficult to see presents unique challenges. The primary obstacle is convincing readers that policymakers' ideals and preconceptions are embedded in the structure of the policies they create. Like scholars who look at ideas as a motivating force in American politics, I argue throughout this book that values, or abstract principles, and assumptions, historically contingent biases, are key parts of public policies and can be found in a policy's rules, procedures, and requirements. Values are reflected in the kinds of ideals policy actors believe *ought* to be included, and assumptions are reflected in the preconceptions policy actors hold that *do* get included.

Values and assumptions both fall in the realm of ideas but they play distinct roles: values account for broad consensus over time whereas assumptions are routinely contested. This distinction ties together two different interpretations of ideas best illustrated by comparing the work of Samuel Huntington and Rogers Smith. Both Huntington and Smith place American ideals at the center of their analyses, but Huntington's American

Creed is timeless whereas Smith's multiple traditions vary throughout history.[20] Huntington's and Smith's different approaches to the role of ideas illustrate the difficult task one has of reconciling the timeless character of American ideals—like liberty—with an acknowledgment that what liberty means in practice changes. Political scientist Robert Lieberman sums up the dilemma:

> Certain ideological constructions, at the level of Huntington's Creed (or culture, or ideology, or tradition)—the ideals of liberty and equality for example—have a very long life span and can define enduring boundaries that a nation's politics will rarely, if ever, cross. But ideas at this level do not offer a concrete guide to understanding the more precise pathways a country's political development might take. Many particular programmatic beliefs might be consistent with these broad boundary conditions, and these ideas might change more quickly. Moreover, the interpretation and framing even of deeply rooted ideas might change over time, so that concepts such as "liberty" or "equality" might be invoked to support very different practices in different contexts by people who all the while believe themselves to be upholding a timeless and unchanging political tradition.[21]

In this book, I refer to those ideals that are fixed and enduring in the manner of Huntington's Creed as *values*. Values are widely shared beliefs in American culture that are above reproach. These values, drawn from American culture, may be traced to seventeenth-century liberal thought and take root in the founding documents of the United States, such as the Constitution, the Declaration of Independence, and the Federalist Papers.[22] Although the values determined by scholars never overlap completely, they almost always include American beliefs in liberty, equality, property rights, and religion.[23] Even critics of the liberal interpretation of American political culture do not question that Americans hold the values articulated above, merely that American values are not derived *only* from liberal ideology.[24]

Yet as Lieberman notes, the actual practice involved in determining what values mean, who is eligible for them, and how far the boundaries lie varies considerably over time. Values provide the stability in American politics by remaining mostly consensual while the concrete practice of them, what I refer to as *assumptions*, account for historical contingency and change over time. In other words, assumptions are the vehicles that translate abstract values into historical and political context. In the face of crises, such as the September 11 attacks, a commitment to liberty remains strong. Nevertheless, the interpretation and framing of what liberty entails, and more importantly the priority of liberty in relationship to other values such as security, may change. "Liberty" has a very different meaning for airline passengers before and after September 11, 2001. The very way that we understand a value like liberty—who receives its protections, how much they get, and the state's role for ensuring it—varies over time and across policy areas. Assumptions allow us to see that public policies reflect very different and contextual prejudices and preconceptions.

When policymakers create public policy, they are guided by values at the same time their preconceptions and biases shape the assumptions of what those values entail. Too often values and assumptions are seen merely as cultural ideas, having little or nothing to do with the creation and maintenance of public policy. In reality, policymakers cannot and do not separate themselves from personal and cultural values.[25] This is not a failing of the American system but a realistic perspective on how policymaking actually occurs. Values and assumptions inform the unspoken norms brought to the policymaking table, limiting the options under consideration and drawing support to preferred alternatives.[26] When policy actors sit down to create a new public policy, they do not draw from the entire universe of possibilities. Rather, they start with a limited range of possibilities, using shortcuts to make their job manageable.[27] They often rely on American values that are either consensual or perceived to be such.

Just as they do with assumptions, which are historically and contextually contingent, critics easily find American practice does not match up to American ideals. Rogers Smith, among others, points out that the rosy portrait of American values is marred by a strong tradition of inequality and intolerance toward large segments of the population.[28] Smith's careful examination details the serious contradictions that seem to plague American history. He characterizes American traditions—of equality and inequality for example—as coexistent, running parallel to one another throughout history. Smith focuses on traditions, actual practices, rather than the ideals.

The distinction I make when differentiating values from assumptions is slightly different than Smith's. As ideals American values are generally agreed upon, but it is the concrete understanding of what they entail that is often the source of political contestation. For example, Americans profess a deep commitment to equality even as it seems to be denied or limited for certain groups. Smith, for one, points out that even though Americans tout liberal principles, "for at least two-thirds of American history, the majority of the domestic adult population was . . . ineligible for full citizenship" due to race, nationality, or gender.[29] Rather than evaluating two competing traditions, I argue that values like equality can be perfectly compatible with what observers label great inequality because values are not lived in the abstract but in historical and contextual ways. In the case of suffrage, both African Americans and women had the right to vote, if propertied, in several states. Women were denied that right in the early nineteenth century as their interests were defined as family interests.[30] From a removed historical or cultural perspective it is easy to see the great inconsistencies between the ideal and practice of equality. The persistent inequalities in American society that Smith points out are often evidence of historical biases and presuppositions.

Assumptions, however, are not always problematic. At times they may result in unfair and unjust traditions, as Smith points out. At other times, assumptions do nothing more than allow policy to function. Whether an assumption is benign or problematic ultimately depends on two factors: how fair and accurate an assumption is and how enduring an assumption is over time. If policies are adopted with unrealistic assumptions that do not reflect the population or the policy constituency, problems arise almost immediately. Yet even fair and accurate assumptions may not be long lasting. Many policy problems that Americans are grappling with in the twenty-first century are a result of policymakers' outdated assumptions from decades earlier: postwar policymakers' inaccurate assumptions about married women's participation in the paid workforce created the so-called marriage tax penalty in national income tax;[31] Great Society policymakers' mistaken assumptions about how common medical conditions are treated (through hospitalization rather than prescription drugs) exacerbated the Medicare prescription drug crisis;[32] and New Deal policymakers' incorrect assumptions about the life span and work habits of the average American has the potential to bankrupt the Social Security system.[33] Policymakers make assumptions based upon the information and prejudices of the time. What may have been "common sense" at one point has the potential to undermine policy decades later.

An understanding of American politics and especially public policy that takes into account universal values and historically grounded assumptions creates space for understanding change. Clearly, American values have provided a great deal of continuity over United States' history, even as what those values mean in practice has been transformed dramatically. Historically grounded assumptions embedded in public policies that either do not match or become outdated so that they no longer match empirical practice will increasingly come under pressure for change. The size and scope of that change is determined by the location in policy in which these assumptions fall—either at the core or the periphery.

Core and Periphery

Public policies are made up of component parts that are not equally important to the continuity of policy, just as changes to the component parts are also not equally likely to occur—or to occur in the same fashion. At bottom, it matters whether policies are challenged at their foundation or in more adaptable details. Giandomenico Majone, in two short pages, lays out the distinction between the two parts of public policy, core and periphery. Building on his original distinction, I argue that the scope of change is related to the location in policy where it occurs.

At the most basic level, public policy is divided into a core, which contains central elements, and a periphery, which has the more mundane details. The relationship between the core and the periphery is best thought of visually, where the core is the center of public policy and is surrounded by the periphery. Instead of a bright line separating a tightly clustered core and a far-removed periphery, the further one moves from the core of the policy toward the periphery, the more mundane and flexible the policy becomes. It is the relative distance rather than an absolute divide that distinguishes the two.[34]

The core of public policy, as the name suggests, holds the central ideas and tenets of public policy. Jacob Hacker notes that the core elements of Social Security are "its contributory structure, its tight link between contributions and benefits, [and] its conservative financing."[35] These three elements are essential to how Social Security in America operates, and changing any one of the three, as President Bush proposed to do in 2005 by privatizing retirement accounts, would have radical consequences for the program. The core of policy is resistant to change and, hence, essential for continuity over time. Majone explains that the core is "only to be abandoned, if at all, under the greatest stress and at the risk of severe internal crisis."[36] Because the ideas of the core are central to the policy itself, the goals of the core inform all parts of the policy. A core change, then, is not only difficult to achieve but it has significant consequences.

Though the literature on the welfare state does not engage the concepts of core and periphery as I have set them out here, scholars' use of the exact or similar terms demonstrates the need to think more about the organization of public policy. Michael Brown, for example, explains the failure of the welfare state to reduce or diminish racial discrimination in the 1960s this way: "Great Society liberals did not challenge the core assumptions of the American welfare state, the middle-class devotion to stable work and its relation to contributor insurance."[37] If they had, Brown's statement leads the reader to conclude there would have been very different welfare policies. Policymakers in the 1960s chose to tinker with the welfare system in Brown's account rather than address the core assumptions that would make a difference.

The 1996 overhaul of Aid to Families with Dependent Children (AFDC) is particularly illustrative of what happens when core elements are challenged. The core of AFDC—the means-tested lifetime commitment to take care of poor families and direct financial aid for mothers to stay home with their children (and out of the paid workforce)—had been roundly criticized since the 1960s. But by the early 1990s, thin public support and pointed attacks called into question the effectiveness of governmental welfare provisions both to lift disadvantaged Americans out of poverty *and* to contribute to stable family lives. It is precisely the core elements of AFDC—work and family—that were challenged. Because the very core of the program was called into question, there can be little doubt that the 1996 reform would be anything other than large and sweeping. At that point in time there was no way to tinker with the system to make incremental changes when discontent was aimed at the very heart of the program.[38] Constituencies that a generation earlier never would have supported "ending welfare as we know it" nonetheless found themselves agreeing to dismantle the public support system and replace it with something very different.

Unlike the core, which holds the key elements of public policy and is essentially stable, the periphery encompasses the less essential values, assumptions, methods, goals, and programs. These more mundane decision rules and administrative directives are based on what is embedded in the core. That is, the periphery is not free floating or divorced from the core; instead, it is made up of activities that emanate from the embedded core values and assumptions. For example, the particular formulas the Social Security Administration (SSA) has developed to determine the amount of money that retirees will receive are located in the periphery, but they are based on core assumptions that link individual contributions to individual benefits. In short, the more money one puts into the system, the more one is eligible to receive upon retirement. In 2005, SSA calculations showed that low-wage earners received monthly benefits of $775, medium-wage earners received $1,277, and high earners received $1,939.[39] These formulas can be and are updated. Most notably, in 1971 Social Security benefits were indexed to inflation, taking increases out of the hands of Congress. Though this was a big change for partisan politics, it had relatively little impact on the policy because Social Security is still structured around the "contributory structure" and "tight link between contributions and benefits" that Jacob Hacker notes are the core of the program.

Change in the periphery is both more common and less dramatic than change in the core. According to Majone: "If the core provides continuity, the periphery . . . provides flexibility. The need to adapt the particular programs through which the policy operates to ever-changing economic, social, and political conditions keeps the periphery in constant flux."[40] Day-to-day politics surrounds making and altering peripheral elements of public policy. On any given day, policymakers vote on budgets, alter departments, and create new legislation to make up for perceived deficiencies in existing programs.

Understanding the distinction between the core and the periphery helps to explain why some changes threaten the continuity of policy while others may go relatively unnoticed. Even in the tax code, which is watched particularly closely by individual and corporate taxpayers alike, the vast majority of changes never grab public attention. Instead, marginal adjustments as small as a fraction of a percent dominate the landscape: "Applicable rates, bracket ranges, exemption levels, standard deductions, depreciation percentages, investment credits, depletion allowances—the list of changes that can be accomplished by simply altering a number is very long."[41] Over time, minor changes often take place in the periphery because such change does not threaten the structure of the policy itself. Change in the core, on the other hand is large and dramatic. When core values are challenged, such as by replacing the current income tax with a flat tax, the policy itself is fundamentally overhauled. Essentially, a new tax system is put into place.

In distinguishing between core and periphery, scholars who employ the ideas (if not the actual terms) use many different words to talk about what makes up these two parts of public policy. To illustrate, Jacob Hacker employs core "elements" in his discussion of Social Security while Michael Brown talks about core "assumptions" in the welfare state. Giandomenico Majone tells us that the core and periphery consist of "values, assumptions, methods, goals and programs."[42] In this book, I focus specifically on values and assumptions because these are the often hidden or subterranean structures on which public policies are built. Behind the rules, procedures, and requirements are the values and assumptions about American social life as well as what it is that government should be doing, how to do it, and with what effect. By shedding light on these often hidden parts of policy, one can see both the very real (and sometimes problematic) ways that policies seek to achieve their goals and the obstacles to reform.

Policy Gaps

Even if values and assumptions are a perfect picture of American society when policies are created, over time social practice may change in ways that deviate from them. In the words of Paul Pierson, "the world does not stand still once new institutional arrangements are selected."[43] If society changes in ways that diverge from policy, it creates a *policy gap* or the difference between the structure of policy and social practice.[44] An ever-widening gap destabilizes support for the policy and opens up "windows of opportunity" for policy entrepreneurs to exploit the gap and trigger sizeable restructuring.[45] Importantly, not all social change will create a policy gap and not all gaps will lead to policy change. Only social change that contradicts the values and assumptions in the structure of public policy will create a policy gap. For example, changing work practices of American women are more likely to create gaps in Social Security or taxation than agricultural subsidy programs. Further, as discussed in the next section, social change does not necessarily lead to policy change, even when there is a gap. Gaps are political *opportunities* to enact change and not guarantees that change will take place. Gaps are identifiable places in public policy where political contestation is likely to take place either because advocates want to close the gap so that public policies better meet the needs of potential recipients or because opponents want to exploit the gap for their own political purposes. Policy gaps are an important conceptual tool because they show that the impetus for change—which problems get defined, which solutions are floated, and whether the political conditions are ripe—can be found partially within policy. Policy actors sow the seeds for potential change into the structure of policies they create.

Policy gaps are an important source of policy contestation when they arise. However, gaps are not equally likely to form in the component parts of public policy. Indeed, gaps are least likely to form in core values, which are less common and more general, and most likely to form in peripheral assumptions, which are the most common and specific parts of public policy. Table 3.1 illustrates the relationship between policy gaps and values and assumptions in the core and periphery. Bringing together the concepts from this chapter, it shows the likelihood of gaps forming in

TABLE 3-1
Policy Structure and the Likelihood of Policy Gaps,
Social Security as an Example

		Substance	
		Values	Assumptions
Location	Core	Extremely rare. Values are consensual, core is stable.	Unlikely. Assumptions have limited flexibility in the core. Amendment occurs in total restructuring of the program.
		Work and Merit	*Contributory structure, link between contributions and benefits*
	Periphery	Somewhat Likely. Values are important but they are located in the periphery where their relative importance may change. Amendment results in minor changes to policy.	Very likely. Assumptions are flexible and numerous. Amendment results in minor (albeit important) changes to policy.
		Family	*Benefit formulas*

any component of public policy and the relative ease or difficulty in closing those gaps, using Social Security as an example (in italics).

Looking at each of the boxes, one can see when and where gaps are likely to occur. Starting at the top left, core values are extremely stable. As Robert Lieberman notes above, values "define enduring boundaries that a nation's politics will rarely, if ever, cross."[46] And in the core of a public policy, they shape the entire direction of policy. Thus, values in the core are both consensual and provide the foundation on which the rest of the policy is built. In the case of Social Security, the core values of the program are work and merit. If one were to replace those values with luck and chance the whole pension system as we know it would change dramatically. It would, in effect, become an entirely different program operating within a very different context. Core values rarely come under fire or change. They are the most stable element of public policy.

Core assumptions have greater flexibility—they are not as consensual as values—yet they are largely stable. Though assumptions are more particular and more likely to become outdated, because they are in the core, these assumptions are also a foundational component of policy. That is, core assumptions translate the broad values of policy into more specific principles around which policy is formed. Core assumptions operate between broad values on the one hand and more specific details in peripheral assumptions on the other. They make midlevel distinctions. Even if gaps occur in the core, they often remain because large change would be politically difficult to accomplish. That is, even when policymakers recognize gaps in core assumptions it takes a large coalition to make serious changes to established programs. Actors in a policy monopoly have an interest in maintaining the status quo.[47] In the case of Social Security, the core assumptions are its contributory structure and the link between contributions and benefits.

Moving out of the core and into the periphery, gaps are much more likely to occur. In the case of peripheral values, the values are still generally agreed upon but because they are in the periphery they are more likely to come into conflict with other values or be reprioritized. Core values are at the foundation of public policy, but peripheral values anchor the more mundane details. They can be added, removed, and reordered more easily than the core. Social Security added the peripheral value of family in 1939 when widows of wage-earners became eligible beneficiaries. Including widows, who did not participate in the workforce, did not remove the core value of work and merit. Instead, the value of family became an important addition in providing benefits in the periphery of the policy. Peripheral values do not form the foundation on which a great many other components of policy are built. They can be changed and reprioritized more easily than values in the core. In the four cases I examined (in three broad areas of policy), I found that family, as a value, operated in the core of policy. Thus, in the analysis presented in the following chapters I do not separately address other peripheral values.

Peripheral assumptions are flexible and numerous and a place where we should expect to see gaps form. Even with the best intentions, policymakers cannot possibly create policy that best suits everyone and especially everyone over time. Peripheral assumptions, which translate values and assumptions throughout policy into concrete and specific policy prescriptions, are bound to be contentious and gaps frequent. The benefits formula for Social Security recipients is a good example. Because the price of goods and the needs of beneficiaries change over time, gaps in the formula are likely to occur, and to occur frequently. Policymakers often change peripheral assumptions.

Table 3.1 shows when and where gaps are likely to occur. It is an important addition to theories of change that look at the actors, institutions, and ideas of the policy process. However, the mere existence of a gap does not mean that policy change will occur. Whether gaps will be contested and successfully closed depends on the policy process. Here I draw on models of policy change developed by political scientists.

POLICY STRUCTURE AND POLICY PROCESS

If, as Pierson says, the world does not stand still once new institutional arrangements are selected, when and how do institutions respond? Policy gaps suggest where contests over public policy are likely to occur, but the mere existence of a policy gap does not mean that actors will contest it or that change will follow. The actors and institutions of the policy process are vitally important for understanding under what conditions policy gaps are likely to remain open and when they are likely to close. Political scientists have done an admirable job in looking at this question. John Kingdon shows there are three important streams in the policy process to bring an item to the agenda: (1) problem recognition, (2) policy solutions, and (3) politics.[48] For Kingdon, the three streams operate relatively independent of one another and come together at critical junctures when policy entrepreneurs are able to couple them. Combining my analysis of policy structure in immigration, tax, and agriculture with Kingdon's three streams provides insight on how elements within policy play a role agenda setting.

First, in the problem stream Kingdon notes a number of ways in which problems are identified, such as important indicators, focusing events, and feedback.[49] For many traditional policy issues (such as health and transportation) this is likely the case. But when looking more closely at the structural means of achieving policy goals, I have found that feedback plays a very large role. Though it may be clear that data on rising health-care costs may push policymakers to address health care, it is not so clear that data on changing family demographics (as the Census puts out) will lead them to revisit "nonfamily" policies like immigration and tax. Likewise, focusing events that grab national attention are likely to paint the problem as one of "immigration" or "taxation" rather than understanding the role that family plays. In the three areas examined here, the problem stream is defined in large part by feedback. Problems are brought to the attention of members of Congress by citizens and residents who feel the squeeze between what is socially expected and what policy allows them to do. For single parents who wished to adopt children from abroad, the law's outdated assumptions about parental standing prevented them from doing so. Even though single parenting was on the rise and single individuals could adopt children *within* the United States, outdated immigration policy prohibited them from adopting abroad and led them to lobby Congress. Problems are also defined by opponents of particular policies who exploit growing gaps to propose reform. For immigration restrictionists, who wish to limit the number of individuals admitted to the United States, visas for adult brothers and sisters have been the main focus of attack. Because Americans are least likely to include adult brothers and sisters in their family life, they are the category that most often comes under fire. The gap between immigration preference and social practice offers opponents a toehold to define the problem in a way that will resonate more nearly with Americans.

Though family plays an important role in immigration, tax, and agriculture policy, it is not always obvious that family is explicitly associated with any of the three, and policy actors work to frame issues as "family problems." In all three areas, policy actors framed the issue as modifying government involvement to better meet the needs of American families. Regardless of one's position, in immigration, tax, and agriculture debates bettering or, at the very least, not harming American families was a key part of the problem policymakers had to address. In the case of single parents wishing to adopt abroad, the problem was defined as one of outdated federal policy unnecessarily preventing family unity. In tax policy, everyone agreed that the marriage tax penalty must be eliminated so as not to penalize American families; it was only a matter of how much relief and directed toward which income group. In the case of American agriculture policy, supporters painted agriculture subsidies as protecting the family farm, an important way of life regardless of their overall position on the bill.

Second, the policy community must have ready solutions. As Kingdon demonstrates, policy communities often have solutions ready and waiting for the right problem to attach to it. Certainly, defining immigration, tax, or agriculture policy as unnecessarily harming American families allows policymakers to propose their favored solution—expanding or restricting provisions in all three. Though Kingdon focuses on particular descriptive policy communities, such as "the health-care community" or the "transportation community," a focus on policy structure also looks at those individuals concerned with the means of accomplishing policy goals. In the three policy areas evaluated in depth in this book, Kingdon's policy communities certainly were in evidence. I observed a distinct immigration community, tax community, and agriculture community. However, in addition to these, there were communities actively involved in many different policy areas with an objective of defining and using family in particular ways. These "bridging communities," including the conservative Heritage Foundation and liberal Human Rights Campaign, are active in promoting policy means across policy areas. The Heritage Foundation, whose mission is "to formulate and promote conservative public policies" and the Human Rights Campaign, which works to "achieve gay, lesbian, bisexual and transgender equality," are interested in shaping the definition of family and the resources devoted to family in a variety of public policies, including immigration and tax.[50] They work with descriptive policy communities to achieve their goals.

Third, political conditions must be right: the national mood is ripe, organized interests advocate, and a new administration is installed. All three of these factors play a role in bringing issues to the agenda for political contestation. For many of the cases I examined here, Republican takeover of the House in the mid-1990s and of the executive branch in 2000 allowed many issues that had been stymied or vetoed earlier to get back on the agenda. Though immigration visas for adult brothers and sisters had been debated for years, in 1996 with the release of the Jordan Commission's Report, support from the White House, and strong public opinion, immigration reform made it to the national spotlight. Likewise, with a Republican president in the White House in 2000, Congress had tremendous support for reducing taxes, especially when it came to the so-called marriage tax penalty. Further, American agriculture policy came up for major revision with support from fiscal conservatives in Congress and members from farm districts. Strong markets made new options more attractive than they had ever been.

According to Kingdon, policy actors who are able to couple the streams can bring issues to the agenda. Yet, three additional factors come into play when assessing their ability to enact policy change. First, I found that coalition building was a key factor for success or failure. In particular, when coalitions were formed with members concerned about the ends of policy (immigration quotas) combined with those concerned about the means (family), they were very successful. Indeed, such coalitions resulted in strange bedfellows—often liberal ends coupled with conservative means. For example, in the fight over immigration visas for adult brothers and sisters, immigration advocates such as the Mexican American Legal Defense and Education Fund combined with pro-family advocates, notably Ralph Reed of the Christian Coalition, to defeat any attempt to limit these visas. Likewise, in the case of ridding the Earned Income Tax Credit of its marriage penalties, supporters included Democrats and liberal interest groups (i.e., the Center on Budget and Policy Priorities) who wanted to help *needy* families as well as Republicans and socially conservative groups (i.e., the Heritage Foundation) who wanted to aid needy *families*. These actors brought attention to their issues and also were successful in stopping or promoting policy amendments.

Second, as political scientists have discussed at length, entrenched interests are better able to safeguard their territory than challengers who wish to take it away.[51] Thus, it is easier to create a new program or expand an existing one than it is to cut back. In the two areas where opponents wished to retrench—immigration visas for adult siblings and agriculture subsidies—long-term policy change was unsuccessful. In those cases where benefits were expanded—allowing single people to adopt abroad and eliminating the marriage tax penalty—long-term policy change succeeded.

Third, depending on where policy gaps occur change becomes more or less difficult. Closing policy gaps in core assumptions would result in a radical overhaul of the system, as President George Bush attempted in 2005 with Social Security. Such a massive change is not impossible; indeed it does occur (as in the case of the 1996 welfare reform) but it is difficult to accomplish and often long in coming. Closing gaps in peripheral assumptions, on the other hand, results in changes that are relatively minor to the functioning of policy, such as tying formula for Social Security benefits to inflation. Because the legislative process requires (at a minimum) majority coalitions and members of Congress are blame avoiders as much as credit claimers, it is much easier to pass small changes than it is to raise the stakes and enact major overhauls, which disrupt the status quo and the organized interests that support it.[52] Changes in the periphery may be important and hotly contested, but they generally are also smaller and have smaller long-term impact. The case studies here reinforce how powerful the status quo is for entrenched interests and the difficulty enacting change in the core elements of policy.

Overall, when policymakers use family in particular in problem definition, in the solutions they propose, and as a politically important way to
build coalitions, it has a strong influence on politics. Supporters and opponents are able to expand the scope of conflict to make arguments about
the harmful effects of state action not only on a particular constituency but
on society more generally.[53] Single parents who wished to adopt children
abroad and married couples negatively affected by the tax code were able
to change legislation and make it more amenable to their needs. They faced
little opposition in part because they were not taking concentrated benefits away from an established constituency, and in part the change they
sought was relatively minor. Yet because they were talking about *family*,
the change they were asking for seemed "natural" and "normal," a better
way to meet the needs of Americans. Beyond political justifications, they
had demographic practices on their side. They pointed to the ways that
everyday families in America work and made it politically very difficult
to oppose them. On the other side, opponents of immigration visas for
adult brothers and sisters and agriculture subsidies had to face not only
entrenched interests who benefited from the status quo, but a strong argument about family practices in America. In these two cases where policy
change failed to occur, the successful actors portrayed the policy change
as having costs to be borne not by the concentrated beneficiaries but by
American society as a whole. Eliminating visas for adult brothers and
sisters was painted as harming American family life more generally. And
for agriculture subsidies, proponents argued that eliminating subsidies
would rid America of an important cultural institution (the family farm)
and a connection to a shared past.

The chapters that follow address the question of family and policy
change by investigating immigration, tax, and agriculture—three "nonfamily" policy areas. Each chapter builds on the theoretical framework
discussed in Chapter 2 by focusing on a means of employing family in the
policy process along with one "nonfamily" policy area. Chapter 4 examines family as a criterion of eligibility in immigration policy; Chapter 5
examines family as an administrator in tax policy; and Chapter 6 examines
family as a normative ideal in agriculture policy.

CHAPTER FOUR

Family Criteria in Immigration Policy

Urging Congress to enact one of the most sweeping reforms in the history of immigration policy, President John F. Kennedy wrote to the president of the Senate and speaker of the House in 1963 asking them to remove barriers to immigration eligibility based upon race. Kennedy disliked the race-based admissions of the national origins quotas because "such a system . . . discriminates among applicants for admission into the United States on the basis of accident of birth."[1] Particularly striking in Kennedy's remark is the association of race or ethnicity with an "accident of birth"—a category born into, not chosen—but not family. Even as he stressed the American ideal of individual merit, his reforms ultimately increased the reliance on birth and family as a criterion of eligibility in immigration policy.

Scholars have demonstrated the importance of immigration and natality for the state construction of citizenship.[2] This chapter builds on these findings, examining the increasing importance of family as a criterion of eligibility in immigration policy and its consequences. Family has been a part of immigration policy since 1924 when Congress first passed permanent numerical restrictions on immigration.[3] In the wake of limited admissions, family became the primary criterion by which foreign nationals qualify to immigrate to the United States. Family connection now accounts for the vast majority of all legal immigration to the United States, making values and assumptions about family embedded in America's immigration laws increasingly important. However, gaps between what policymakers expected families to do and the way they now actually behave have given actors the opportunity to amend immigration policy. In the case of immigration, populations who sought to close the gaps in assumptions about single-parent adoptions have been successful. Those actors who have advocated closing gaps in assumptions about the proximity of extended family relations have faced tough obstacles without much success.

The first part of this chapter outlines the nuts and bolts of immigration policy, both what it entails and how it operates. The second part looks in-depth at the details of policy, examining assumptions in both the core and the periphery. Using census data as a measure of demographic change, I show when and where policy gaps should arise. In the third and final part, I bring both family and policy structure together with cases studies of single-parent adoption and extended family preference to show how the structure of policy influences the politics surrounding immigration criteria, defining problems and creating coalitions.

IMMIGRATION NUTS AND BOLTS

Immigration policy is an umbrella concept for the entry and exit of foreign nationals. The formal legal definition of "immigration laws" set out in the *U.S. Code* includes the Immigration and Nationality Act "and all laws, conventions, and treaties of the United States relating to the immigration, exclusion, deportation, expulsion, or removal of aliens."[4] In practice, immigration policy, broadly defined, is composed of five more specific functions: *temporary admissions*, or the admission of foreign nationals for a specific purpose and a finite amount of time (such as tourists, business travelers, diplomats); *legal immigration*, the process by which aliens are selected for admission or gain status to become legal permanent residents; *naturalization*, the process of granting U.S. citizenship; *refuge/asylum*, granting refuge to foreign nationals outside the United States or asylum to aliens inside the United States who, because of well-founded fears of persecution, are unable or unwilling to return to their home country; and *enforcement*, apprehending and deporting aliens entering or residing illegally in the United States.[5]

Though defining immigration policy broadly to encompass many functions and federal administrators reflects the actual complexity of immigration policy,[6] for the purposes of this chapter I use a more specific functional definition. Immigration is the process by which aliens are selected for admission or adjustment of status to legal permanent residents of the United States. This more narrow meaning gets to the heart—who is admitted, how, and why—of immigration policy. In particular, I focus on legal immigration since 1952 when Congress passed the Immigration and Nationality Act (INA), which substantially rewrote previous immigration laws in one comprehensive act. Beyond laying out specific formulas and criteria for admission, the INA tells a story about the concerns and priorities facing legislators, both those they dealt with directly and those they dealt with through omission. The INA, along with its subsequent amendments, is a reflection of particular American values, carried forward from earlier immigration legislation, and specific assumptions of modern politicians trying to come up with a system that would allow for immigration of the number and kind of persons who could become Americans.

Immigration law since the Alien and Sedition Acts of 1795 had limited the characteristics and qualities desired, the *kind* of alien allowed to immigrate. But it was not until the 1924 Immigration Act that legislators enacted a permanent policy restricting the *number* of immigrants as well. The 1924 Act limited immigration by setting criteria for admission that favored family (to be humane) and agricultural workers (to meet the needs of the farm community). The twin restrictions of number and kind made the criteria for eligibility for admitting foreigners a central part of immigration policy.

In designing the INA of 1952, policymakers kept the distinction of the 1924 Immigration Act between unrestricted immigrants (not subject to numerical limitations) and restricted immigrants (those subject to numerical limitations). Unrestricted immigrants included natives of the Western Hemisphere, immediate family members of U.S. citizens, and lawful residents returning to the United States. Everyone else wishing to immigrate to the United States was subject to the priorities of American immigration law. For these numerically restricted immigrants, immigration preferences were set out in the second of four titles of the INA. Within the bounds of controversial numerical country quotas, which effectively promoted immigration from Northern and Western Europe at the same time that they depressed immigration from Asia, Africa, and Eastern Europe,[7] the preference system determined who was granted priority to immigrate. As enacted, there were four preferences based entirely on job skills and family relationship.

The INA of 1952, as amended, is the current immigration law. It retains many of the structural features contained in the original 1952 version, such as the distinction between unrestricted and restricted immigrants and the division of scarce restricted visas by preference categories. Over time, both unrestricted and restricted immigration have been continually altered, adjusting preference categories and reallocating visas. For a blunt comparison of immigration policy as it was initially passed, and its current status, Table 4.1 lists the number of visas allocated and granted for immigration in fiscal year 1954, the first year that the INA was fully in effect, and 2005, the most recent record of immigration.[8] Although the law has changed in many ways, a few important differences can be discerned from Table 4.1.

First, the length of the right-hand column compared to the left shows there has been a proliferation of visa types and subtypes. By 2005, rather

TABLE 4-1

Categories of Immigration and Number of Immigrants Admitted in 1954 and 2005

1954 Immigration	Granted	2005 Immigration	Granted
Total Immigration	208,177	Total Immigration	1,122,373
Unrestricted Immigration	113,258	Unrestricted Immigration	464,301
Natives of Western Hemisphere, their spouse and children	80,526	Immediate Relatives of U.S. citizens	436,231
Immediate Relatives of U.S. citizens	30,689	Children Born Abroad to Alien Residents	571
Former U.S. Citizens	427	Nicaraguan and Central American Relief Act (NACARA) Section 202—Nicaraguan and Cuban Nationals	1,155
Ministers of Religious Denomination, their spouse and children	385	NACARA Section 203—Salvadoran, Guatemalan, and Former Soviet Bloc nationals	15,597
Employees of U.S. Government abroad, their spouse and children	4	Haitian Refugee Immigration Fairness Act (HRIFA)	2,820
Other Non-quota Immigrants	1227	Parolees, Soviet and Indochinese	7,710
		Other	217

	Granted (Allocated)		Granted (Allocated)
Restricted Immigration	88,016	**Restricted Immigration**	515,110
First Preference: Selected immigrants of special skill or ability and their spouses and children	2,456 (50% of quota for each quota area)	**Family-Sponsored**	212,970 (226,000)
		First Preference: Unmarried sons/daughters of U.S. Citizens	24,729 (23,400)
Second Preference: Parents of U.S. Citizens	2,783 (30% of quota)	Second Preference: Spouses and children (minor or unmarried adult) of resident aliens	100,139 (114,200)
Third Preference : Spouses and children of resident aliens	6,004 (20% of quota)	Third Preference: Married sons/daughters—and their spouses and children—of U.S. citizens	22,953 (23,400)

TABLE 4-1 (continued)

1954 Immigration		2005 Immigration	
Fourth Preference: Un-used visas by first three preferences granted to brothers, sisters, sons or daughters of U.S. citizens	1,930	Fourth Preference: Broth-ers and sisters—and their spouses and children—of U.S. citizens	65,149 (65,000)
Nonpreference Quota: All other qualified immigrants subject to numerical restriction	74,843	Employment-Based	246,877 (148,449)
		First Preference: foreign nationals with extraor-dinary ability and their spouses and children	64,731 (42,456)
		Second Preference: Professionals holding ad-vanced degrees and their spouses and children	42,597 (42,456)
		Third Preference: Skilled/ unskilled workers, professionals and their spouses and children	129,070 (42,456)
		Fourth Preference: Spe-cial immigrants and their spouses and children	10,133 (10,543)
		Fifth Preference: Employment creation, along with spouses and children	346 (10,540)
		Diversity (with spouses and children)	46,234 (50,000)
		Other	9,029
	Granted		Granted
Refugees/Asylees (w/spouse & child.)	6,903	Refugees/Asylees (w/spouse and child)	142,962

SOURCE: Author's analysis of data from: "Annual Report of the Immigration and Naturalization Service." (Washington, D.C.: United States Department of Justice, Immigration and Naturalization Service, 1952); "Yearbook of Immigration Statistics: 2005," (Washington, D.C.: Department of Homeland Security, 2006)

than four simple preferences, there are three general categories—fam-ily, employment, and diversity. Family and employment visas are further broken down into more specific preference categories. Diversity visas, which make up only a small percent of total immigration, are granted to individuals from countries adversely affected by changes to immigration law since 1965, mainly Europeans. Unlike the original 1952 legislation, which allotted 50 percent of restricted immigration for employees with job skills and their families, current law allocates more to family preferences (226,000) over employment (148,449) and diversity (46,234).

Second, between the time the Act was first passed and 2005, flexibility in immigration policy has been significantly curtailed. With the elimination of unrestricted immigration by Western Hemisphere nationals (39 percent of all immigration in 1954) and restricted nonpreference immigrants (36 percent of all immigration in 1954) the flexibility of "first come, first served" immigration has been replaced by strict family criteria. In 1954, immediate family members and family preference visas accounted for only 20 percent of all immigrants, but by 2005 these two categories alone climbed to 58 percent.

Ultimately, even though family has been a priority for admission as long as there has been a need to prioritize who may immigrate, the relative importance of family connection has not remained constant. Though family has been a part of immigration law since 1924, over time, as discrimination on the basis of race or ethnicity (the grounds of the national origins system) became unacceptable and untenable, lawmakers needed another criterion to determine eligibility for immigration and turned to family connection.

After years of struggle and constant requests by successive presidents of the United States, in 1965 Congress finally eliminated the national origins preferences that assigned individual country quotas heavily favoring Northern and Western Europe at the expense of Asia, Africa, and Eastern Europe. However when legislators eliminated racial criteria, they removed barriers that had artificially depressed both the number and kind of immigrants allowed to enter the country for decades. These policymakers inadvertently opened the floodgates for new immigrants, changing the face of immigration and putting additional strain on the system that would fully manifest decades later. As the demand for immigration visas has grown, immigration policy has sacrificed its flexibility, granting visas on a first come, first served basis, for tighter and more structured immigration categories and preferences. Core assumptions about "American identity" in immigration policy shifted from a racial/ethnic identity to one based on shared values of democracy and family. After World War II, American immigration policy embraced democracy, opening the door to refugees and asylum seekers through regular admittance as well as special legislation designed to aid persons displaced from politically unpopular states; for example, Congress granted immigration admission for certain former Cubans and Soviet bloc émigrés (see Table 4.1). But immigration policy also turned to the shared value of family. With the end of national origins a racialized American identity faded from the forefront of immigration admissions policy, and family connection took its place.

Visually, the change in immigration priorities over time is quite stunning. Figure 4.1 charts the number of admissions attributable to the five criteria from 1945 to 2005.[9] It demonstrates that values underlying policy shift in importance over time. Particularly striking in Figure 4.1, is the pivotal change that took place in 1968, when the 1965 amendments to the

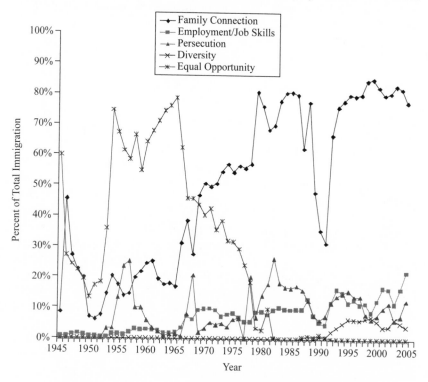

FIGURE 4-I
Immigration by Criteria 1945–2005

SOURCE: Author's analysis of data drawn from: years 1945–1986 "Annual Report," (Washington, D.C.: Immigration and Naturalization Service), for years 1987–2001 "Statistical Yearbook of the Immigration and Naturalization Service," (Washington, D.C.: U.S. Department of Justice, Immigration and Naturalization Service), and for 2002–2005 "Yearbook of Immigration Statistics," (Washington, D.C.: Department of Homeland Security, Office of Immigration Statistics).

NOTE: Category totals are summed by criteria and add to more than 100% because multiple criteria account for a single admission. Data prior to 1953 do not differentiate between quota immigrants—those that are family versus those that are admitted for job skills. Likewise, refugees and asylees are missing from these early data. Thus, all three categories are seriously under-reported. Sufficiently detailed data are available after 1953 to make reliable comparisons across years. Family connection includes both the explicit use of family visas (such as unrestricted immigration for immediate family members and restricted immigration by family preference category) as well as the implicit family connection (family members of an immigrant eligible for employment, diversity, and refugee admissions).

INA went fully into effect. Though the amendments are usually considered important for what they removed (race), the figure demonstrates that they should also be considered important for what they included in their wake (family).[10] Even though employment, persecution, and diversity visas have fluctuated over time, these categories have peaked at no more than 30 percent of annual immigration. Family connection, on the other hand, has increased markedly over time, and it has expanded at the expense of the unstructured category. More than any other criterion, family connection has eroded the unstructured, or "first come, first served," category and become the primary determinant of eligibility.

FAMILY, IMMIGRATION, AND POLICY GAPS

The 1965 amendments to the INA, which replaced the race-based national origins quotas with more "neutral" criteria, bolstered the importance of family. In part, family was used because it was judged an effective criterion, but in part it was used because it was politically painless. Family faced no organized opposition, unlike employment criteria that encountered stiff resistance from labor unions.[11] On average, 65 percent of all annual immigration since the amendments went into effect in 1968 is due explicitly or implicitly to family connection.[12] Yet at the same time that family, as a criterion of eligibility, has become more important in immigration policy, the social practices of Americans have changed substantially since the 1952 INA was originally enacted. Though Americans continue to hold family life as very important value, dramatic legal, social, and demographic shifts in the 1960s and 1970s left Americans with more options and more freedom to define their individual family life.[13]

Have changing social practices affected immigration policy? To answer this question, one needs to look carefully at the structure of the policy. In other words, how immigration policy uses family to accomplish its goals and how nearly this use mirrors family practices in American society more generally. Because family as an abstract core value is relatively uncontroversial, Americans do not challenge the place of family in immigration policy. Indeed, using family appears a natural way to determine preferences, which is both compassionate and politically popular. As President Kennedy so clearly illustrates at the beginning of this chapter, family criteria are equated with the absence of illiberal traditions. However, specific assumptions about what constitutes a family and what roles family members are expected to play are subject to greater debate. It is in these assumptions where gaps are likely to form. In the subsections that follow, I evaluate core and peripheral assumptions of immigration policy. For each type of assumption, I discuss the role family plays in the policy, the corresponding family practices, and the likelihood of policy gaps arising. I find that social practices in immigration policy, so far, have diverged from specific structural assumptions in the periphery but not the core.

Core Values

Core values form a broad frame that sets the scope of problem definition. These values are important because they form the foundation for any given policy. When a policy's main purpose is selection, as with immigration policy since 1924, the criteria for selection are indicators of important underlying values. That is, the criteria of eligibility provide a means to evaluate the values in immigration policy over time. The core values in immigration policy include national needs, humanitarian assistance, American identity, equal opportunity as well as a strong commitment to family unity, or the principle that families should not be artificially separated. Though all of the core values play an important role, here I focus on family, which defines the basic unit eligible for immigration underlying all immigration categories.

Immigration policy does not operate in a vacuum, and family is certainly not the only value that shapes U.S. immigration. Yet, even as American intervention around the globe pushed policymakers to alter the relative number of visas at any given point in time, the basic structure that privileged families in all types of visas remained remarkably stable. American policymakers responded to the massive dislocations of World War II with the Displaced Persons Act (1948) and to the needs of returning American soldiers with the War Brides Act (1945) and the Fiancées Act (1946), all of which sought to provide relief not only to particular target populations—refugees and soldiers—but also made provisions for their immediate family. Not surprisingly, cold war politics also significantly altered immigration practices. Congress passed measures such as the Refugee Relief Act of 1953 that gave visas to refugees from communist countries, aid to Hungarian escapees in 1956, and to Cuban refugees in the early 1960s. American foreign policy has and continues to shape American immigration. In 2005, in addition to the standard allotments for refugees, special legislation dealt with the plight of immigrants from Nicaragua, Cuba, El Salvador, Guatamala, the former Soviet bloc (Nicaraguan and Central American Relief Act, PL 105-100), and Haiti (Haitian Refugee Immigration Fairness Act, PL 105-277) as well as parolees from Poland and Hungary. Immigration policy responded to foreign policy by increasing the number and adjusting the countries from which immigrants would be selected, but it did so within the traditional structures—which privileged family—as a key determinant for eligibility. The importance of family as a criterion of selection is evidenced in its role in nearly every type of visa: employment, diversity, and refugee.

To show the importance of family as a core value, Table 4.2 lays out the criteria and underlying values in American immigration policy from 1924 to 2001. The second column lists the four main selection criteria that legislators explicitly identify: family connection, job skills/employment, legitimate fear of persecution, and quota laws/diversity preferences. These four selection criteria can be assigned to four values listed in the first column: family, national needs, humanitarian assistance, and American identity.[14] In addition to those criteria, which legislators specifically sought to manipulate over time, I have added a criterion termed "first come, first served" and a value, "equal opportunity," that accounts for immigration that legislators dealt with through omission. In other words, these are admissions for everyone else who does not qualify for the specified formal preferences. As Table 4.2 shows, though there are many values on which immigration is built, family is significant.

Looking at the most recent immigration admissions from fiscal year 2005 illustrates just how important the value of family is to immigration policy. In 2005 family accounted for over 58 percent of all immigrants. In comparison, employment-based and refugee admissions, the next two largest categories, totaled only 33 percent combined. Yet, because these numbers consider only the category or type of visa granted and not to whom and why they are given, they actually minimize the number of admissions attributable to family connection.

Above and beyond the specific "family categories," family unity is a value that is reinforced throughout almost every aspect of immigration policy, including "nonfamily" admissions like employment visas. For almost every category, immigration law grants admission to qualified individuals as well as their spouses and children.[15] In other words, when an individual qualifies for a visa through family connection, employment skills, or well-found fear of persecution, his or her immediate family qualifies for the same preference visa. To illustrate, employment-based visas, the largest "nonfamily" category in 2005, are given not only to the particular individual, but to his or her accompanying spouse and child. In 2005, ironically, professionals, skilled employees, and unskilled workers made up the *minority* of employment-based admissions. More than half of the nearly 246,877 employment visas were given to the spouses and children of qualified employees immigrating to the United States.[16]

The prevalence of family as a criterion of eligibility for both "family visas" and visas that do not have a specific family connection, like employment or asylum, demonstrates the very important way that family is embedded as a core value in immigration policy. Yet, it also is cause for some concern. When policymakers embed family in public policies they

TABLE 4-2
Core Values and Selection Criteria in Immigration Policy

Core Value	Selection Criteria	Unrestricted Immigration	Restricted Immigration
Family	Family Connection	1924: Immediate family of U.S. citizen residing in the United States. 1952: Immediate family (spouses and children) of U.S. citizens 1965: Immediate family now includes parents of adult citizens	1924: Unmarried child, father, mother, husband or wife of U.S. citizen 1952: Preferences for parents and extended family of citizens, immediate family of lawful permanent residents
National Needs	Job Skills, Employment		1924: Skill in Agriculture 1952: Skills needed determined by Attorney General 1965: Preference skills defined in law 1990: Increased number and kind of employment admissions
Humanitarian Assistance	Legitimate fear of persecution from ideologically opposed countries		1948, 1950: Displaced persons admitted 1965: Conditional entries for persecution 1980: First systematic refugee admissions. Non-preference status for refugees ceiling set by president
American Identity	Quota laws Diversity preferences		1924 Quota Laws restrict immigration to 1/6 of 1% of the number of inhabitants living in the United States in 1920. 1965: Quota laws abolished 1990: Diversity preferences added
Equal Opportunity	First come, first served	1924: Western Hemisphere exempt 1965: First limitations placed on W. Hemisphere	1952: Non-preference immigrants subject to quotas but not preferences 1976: Preference system applied to W. Hemisphere 1978: Ceilings combined and difference eliminated.

rely not on abstract ideals or freedom of self definition, rather they use very specific structural assumptions to determine who may enter the country. Even though the value of family may be relatively uncontroversial, more specific assumptions about what constitutes a family and which particular individuals qualify as "mother" or "child" have been more difficult to agree upon.

Core Assumptions

A general commitment to family necessarily includes more specific assumptions as to what constitutes a family and what may be expected of one. If values are the foundations, assumptions are the framework that structures public policy. Core assumptions take an intangible commitment to family and transform it into general rules of thumb as to what constitutes family and what these families need. Core assumptions, then, operate between abstract and general values on the one hand and detailed and specific peripheral assumptions on the other hand. They become the broad basis for further specific rules and regulations, and they set up the categories and the way of conceptualizing family that will be used to structure the policy. Core assumptions in immigration policy take "family" and break it down into two broad types—nuclear and extended.

To find the core assumptions in immigration policy, I listed individual family members and what privileges each qualifies for since the 1965 amendments. Table 4.3 shows core assumptions in which *individuals* are inherent parts of family *units*, and at each and every stage nuclear families are most privileged. Alternative approaches to categorization—such as by gender, age, or blood relationships—do not result in meaningful groupings. For example, gender does not act as a consequential category in determining eligibility at the level of core assumptions. Looking at the criteria, the specified family relations ("spouse," "parents," "adult children," and "adult siblings") at this level are all gender neutral. The law does not explicitly favor women's families over men's or female relatives over male relatives. The same holds true with age or blood relations. The law does, however, explicitly prioritize nuclear families. Table 4.3 illustrates the benefits for parents and their children. Whether a U.S. citizen or a foreign national, the most generous immigration categories are for spouses and their minor children. As one moves away from a nuclear family model, the categories become less generous and, in many cases, prohibitive. The House Report on the 1965 amendments to the INA summed up the thinking behind admissions categories as, "The closer the family relation, the higher the preference."[17] Immigration policy makes assumptions about the emotional proximity and dependency of close relations.

TABLE 4-3
Eligibility of Individual Family Members Since 1965

	U.S. Citizen Principal				Foreign National Principal			
	Unrestricted	Restricted Equal Classification	Restricted Unequal Classification	No Priority or Not Eligible	Unrestricted	Restricted Equal Classification	Restricted Unequal Classification	No Priority or Not Eligible
Spouse	X					X		
Minor Child	X					X		
Adult Parents	X							X
Adult Son or Daughter (unmarried)			X				X	
Adult Son or Daughter (married)			X					X
Adult Siblings			X					X
Grandparents				X				X
Aunts/Uncles				X				X
Cousins				X				X

NOTE: Restricted Equal Classification means the family member was granted the same priority and preference as the principal. Restricted Unequal Classification means the family member was granted a different priority and preference than the principal.

The privileges accorded to nuclear families were further strengthened by the 1965 amendments to the INA. Under the amendments, as the total number of immigrants increased, Congress took a more expansive view of family. Congress redefined the unrestricted category to incorporate parents of adult U.S. citizens, while family preference categories expanded the reach of family connection. Formerly fourth preference family members (those who received whatever was unused by the other three) were given distinct status with their own preference categories. These changes in the law reinforced core assumptions about the nature of family already embedded in immigration policy: both treatment of individuals as part of family units and a categorical difference between nuclear and extended families.[18]

Though the amendments reinforced the value of family in immigration law, they were put in place in the midst of changing family norms. At the same time that lawmakers were buttressing the importance of nuclear family in immigration policy, traditional nuclear families in America were starting to decline. Indeed, the 1960s marked the beginning of a steady drop in traditional married households and households with children. If the American nuclear family lost salience there could be potentially far-reaching implications for an immigration policy predicated on the distinction between nuclear and extended family. Has the declining number of nuclear families created a policy gap in the core assumptions in immigration policy?

Declining numbers of nuclear family households do not necessarily lead to a policy gap or the difference between social practice and the assumptions embedded in public policy. The social practice must be at odds with core assumptions embedded in immigration policy. As I have shown in this chapter, a core assumption in immigration policy is the differentiation and privileging of nuclear over extended family relations. For a policy gap to form, social practice in the United States would need to challenge these core assumptions. That is, even though nuclear families had started to decline in the 1960s, an extended family model would need to stay steady or increase to show that American practices are at odds with the assumptions in this particular policy.

One way to measure American's behavior is to look at household composition. Census data that measure household composition provide an important means to evaluate Americans' behavior and to test whether the distinction between nuclear and extended family members holds. If a gap has formed, nuclear families would not take priority in social practice. American households would be equally or even more likely to consist of extended rather than nuclear family relations. Census data, however, show that this is not the case. Declines in nuclear family households have been met with declines in extended family households as well.

Figure 4.2 shows the percent of nuclear (defined as both married and single parents along with their children) and extended family households in the United States from 1950 to 2000. Clearly, both types of family living situations have declined over time. Even though there has been significant decline in the lines associated with traditional and extended family households, these trends have not caused a policy gap because a decline in both types of households has not challenged the core assumption that there is a categorical difference between the two. In other words, for a policy gap to form in the core assumptions that privilege nuclear family, Figure 4.2 might instead display a sharp decline in nuclear families and a corresponding increase in extended family members, not the parallel decrease. In fact, Figure 4.2 illustrates two key points about the decline in nuclear and extended families. First, there are still far more nuclear family households than extended family households. For every extended family household in America there are three nuclear family households. Second, although both types have declined, the small percentage of extended fam-

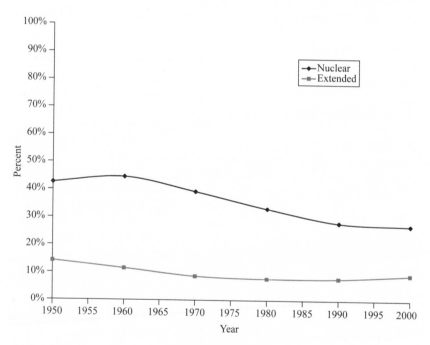

FIGURE 4-2

Nuclear and Extended Family Households, 1950–2000

SOURCE: Author's analysis of census data provided by Steven Ruggles, Matthew Sobek, and et al., "Integrated Public Use Microdata Series: Version 3.0," (Minneapolis: Historical Census Projections, University of Minnesota, 2003.)

NOTE: Nuclear families households are made up of head of household, married spouse, and children only; extended family households are defined as households with any additional family members.

ily households means that even a small number drop accounts for a large percentage of households

To date, the demographic changes in nuclear and extended family households have not created a policy gap in the core assumptions about the emotional proximity of close relatives in immigration law. There is still a large difference between norms for nuclear versus norms for extended family households, at least when it comes to living arrangements. Extended family households have not become more prevalent while nuclear family households have decreased, rather both have experienced decline.

Peripheral Assumptions

Though the basic categorical distinction between nuclear and extended families in America still holds strong, assumptions about the individuals who fall within each of those categories are more specific, numerous, and controversial. Peripheral assumptions break down broader categories into workable definitions. In the case of immigration policy peripheral assumptions tell us not just that nuclear families are prioritized but who qualifies as a mother or father in a nuclear family. Because peripheral assumptions are both more specific and more numerous than either core values or core assumptions, peripheral assumptions are also most likely to diverge from social practices creating a policy gap.[19] Unlike the core value of family or core assumptions distinguishing between nuclear and extended families, peripheral assumptions, which make finer distinctions, require smaller changes in social practices for gaps to occur.

Though there are numerous peripheral assumptions about family in immigration policy, in this section I analyze assumptions about what constitutes a "child" in immigration law over time. The definition of child is a particularly useful example for three reasons. First, even though immigration law gives standing to a number of family relationships, with the exception of spouses, it specifies these relationships through the definition of child. Siblings, for example, are identified as children of a common parent, and parents are identified through criteria that define child. Second, shifting social practices, presented in Chapter 2 (see Figure 2.5), suggest key demographic changes that would directly affect relationships between children and their parents. Third, and finally, the definition of child has been amended several times since the INA was first enacted. It provides insight to how policymakers respond when they decide to take action.

Unlike a general commitment to family, or a distinction between extended and nuclear families, the relationship between children and their parents has changed significantly over time. Gaps have developed between the assumptions about families policymakers had in mind when they defined "child" in immigration policy in 1952 and social practices over the next five decades. The idyllic model of a nuclear family, with two married parents and children biologically related to both, that was part and parcel of the original definition of child has given way to an increased number of parents who are either not married or not married for the first time. These patterns in marriage also influence children. The children in households are now less likely to be biologically related to one or both parents.[20] These changes in the makeup of American family households suggest real dilemmas for immigration policy composed in the early 1950s with a different set of family norms.

As enacted, the INA of 1952 defined "child" as follows:

The term "child" means an unmarried person under twenty-one years of age who is—

(A) a legitimate child; or

(B) a stepchild, provided the child had not reached the age of eighteen years at the time the marriage creating the status of stepchild occurred;

(C) a child legitimated under the law of the child's residence or domicile or under the law of the father's residence or domicile, whether in or outside the United States, if such legitimation takes place before the child reaches the age of eighteen years and the child is in the legal custody of the legitimating parent or parents at the time of such legitimation.[21]

The definition of child adopted by policymakers reflects both the common law understanding of parentage and legitimacy and 1952 expectations of families. The definition extends beyond the traditional nuclear family, with biologically related children, by including provisions for step-children, but it falls within the constraints of the traditional definition in three key ways. First, the definition of child provided originally in 1952 makes no mention of orphans, or children without any biological connection to parents in the United States. Second, the definition is strictly limited to *legitimate* children, whether born in marriage or legitimated afterward. Third, and related to the previous point, the definition is male centered. "Legitimate" offspring are those born within a traditional marriage or, in American immigration law, legitimated afterwards by their fathers.[22]

To be sure, policy gaps have been part and parcel of the definition of child from the very first day. However, unlike core values or core assumptions discussed earlier, gaps have grown in peripheral assumptions about parents and their children. All three of the specific traditional nuclear family norms in the paragraph above have been eroded. Further, policymakers have acted on policy gaps by amending the legislation with respect to orphans, legitimate children, and gender norms. Since the INA of 1952 was enacted, Congress has tinkered with the definition of child on twelve separate occasions (in 1957, 1961, 1965, 1975, 1981, 1986 [twice], 1988,

1989, 1995, 1999, and 2000). Appendix C summarizes these amendments. Congress has acted four times to alter the definition of "child" in respect to orphans, twice with respect to legitimacy, and once concerning gender norms.

Soon after the INA was passed, Congress amended it to include eligible orphans as part of the definition of child exempt from numerical limitations. In 1957, Congress added a paragraph allowing alien children to be considered immediate relatives as long as they had been in the custody of the adopted parents for a minimum of two years. In 1961, Congress once again amended the definition of child, giving permanent status to a temporary adoption program. American citizens *and their spouses* who wished to adopt abroad were now able to do so. In 1975, Congress acted again to expand the eligibility for American citizens wishing to adopt abroad. Deviating substantially from the nuclear family ideal, Congress allowed single persons over twenty-five to adopt alien children.

Congress addressed the question of legitimacy twice, but only once did it have a substantive impact on the definition of child. In 1957, Congress gave standing to two specific categories of illegitimate children: stepchildren born out of wedlock and mothers' illegitimate children. Notably, fathers' illegitimate children still lacked standing. In amending the status for illegitimate children, Congress reinforced conventional gendered norms.

Gendered assumptions about parents, which articulate separate criteria for mothers and fathers, reflect the expectations of men and women in society more generally. Congress addressed the gender distinctions in definitions of children and parents once. In 1986, Congress modified—but did not eliminate—gender distinctions. It amended the definition of child so that in addition to allowing illegitimate children of citizen-mothers unconditional standing, illegitimate children of fathers could have standing, *provided* they could prove a "bona fide parent-child relationship."[23]

Peripheral assumptions in policy, like the definition of child that failed to include children born out of wedlock or disallowed single persons to adopt abroad, reflect specific assumptions in immigration policy about expectations of families and individual family members. These assumptions were either made explicitly, with the intention that certain classes of individuals were not wanted or did not qualify, or they were made implicitly, by neglecting to consider certain categories. In either case, policymakers have closed the gaps in the definition of child through statutory amendment.

Immigration policy has evolved in the periphery with changing family norms—albeit irregularly. Congress has acted to amend the definition of child. Yet, the mere presence of a policy gap does not automatically mean that change is immediately forthcoming. Policy gaps suggest sites for political contestation, and they alter the politics surrounding attempts for change. Actors and institutions in the policy process remain the causal forces for change. In the next section, I explore in more depth the process by which policy contestation and (sometimes) change occurs.

FAMILY, IMMIGRATION, AND CHANGE OVER TIME

Explanations of change that incorporate both the structure of policy and the actors and institutions of the policy process can identify parts of policy vulnerable to change as well as what that change might look like. According to the analysis here, when social practices diverge from the values and assumptions in policy, a policy gap forms. This gap may be exploited by entrepreneurs who wish to expand and enhance policy or those who wish to eliminate it. Closing gaps in the periphery results in incremental policy adjustment whereas closing gaps in the core results in major policy overhaul. In this section, I evaluate what this analysis adds to two cases of peripheral policy gaps. In the first case, taken from the discussion of peripheral assumptions above, I examine why and how the definition of child was amended in 1975 to include single parents. In the second case, I look at the provision of visas for extended family members. In this second example, change has not occurred *despite* the presence of a policy gap and determined efforts by entrepreneurs. These two examples illustrate how the aspect of change I emphasize, the structure of policy, complements traditional process-based explanations.

Amending the Definition of "Child"

By the mid-1970s social practices for single-parent families had begun to change, in some cases quite dramatically. Taboos surrounding single-parent households and childbirth out of wedlock had eased, contributing both to an increase in the number of single parents as well as to a decrease in the number of children born out of wedlock put up for adoption.[24] Changes in adoption norms toward single parents in the fifty states followed suit. Harry Krause writing on family law in 1977 noted: "The typical standard for an appropriate adoptive placement well into the 20th century was a happy, upstanding, young married couple. This has changed considerably as a result of societal views, statutory changes, and the need to enlist adoptive parents ... to deal with the broadened constituency of children who now enter the adoption pool."[25] In the mid-1970s, state adoption statutes generally allowed single people to adopt. However, federal immigration law lagged behind.

Unmarried individuals, who by state law were permitted to adopt in the United States, were unable to bring foreign children to the United States as immediate relatives. Instead, they had to petition for a preference visa, which could take an extended period of time and involve an unacceptably long separation from their children, making it practically impossible for single parents to adopt abroad. In September 1972, Representative Edward Koch (D-NY) proposed legislation, in his own words, "after the injustice of the present law was brought to my attention by a constituent."[26] The bill was unanimously approved by the House Judiciary Committee and passed the House in September 1973, but it languished in the Senate Judiciary Committee. In the spring of 1975, as American military involvement in Vietnam was about to end and the government of South Vietnam was in its final hours, Koch proposed the bill (HR-568) again, but this time with a different result.

On March 26, 1975, the House Judiciary Committee favorably reported HR-568 out of committee. Less than a month later, on the very day that South Vietnamese President Nguyen Van Thieu resigned from office, the bill was read before the House and passed on a voice vote. The Senate Judiciary Committee favorably reported the bill out of committee on November 20. It was approved by the full Senate on December 4 and signed by the president on December 16.

Though potentially controversial (the amendment formally recognized single-parent families in federal law), there was no vocal opposition to the amendment. Not one person spoke against the measure in the House or Senate, and there are no dissenting views in the House or Senate Committee reports. The law received even less negative attention in the general public. The extent of national *New York Times* coverage was a two-sentence AP article tucked away on page 32, after the Senate Judiciary Committee approved the bill on November 20, 1975.[27]

Amending the INA to allow unmarried persons to be categorized officially as "parents" and their adopted children as "children" under the law is an example of change in a policy gap where problem definition, policy solutions, and political will all came together to put the issue on the agenda. First, proponents identified the policy gap between social practices and the assumptions about family embedded in the periphery as a compelling problem to be fixed. American families were increasingly headed by single parents, and state law had already recognized the need to allow single parents to adopt by the mid-1970s but federal law lagged behind. Both House and Senate Committee reports reference state statutes that permit unmarried persons to adopt.[28] In addition to the general demographic changes, Koch references the need to change the law due to the specific political needs to resettle Vietnamese orphans. He explains:

"there are many unmarried persons who would like to adopt Vietnam orphans" and goes on to note later in his remarks that "there are so many more orphans from Southeast Asia that are available for adoption by single parents."[29]

Second, a political entrepreneur (in this case Rep. Koch) brought the issue to policymakers' attention with a solution that—in addition to alleviating a pressing political problem—would update federal law to match social practice. Representative Patsy Mink (D-HI) explains that federal law must adapt to social needs. She says: "Our immigration laws must keep pace with our domestic adoption procedures. Single-parent adoptions are accepted and increasing at home." She continues by making the connection between social practice and policy change explicit: "Our domestic laws reflect changes in adoption patterns and the recognition given single-parent adoptions. We must now amend our immigration laws to acknowledge and implement this fact."[30]

Third, and finally, fallout over Vietnam gave Congress the incentive to act both quickly and in a coordinated manner. Policymakers who wanted change had political circumstances that bolstered their case. As the House and Senate were considering changes to this peripheral assumption in immigration policy, they were overwhelmed by the fall of Vietnam and the withdrawl of American troops. In the spring of 1975, the rapid pace of events in Vietnam and need to evacuate American personnel and Vietnamese orphans, along with creating a sustainable refugee policy, was at the forefront of the political agenda. At the same time that HR-568 was under consideration, the cover story of every *Congressional Quarterly Weekly Report* for the month of April was foreign policy and aid to South East Asia.

Any hesitancy on the part of members of Congress to oppose this measure was surely quelled by overwhelming public support for Vietnamese orphans (referred to as "war orphans"). In an April 3 news conference in San Diego, President Gerald Ford was grilled about eliminating red tape for Americans who wanted to adopt Vietnamese orphans. Ford responded "I am assured that all bureaucratic red tape is being eliminated to the maximum degree and we will make a total effort . . . to see that South Vietnamese war orphans are brought to the United States."[31] But in addition to the president's encouragement, *Congressional Quarterly Weekly Report* states that thousands of citizens' letters, calls, and telegrams, which offered financial support or a good home to the orphans, "swamped the offices on Capitol Hill," as well as government agencies.[32]

Policymakers who favored the change were able to enact it because there was broad support. The net effect of this change in law was miniscule, less than .05 percent of total immigration. It was a victory for a small group of single Americans who wished to adopt abroad or who wished to have the ability to adopt abroad. Any opposition to recognizing single-parent families was second to the necessity of refugee assistance for Vietnamese children who had gained the sympathy of the American public.

In this example, actors agitated for changing immigration preferences because they felt excluded by the assumptions in immigration policy that defined parents as a married couple. Single parents had gained the right to adopt in many states in the United States and, as Representative Patsy Mink makes clear, it was time for federal law to keep up. It is no surprise that there would be a gap in this piece of immigration law and that during the 1970s potential single parents would work to change it. Policy gaps set the stage for more immediate political imperatives. Allowing single people to adopt would solve two problems: it would bring federal law in line with state adoption laws and, even more, it would aid displaced Vietnamese orphans. Koch was successful in captivating political will in 1975, though he was not able just a few years earlier, in part because of the U.S. obligation to resettle thousands of refugees (including orphans) very quickly. There was limited opportunity to oppose the measure. The net result was a change in immigration policy that was quite minor. It had little substantive impact on the way that immigration policy works and the actual number of individuals affected by it.

Immigration Visas for Extended Family

If the 1975 amendment to the INA, which allowed unmarried persons to adopt foreign orphans, is a case where a policy gap made it to the agenda and was successfully changed, the multiple unsuccessful attempts to eliminate visa preferences for extended family illustrate the difficulties when coalitions and constituencies form to protect a gap. Given pressures to reform the immigration system, and especially to rein in ever-increasing numbers of immigrants, the priorities that would appear to be the most vulnerable to reduction and elimination are preferences granted to extended family members. The assumptions about family, which rely on the emotional proximity and dependency of nuclear family members, are increasingly remote for actual extended family members. Not only are Americans comparatively distant from extended family (as opposed to nuclear family members), this trend has only grown stronger over time.

Figure 4.2, presented earlier in this chapter, shows a decline in the number of extended family households. In 1950, 14.2 percent of American households included extended family members, but by 1980 the percent had fallen by nearly half to 7.8 percent. It rebounded slightly in 2000 to 9.2 percent. The decline of an already small number of extended family households further opens a policy gap in immigration preferences. Ever since the 1950s, when the INA was enacted, Americans have not been especially close to extended family relations. There has always been a gap between this assumption and broader social practice, but this gap remains and has even grown. Gaps are sources of likely political contestation and it takes actors and institutions of the policy process to contest those gaps. If American citizens and policymakers were satisfied with the number of immigrants coming to the United States, and the system worked without major flaws, the gap between assumptions about extended family and social practice could potentially remain without organized opposition or pressure for change. Just the opposite has happened. Americans support changes to immigration policy, and the piece of policy that has come under fire repeatedly is that part that looks least like "family" as Americans know it—extended family visas.

With the exception of California's Proposition 187 in 1994 and pro-immigration protests across the country in 2006, public opinion literature generally points to the low salience of immigration policy.[33] Nevertheless, when asked, Americans have consistently favored *decreased* levels of immigration. In response to a Gallup poll in 1965, 33 percent of respondents reported that immigration should be decreased. Since then, the number of people seeking to decrease immigration peaked in the mid-1990s: 42 percent in 1977, 49 percent in 1986, 61 percent in 1993, 49 percent in 1999, and 47 percent in 2006.[34]

Americans express dissatisfaction with American immigration, and there is clearly a need to reform the system. Regardless of one's position on the total number of immigrants that should be admitted annually, the way they are admitted, through backlogged preferences, fosters neither the goals of family unity nor national needs.[35] Because family is the major criterion for immigration, and admitting a single person potentially entails dozens of family members, family preferences are easily oversubscribed. Massive backlogs are the rule rather than the exception for second preference (immediate family of legal permanent residents) and fourth preference (adult brothers and sisters) immigrants. Testifying before the Senate Immigration Subcommittee in 2001, Warren Leiden, a San Francisco lawyer, summed up the situation this way: "In each and every one of the family categories, there's a substantial backlog ranging from as little as a year to as much as ten years and more."[36] To get a better picture of actual wait times for particular preference categories, the State Department publishes a monthly "Visa Bulletin" that gives the approximate date that applicants now *receiving* visas first *applied* for them. Adult siblings receiving a fourth preference visa in 2006 first applied in June of 1995—eleven years earlier.[37] Applicants receiving second preference visas in 2006 fared a bit better. Immediate family of legal permanent residents waited between seven and nine years.[38]

Clearly, there is a disjuncture in immigration policy and a need to reform the preference system to better accommodate qualified individuals. The mere presence of a policy gap, however, does not mean that change is forthcoming. In addition to the policy, the policy process plays a role as well. Policy actors must bring an issue to the agenda by recognizing the problem of changing demographics, having a potential policy solution, and seizing the right political conditions. Change is most likely to occur when broad coalitions form, when policy expands rather contracts, and when the change is relatively minor. In the case of preferences for extended family, legislators on both sides of the aisle (though heavily favoring Republicans) brought the issue to the national agenda, but they were unable to muster a political coalition to cut visas for mobilized groups of electorally influential constituents.

Preferences granted to extended family members, especially adult brothers and sisters along with their spouses and children, have been the most contentious of the preference categories created by the 1965 amendments to the INA of 1952. Unlike dependent orphans in the earlier example, adult brothers and sisters can and are able to act independently of their American family members. Further, because of the privileges accorded to nuclear families, adult siblings come along with their own nuclear families—potentially increasing the number of visas given exponentially. Every major attempt to reform legal immigration has addressed this category with amendments to limit the visas to *single* brothers and sisters or eliminate the category altogether. As early as 1972, in a bill to authorize special immigration visas to countries adversely affected by the 1965 amendments, Representative David W. Dennis (R-IN) introduced an amendment limiting visas to unmarried brothers and sisters, explaining "Those people who are married have families of their own . . . They have formed another family unit and they do not need to come in."[39] Dennis's strong words about what it means to be a family—clearly nuclear—are not that far off from immigration policy as it was originally constructed nor the ways that Americans experience their own family life. In the 1980s and 1990s, pressure to reform immigration came round again and again to limiting extended family preferences.

As the number of total immigrants (legal and illegal) spiraled upward, pressure mounted for reform. In 1982, Senate Immigration Chair Alan Simpson (R-WY) and House Immigration Chair Romano Mazzoli (D-KY) introduced legislation to address the backlog in immigration visas. Their amendment called for the elimination of the adult brothers and sisters category in order to reallocate visas for more immediate relatives. Unsuccessful in their first attempt, Simpson and Mazzoli tried again in 1983 with similar results. In 1989 Simpson paired up with liberal Democrat Edward

Kennedy (D-MA) to curtail extended family immigration by eliminating visas for *married* adult brothers and sisters and their spouses and children, *unmarried* brothers and sisters would still qualify. According to the *Congressional Quarterly Almanac* "while family reunification was an important theme in the legislation, the sponsors said immigration law did not make enough distinction between close and distant relatives."[40] The measure was unsuccessful.

In 1995, thirty years after the 1965 Amendments to the INA, American dissatisfaction with the number of immigrants peaked. Sixty-two percent of Americans polled favored decreased levels of immigration.[41] Similarly, when asked specifically about reforming federal law in regard to *legal* immigrants, "Would you favor or oppose changes in federal law to reduce the number of immigrants who enter the country legally?" 62 percent of respondents in a *Time*/CNN poll in 1994 indicated they would favor changes in federal law.[42] A much anticipated report by a bipartisan commission headed by the late Barbara Jordan (D-TX), made a series of recommendations for reforming the nation's immigration policy. The Jordan Commission recommended cuts in overall immigration and the elimination of all preferences for nonnuclear family members. Barbara Jordan's Democratic party affiliation and strong civil rights record boosted the legitimacy of the Commission's findings. Building on the Jordan Commission recommendations, House Immigration Subcommittee Chair Lamar Smith (R-TX) introduced a comprehensive immigration reform bill that would eliminate nonnuclear family preferences, claiming his bill focused on reuniting nuclear rather than extended families. Simpson introduced a similar bill in the Senate. The debate over legal immigration was particularly intense but these bills, like their predecessors, were eventually defanged of all provisions that eliminated or severely curtailed immigration by extended family members.

By the time the issue of legal immigration came to a head in mid-1990s, legislators had recognized demographic trends in American society that had created a policy gap and defined them as a problem to be fixed. Susan Martin, the executive director of the Jordan Commission, explained that extended family preferences were a luxury that the country could not afford anymore. For Martin, married children and adult brothers and sisters "are not bad or unnecessary, but the nuclear family comes first."[43] Then-Commissioner of Immigration Doris Meissner noted clearly the cultural pull of the nuclear family. "It's very hard to quarrel with children and spouses. It's even pretty hard when parents are concerned . . . But siblings add up in terms of numbers and values, there is a difference between nuclear and extended family. It's a cultural thing. The nuclear family orients our thinking about family. It's the operating model in the United States."[44]

Restrictionists, who long advocated limiting immigration, seized on the Jordan Commission's recommendations, explaining the "nuclear family is what the bi-partisan Jordan Commission recommends. It's a return to our heritage."[45] But pro-immigration advocates, defending their ground, made arguments that exploiting the gap was unfair to minority families. Antonia Hernandez, president and general counsel of the Mexican American Legal Defense and Education Fund argued "as reflected in the U.S. Census, families are integral to the Hispanic community. . . . changes in family preferences will have an unduly burdensome impact on communities such as the Hispanic community."[46]

Policymakers of all stripes further proposed solutions to "fix" immigration by looking specifically at fourth preference immigrants, the favored solution at least since the 1970s. Though legal immigration reform had long been in the camp of conservatives, Kennedy's involvement in 1989 and the recommendations of the Jordan Commission in 1995 opened the door for more liberal politicians to explicitly recognize the need for change. Jordan testified that it was necessary to eliminate all extended family preferences saying, "the numbers not used to admit these individuals in more extended family relationships could be used instead to reduce the waiting time for closer family members."[47] The plan had support from the White House when the Clinton Administration endorsed the Jordan Commissions findings in somewhat modified form.

In 1995, public opinion polls showed high dissatisfaction with immigration (from a normally quiescent public), Republicans controlled both houses of Congress, the Jordan Commission released strong recommendations, and the White House offered support. As with the previous attempts to eliminate visas for adult brothers and sisters, however, this reform failed too. Even though members of Congress recognized that there is a categorical difference between nuclear and extended families (certainly, there has been no serious consideration given to reducing or eliminating nuclear family preferences), and though they acknowledged the need to fix the oversubscribed extended family categories, Immigration Subcommittee chairs since the early 1980s have been unable to actually reduce or restrict extended family preferences. Unlike expanding immigration for single persons who wished to adopt abroad, restrictionists have been unable to marshal the political coalition necessary to enact change.

There are several reasons why immigration for extended family members has remained surprisingly resilient over the years. First, by the time restricting family preference began to reach a more ideologically diverse audience in the late 1980s and early 1990s, it was particularly salient to subsections of the American public—especially Asians and Latinos—who were exerting growing influence as important voting blocks in electorally influential states. According to one limited-immigration interest group staffer,

"I think it's certainly true today, there is an electoral focus. Republicans and Democrats are trying to capture the Latino vote."[48] Asian American and Latino advocacy groups fought limitations on immigration to adult brothers and sisters as a cultural misunderstanding of family. Melinda Yee, executive director of the Organization of Chinese Americans Inc., told the *Congressional Quarterly Almanac* in 1989, "We consider the nuclear family as also including brothers and sisters."[49] Antonia Hernandez explained, "under no conceivable scenario are sons and daughters, brothers and sisters and parents anything other than an integral part of the nuclear family."[50] The Clinton Administration and other moderate policymakers in Congress found themselves in a delicate political position, and they did not want to appear culturally insensitive. According to Doris Meissner, "Asian and Latino groups made up most of the extended family preferences and policymakers did not want to be portrayed as discriminating against them—as in our families used sibling preferences but now we want to end them. It would be like a return to the National Origins Quota System."[51]

Second, immigration policy creates a natural constituency to lobby on behalf of continued immigration. Political scientists have shown that it is far more difficult to reduce or eliminate programs from interests than it is to create them to begin with. Figure 4.3 shows the remarkable divergence in the percent of extended family households for American versus foreign-born residents. The lines show a similar decrease over time until 1970 when American-born households continued to decline as foreign-born households make a rapid ascent. No doubt the increase in extended family households after 1970 is due in large part to the ethnic makeup of new immigrants (Asians were no longer excluded) and to the feedback from the immigration policy itself.

Third, as one interview respondent noted: "The case of extended family preferences shows the power of the most interesting bedfellows."[52] The odd, but effective, coalition of liberals on the left and both fiscal and social conservatives on the right helped to quash attempts to limit extended family immigration. That coalition formed because of policy communities interested in both the *ends* and *means* of policy worked together. Although pro-immigration and pro-immigrant groups would likely oppose any further restrictions, they teamed up with business community leaders upset by provisions of the bill restricting work visas and religious groups (such as the Catholic Church) and conservatives worried about the "family implications" of the bill. Phyllis Eisen, of the National Association of Manufacturers, showed business concern over immigration restrictions: "We are distressed at the proposed cutback in legal immigration. It's shortsighted . . . Most manufacturing companies . . . need to seek out talent globally."[53] Whereas fiscal conservatives focused on the health of business, social conservatives reached for the health of American families. Ralph Reed of the Christian Coalition

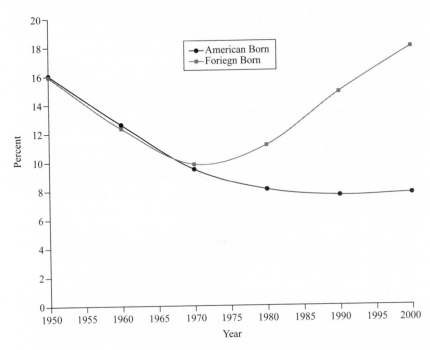

FIGURE 4-3

Extended Family Households For Subpopulations American and Foreign Born,
1950–2000

SOURCE: Author's analysis of census data provided by Steven Ruggles, Matthew Sobek, and et al, "Integrated Public Use Microdata Series: Version 3.0," (Minneapolis: Historical Census Projections, University of Minnesota, 2003).

NOTE: Foreign-born households are comprised of a foreign-born head of household and/or a foreign-born spouse. American-born households are made up of an American-born head of household, and if head of household is married, an American-born spouse.

went so far as to write a letter advocating Republican members take the position that most closely matched traditional family values.[54] One pro-immigration interest group staffer explained that the bill would not have passed without the coalition. In 1996, "both houses were controlled by the Republicans, both committees were chaired by people who supported reductions. We needed the support of the conservative side. Business, a traditional [conservative] constituency, gave us a voice on the other side."[55] Another staffer noted that "religious groups came in defense of the family. They validated the more expansive view of family."[56]

In the case of extended family preferences, assumptions about the emotional proximity of American families suggest that Americans live and operate in nuclear family units followed by extended family relations. Extended family preferences have come under fire over and over again because restrictionists working to limit the number of immigrants, policymakers working to reduce oversubscribed categories, and liberal politicians who want to increase benefits to immigrants by reducing the number of individuals who come into the country all agree that extended family is least like American social practice. Even though both preferences for immediate family of legal permanent residents (LPR) *and* preferences for adult siblings of U.S. citizens were heavily oversubscribed by the early 1980s, immediate family of LPRs was out of the line of fire and off the table when it came to any reductions. In fact, legislators reinforced over and over again that reductions in extended family visas would be used to assist immediate family of LPRs.

Because LPRs formed a group distinct from American-born citizens, it is entirely plausible that legislators could have argued that American citizens deserved more privileges than permanent residents. But this is exactly opposite of what occurred. Over and over again, legislators stressed the need to keep families of LPRs together. Under the Refugee Act of 1980, the LPR preference category was granted an extra 6 percent of restricted admissions, which were formerly given to refugees.[57] And under the Jordan Commission's plan, an additional 150,000 visas would be made available to immediate family of LPRs. The weakness of extended family preferences, I argue, stems from the policy gap in peripheral assumptions. Under pressure to reform the system, the category that least matched the ways that Americans experienced family life were viewed as the least legitimate and hence subject to cuts.

The example of extended family preferences in immigration policy illustrates that assumptions and social practices create policy gaps that can be exploited by political actors who wish to make change. In other words, they create the broader context under which debates about public policy take place. Getting policy gaps on the agenda requires problem recognition, policy solutions, and the right political atmosphere. Successfully closing the gap depends on the constituencies that organize around an area and the part of policy that is to be amended. The ability to act to close the gap in adoption by single parents differed from extended family preferences in three key ways. First, single parents were expanding immigration policy in a way that would not disrupt current stakeholders; they were not taking preferences away from other groups. Restrictionists who wished to eliminate visas for adult brothers and sisters, on the other hand, would concentrate the costs of their changes on particular individuals who were well represented. Second, single parents were asking for a relatively minor change, one that would affect only a small portion of immigration. Restrictionists who wished to eliminate fourth preference visas, would have a huge impact—approximately 65,000 people per year. Third, and related to the first two points, the single parent adoptions generated hardly any attention from organized interests or the media, but elimination of visas for adult siblings was hampered by a broad and nearly unstoppable coalition that included civil rights organizations on the left and social and fiscal conservatives on the right. This coalition was able to shape the debate about immigration by arguing the costs would be borne widely by harming American families, rather than just the particular immigrant families involved.

CONCLUSION

Although it is easy to look at immigration reforms as a battle between parties or interest-group coalitions, the role of family in public policy adds to the understanding of why this particular immigration preference came under fire and how such a ideologically diverse (and bipartisan) coalition could form to defend it. In the words of Susan Martin, "a lot of what happened was a real battle about family."[58]

A focus on the family shows that the assumptions embedded in policy are not disconnected from the broader public. Indeed, the ways that Americans think and live in social family units influences proponents who find themselves on the outside of policy to push to expand and modify assumptions, as was the case in single-parent adoptions. Likewise, it emboldens opponents to target assumptions that have a gap and are vulnerable, as retrenchment advocates did for adult brothers and sisters. Including family in analysis helps one to see the broader historical and social factors that shape the political arena. I have found that policy gaps have developed in peripheral assumptions in the definition of "child" and in extended family preferences. Though the gaps were closed successfully by redefining child, they remain open for extended family visas. The likelihood that a gap will be closed successfully increases as highly motivated groups fight for policy change, as was the case in amending the definition of child. The likelihood that a gap will be successfully closed decreases as highly motivated groups fight to defend their turf, as pro-immigration and ethnic immigrant groups did to save extended family visas. These pro-immigration groups worked hard to build an ideologically diverse coalition that included parties interested in increasing immigration as well as helping families: labor and business, religious organizations and ethnic groups, and Democrats and Republicans. They were tremendously successful in portraying retrenchment in this area as harming family life rather than singling out particular immigrant families. That is, they were able to portray the costs as concentrated and the benefits as diffuse.

Scholars who have looked at immigration policy in particular have focused on the role of parties and policy regimes over time. Gimpel and Edwards, in a thorough look at the role of Congress in immigration policy, explain that change over time is due to the partisan nature of the issue.[59] It has moved from a consensus issue in the 1960s to highly contentious. Daniel Tichenor, in a study of immigration policy over time, argues that changes in policy are not the result of economic, social, or cultural forces alone, but the outcomes conditioned by policy regimes.[60] The analysis offered here offers an alternative and complementary perspective. By looking closely at what is in policy and how nearly it matches the ways in which Americans live, we can see when and where policy gaps form. Policy gaps suggest places where political contestation is likely to occur, even if it does not always succeed.

CHAPTER FIVE

Taxing the Family

"All we hear about is families, families, families," retorted Stephanie Knapik of the American Association of Single People in response to Congressional tax debates surrounding the marriage penalty. "And we're just ready to gag."[1] Though Knapik has a definite political agenda, her observation that tax policy debates are full of references to family is not far removed from reality. Even as American tax policy is anchored by the individual income tax, in actuality, family-households more than individuals are at the center of both the debate and the actual practice of American taxation.

Family's important place in American tax policy was neither inevitable nor always as strong as it stands at the beginning of the twenty-first century. Instead, the history of American taxation points to plenty of "family neutral" taxes in place before the federal income tax of World War II, the basis of the current system of income taxation. However, in order to meet the sustained revenue needs of the American state after the war, the national mass-based income tax became a permanent feature. Tension in the federal system between national revenue needs and state-level definitions of family-property led to the incorporation of family-household as the basic taxable unit in 1948. Moving the taxable unit from individual to family-household cost the U.S. Treasury up to three-quarters of a billion dollars in lost annual revenue at the time, but in the half-century since, the tax code has proven a cost-effective and bipartisan tool of public policy.[2] The tax code allows policymakers who do not want to increase the size of the American state to reward and encourage particular outcomes through tax incentives rather than creating additional bureaucratic agencies. These incentives are given not only to individuals for their own use, but often for their action on behalf of others. When taxpayers are given incentives to provide goods and services for others, they essentially act as policy administrators. The Internal Revenue Code (IRC) puts the onus on individual taxpayers—parents, grandparents, siblings, and adult children—to know and utilize provisions of the tax code. In the end, American families, supervised by the Internal Revenue Service (IRS), have taken on a significant task of administering federal public policies.

This chapter focuses on the role of family as an administrator in the U.S. tax code. I argue that family has grown to become a crucial part of American taxation at the same time embedding structural assumptions about family in the tax code has long-term consequences for the politics surrounding tax policy. Even as the value of family in the tax code has remained strong, assumptions about shared family resources and the contribution of women's income have changed over time creating policy gaps in filing status and benefit structures. Policymakers have sought to adjust the tax code to meet the needs of families that include working wives and mothers in their attempts to fix the so-called marriage tax penalty.

There are three parts to this chapter. In the first, I provide a brief overview and history of American taxation, paying particular attention to the place of family in tax policy over time. The second examines the particular values and assumptions embedded in tax policy and compares them to American family practices. I find gaps have developed around assumptions of shared family resources with the influx of wives into the paid labor force. The third shows how administration of one of the key expenditures of the U.S. tax code—the Earned Income Tax Credit (EITC)—has changed to meet social practice or demographic patterns in America. Even though one congressional staffer claimed, "It's never smart policy when you're dealing with money, and taxes are always about money,"[3] in truth, tax policy illustrates vividly the conflict between policy gaps and real political limitations policymakers face when trying to address them.

A BRIEF HISTORY OF AMERICAN TAX POLICY

The inclusion of family in American tax policy was not a foregone conclusion. In fact, until World War II most taxes were family neutral: they did not incorporate family as a value to promote or assumptions about the needs and expectations of close relatives. Early American taxation, which relied heavily on tariffs and excise taxes, placed levies on goods rather than people.

From the beginning, the Constitution gave only limited powers to the federal government to "lay and collect taxes, duties, imports, and excises."[4] Article I, section 8, allowed revenue collection, but section 9 prohibited direct taxation "unless in proportion to the census."[5] This limitation presented few obstacles to early American state builders who collected all the revenue necessary to run the new national government largely from tariffs and excise taxes.[6] Sustained federal challenge to the constitutional prohibition on direct taxation did not arise until 1861 when the United States government looked for new sources of revenue to fight the costly Civil War.[7] Though the Civil War income tax was upheld by the Supreme Court, the Court turned about face in 1895 when it ruled that a similar tax, the income tax of 1894, was in violation of the Constitutional prohibitions of direct federal taxation.[8] The Court's action set the stage for ratification of the Sixteenth Amendment in 1913, which gave Congress the power to collect revenue without limitation as to the source and type of tax.

From the origins of the federal republic until early into World War I, excise taxes and tariffs accounted for the lion's share of all federal revenue—over 90 percent.[9] These tariffs and taxes, reflected in the purchase price of goods, affected families only in as much as the selection of goods they chose to buy were taxed. Individuals, households, or families were taxed upon their purchases rather than their status as a particular unit. The use of the income tax to generate revenue during World War I, however, began to change the burden of taxation from levies on goods to levies on individuals.[10] The early American income tax, however, had limited effect on American families, largely because the tax was confined only to the upper echelons of society. Prior to World War II, no more than 7 percent of all Americans, 18 percent of the total labor force, filed income tax returns.[11] Few Americans were subject to the income tax, yet the tax proved to be a reliable source of wartime income that would surpass excise taxes and tariffs. This lucrative source of revenue would be exploited further two decades later at the opening of World War II.

The foundations of the contemporary American income tax were laid during World War II. The increasing demand for revenue in the face of grave international consequences led President Franklin D. Roosevelt and Congress to expand the individual income tax significantly so that it became, for the first time, a mass-based tax. Although no more than 18 percent of the labor force filed income tax returns in any given year prior to the outbreak of World War II, on average 64 percent of the labor force filed tax returns annually during the five years the United States was officially at war (1941–45). Figure 5.1 shows income tax returns as a percent of total labor force and population from the origins of the income tax in 1913 to 1950. The figure demonstrates the rise in income taxes during World War I, their relative decline, and the sharp and sustained increase that corresponds with World War II and the postwar period.

Roosevelt's income tax plan reflects two particularly important core values. As designed, it was both equitable and progressive. In other words, the tax treated individuals with similar amounts of income equally, at the same time as those with increased financial means paid a proportionally

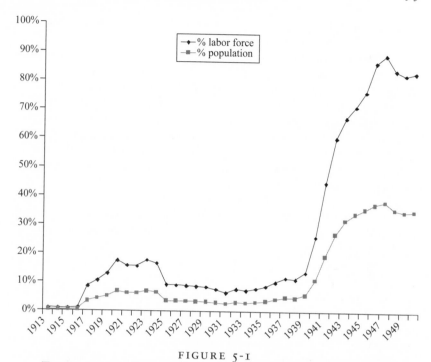

FIGURE 5-1
Tax Returns as a Percent of Labor Force and Population 1913–1950
SOURCE: Author's analysis of data drawn from the "Historical Statistics of the United States: Colonial Times to 1970," (Washington: DC: United States Bureau of the Census, 1976).

higher amount of their income to the state. Though the tax was designed to be both equitable and progressive, its implementation strayed from both of these goals. Because individual states determined property rights, and hence income attribution, married couples in the eight community property states largely in the West (Arizona, California, Idaho, Louisiana, Nevada, New Mexico, Texas, and Washington) were able to skirt higher income rates by defining individual income as split between two married people. In the remaining forty common law states, individual income was attributable only to the individual who earned it, which resulted in greater tax burdens for married taxpayers in the Midwest and East. In practice, equal income did not translate into equitable tax rates, just as those with increased financial means in community property states were able to skirt the proportionally higher tax rates.

The adoption of a national income tax in a federal system created geographic disparity between taxpayers in community property states in the West and common law states from the very first day of the income tax in

1913. Yet both the expansion of the tax to cover the majority of Americans and the increased progressivity of the tax during World War II exacerbated the situation.[12] National policymakers, who looked at income splitting as a strategy of tax avoidance rather than a legitimate interpretation of the law, finally gave up on crafting solutions that required all taxpayers to pay at higher individual rates and instead instituted the joint return with income splitting, which effectively reduced taxes for all married couples, in 1948.[13] With leeway to reduce taxes after the war, families across the United States received the benefits of community property taxation at the expense of the U.S. Treasury, which put cost of the measure at the time at upwards of $800 million annually.[14]

At the time, what was for many policymakers a bitter pill to swallow would turn out years later to be both a beneficial tool and detrimental flaw in the tax code. By moving from individual to family-household as the basic unit of taxation, the tax code firmly embedded family into the core of American taxation. Along with the formal recognition of married couples came the core assumption that families share resources, which would allow policymakers to effectively use the tax code to provide goods and services for individuals who may never have filled out a tax return.

This chapter concentrates on tax policy in the postwar period, when taxation became not only a means to collect revenue but increasingly a means of creating and administering public policies as well. The history of the income tax during this period is marked by two major factors: the relatively stable (and proportionally high) amount of revenue derived from the individual income tax and the rise in family administration through tax expenditures.

The first important feature of the postwar period is the relatively high and sustained revenue derived from the individual income tax. Figure 5.2 illustrates the composition of federal revenue by source. It shows the meteoric rise in federal revenue derived from both individual and corporate income taxes during the war years in the early to mid-1940s. While corporate taxes decline thereafter, individual income taxes remain relatively stable from 1946 to 2006, at about 45 percent of total government revenue. Importantly, Figure 5.2 also demonstrates the steady decline of traditional revenues derived from family-neutral sources like tariffs and excise taxes. Excise taxes, which accounted for 45 percent of government revenue in 1934, shrunk to just over 3 percent by 2006. Perhaps the most striking change between 1934 and 2006 is the sharp increase in revenues derived from social insurance deductions from American workers' paychecks. Taken together, Figure 5.2 shows the burden of taxation has shifted from family-neutral sources like excise, tariff, and even corporate income taxes to individuals and families. Further, as a nontrivial source

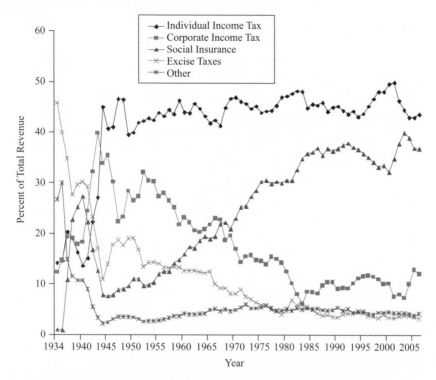

FIGURE 5-2
Revenue by Source 1934-2006

SOURCE: Author's analysis of data from "The Budget for Fiscal Year 2007, Historical Tables," (Washington: DC: The Executive Office of the President, Office of Management and Budget, 2006).

of government revenue, legislators who wish to maintain current revenue streams are limited by what they can do with the individual income tax. Not only are there powerful interests supporting particular provisions but small changes in any one part of the tax code can have a substantial impact on government revenues.[15]

As the individual income tax has developed into the backbone of American national revenue, it has also come to be a central policy device. In other words, the income tax is in part a tool to raise revenue and in part an effective collection of public policies. Then-Assistant Secretary for Tax Policy Stanley Surrey first used the concept of "tax expenditures" in 1967 to describe extraneous federal programs implemented through the tax code. He explained: "the system of tax expenditures provides a vast subsidy apparatus that uses the mechanics of the income tax as the method of paying the subsidies. The special provisions under which this subsidy apparatus functions take a variety of forms, covering exclusions from income, exemptions, deductions, credits against tax, preferential rates of tax and deferrals of tax."[16] For Surrey, the end result of tax expenditures is no different than more traditional governmental expenditures through grants, loans, or interest subsidies.[17] Even though traditional expenditures and tax expenditures may have similar results, their administration is often very different. Policies implemented through tax incentives often rely on family as unseen administrators in a "shadow" bureaucracy.[18]

Since 1974, when Congress first required explicit records of tax expenditures, the number and kind of expenditures have increased dramatically. Looking back, the Congressional Budget Office estimated that in 1967 tax expenditures accounted for $37 billion or 21 percent of total revenue. But by 1984, before congressional overhaul of the tax code, that number had mushroomed to $327 billion, or 35 percent of total revenue.[19] The call for tax reform in 1986 meant that many tax expenditures, often considered loopholes, were subject to reform.[20]

Tax expenditures are more than just a boondoggle on behalf of powerful wealthy Americans. Tax expenditures are a popular way of getting business done because they appeal to legislators on both sides of the aisle. Republicans, who wish to cut the size of government and tax burdens more generally, look upon tax expenditures as a tax cut returning to Americans the income that rightly belongs to them. Democrats, who wish to provide additional benefits or services, are able to accomplish their goals by relying on the tax code to increase "spending" in the form of credits and deductions for childcare or housing rather than more traditional (and controversial) spending programs.[21] Taxpayers who claim expenditures, not surprisingly, also favor the programs. From homeowners who deduct their mortgage interest to corporations that receive incentives for charitable giving, the financial benefits of tax expenditures are attractive to many Americans. Thus, even though the tax code undergoes periodic reforms, individual tax expenditures across a broad range of policy areas have incredible staying power.

Table 5.1 provides a detailed comparison of tax expenditures in 1972— when Congress was first considering monitoring the amount of money channeled through the tax code—and 2006 the most recent record for comparison.[22] The table shows the wide range of policy areas covered by tax expenditures. They are not limited to corporate interests but cover a host of policy areas that touch the elderly, the middle-class, and the working poor.[23] Table 5.1 also shows that tax expenditures are a growing source of federal spending (for many of the reasons cited above). In 1972, tax expenditures accounted for 20 percent of revenue collection. Even though the tax code was reformed in 1986, expenditures have continued

TABLE 5-1
Individual Tax Expenditures in 1972 and 2006, in Millions of Dollars

Tax Expenditures	1972	% of Total Revenue	2006	% of Total Revenue
National Defense	$700	0.30	$3,000	0.13
International Affairs and Finance	$85	0.04	$4,500	0.20
Agriculture	$900	0.39	$400	0.02
Natural Resources & Energy	$370	0.16	$2,100	0.09
Commerce and Transportation	$11,520	4.99	$180,100	7.88
Housing and Community Development	$7,100	3.08	$126,400	5.53
Health Labor and Welfare	$20,130	8.72	$475,400	20.80
Education	$1,040	0.45	$16,200	0.71
Veteran's Benefits and Services	$480	0.21	$3,900	0.17
General Government	$100	0.04	$1,100	0.05
Aid to State and Local Financing	$6,300	2.73	$55,500	2.43
Total	$48,725	21.11	$868,600	38.01

SOURCE: Author's analysis of 1972 calendar expenditure data reported in Stanley S. Surrey, *Pathways to Tax Reform: The Concept of Tax Expenditures* (Cambridge, MA: Harvard University Press, 1973), 2006 Expenditure data from "Estimates of Federal Tax Expenditures for Fiscal Years 2006-2010," (Washington, D.C.: Joint Committee on Taxation, 2005), Total revenue income taken from "The Budget for Fiscal Year 2007, Historical Tables," (Washington: DC: The Executive Office of the President, Office of Management and Budget, 2006).

NOTE: Though each of the budget functions (like National Defense) is summed to give the reader a general sense of the size of the expenditures, the numbers do not equate to revenue loss. Because tax expenditures do or do not affect taxpayer behavior in complicated ways there is no way to reliably estimate the cost.

to grow since then. By 2006, tax expenditures had grown as large as 38 percent of total revenue.

The history of the income tax shows that it is both an important revenue device and an important tool for policy implementation. Most significantly, since World War II the individual income tax has become less and less about individuals and more about the family-households of which they are a part. The following sections discuss how family is a value and an assumption underlying the income tax code and how demographic changes have pushed policymakers to amend the tax code. I focus on the public social policy dictated by tax expenditures, and in particular, the

EITC, which is both one of the largest tax expenditures and also appraised as one of the most successful.

When legislators created the income tax code in the early twentieth century, they did so with values and assumptions that reflected their historical experiences. The values they chose—equity, progressivity, and later family—have remained an important part of the code. Though added after the original income tax was created by begrudging national legislators, family nonetheless plays a nontrivial role in American taxation. Because the basic taxable unit is a family-household, family lies at the core of American taxation, pervading all parts of the code. It determines one's filing status, rate structure used to pay taxes, and eligibility for credits, exemptions, and deductions.[24] Even though family plays a major role in each of these areas, it is uniquely positioned as an administrator of federal policy through individual tax expenditures.

Though public administration scholars have expanded the notion of policy administration beyond traditional hierarchical models of public service agencies to include nonprofits, public-private partnerships, and private companies, they have not looked at how seemingly private social arrangements also operate in much the same way.[25] American families—like these other network actors—act on behalf of the state under the laws prescribed by Congress and the rules developed by the IRS when they take tax reductions and in turn provide goods and services to members. Just as corporations are motivated by favorable tax incentives to provide additional pension and healthcare programs to their employees so, too, taxpaying family members are given incentives that discount the cost of goods and services.[26] For example, parents may contribute $5,000 toward their child's college tuition, but after favorable tax provisions the actual cost is only $3,500.[27]

Even though taxpaying family members are given incentives and often do act on behalf of other members of their family, there are no guarantees that the resources will get to where policymakers hope to target them. A grandmother may choose not to save for her grandchild's education or parents may direct additional funds provided for a second child under the EITC to paying past debts. That is, tax expenditures make assumptions about shared income, shared resources, and the natural bonds of care that motivate individuals to act on behalf of their family. Nancy Folbre refers to the care that families provide as the "invisible heart" in direct contrast to the goods and services that the market provides by the "invisible hand."[28] The problem with assumptions that rely on the invisible heart is that there is little recourse when families do not act in accordance with them. Unlike traditional models of public administration there are no other managers or executives to whom to voice complaint. And unlike corporations, which also utilize incentives in the tax code, family members cannot change their kinship as they can their jobs.

This section explores the values and assumptions that underlie the social policy of American tax expenditures in which families act as administrators. Christopher Howard, in a thorough examination of tax expenditures, limits his analysis to programs that have social welfare as their primary objective arguing that, "virtually everyone can agree to exclude certain government functions like national defense, energy, commerce and transportation."[29] However, leaving out government functions, like national defense, which do *not* have social welfare as their primary function provides a much narrower analysis of social policy. For the purposes of this chapter, social policy is defined broadly to include all programs designed to meet the social needs of its citizens—health, welfare, education, general well-being—regardless of the primary function of the policy where they are found.

In this section, I first examine the value of family and then the core and peripheral assumptions in the administration of social policy in the nation's tax code. Family is relatively uncontroversial in the tax code, but concrete expectations for family members, especially wives, have deviated from broader social practices. Thus, policy gaps have developed in those areas of the tax code that treated families under a single-breadwinner model and have provided entrepreneurs opportunities to enact change. As with immigration policy, gaps in tax policy have formed in the peripheral assumptions.

Core Values

Core values are ideals that set the general scope of policymaking: what should be provided, how, and to whom. Though core values are relatively abstract, they can be found in tax policy by examining the details of public law. Even though the tax code is notorious for its complexity, finding the values that underlie it can be a somewhat more manageable task. Because the focus of this chapter is on policy administration in the Internal Revenue Code, the means by which incentives in the tax code are implemented are indicators of important underlying values. In the case of the U.S. tax code, families and corporations (as taxpayers) shoulder the burden of carrying out the implicit policy in tax expenditures.[30]

Lining up all of the tax expenditures in the individual income tax code reveals there is very little that is systematic about programs accomplished through the tax code. The expenditures benefit various segments of society: business and individuals, wealthy and poor, elderly and children.[31] Restricting the list to social programs, the values underlying what would otherwise appear to be haphazard collection of policies become much clearer. When tax expenditures target the social well-being of Americans, family is a core value. Not only does family relationship determine the criterion of eligibility (*who* gets what), but it also determines administration (*how* goods and services get to particular individuals in society). Rather than create new policy programs or new bureaucratic agencies to monitor them, policymakers are able to target goods and services to members of society through their families. In social provision through tax expenditures, families are the primary administrators.

Because it is not possible to examine each and every tax expenditure, to find the core values of tax expenditures generally, I examined the particular administrative features of three important components of the federal budget: education (4 percent of all federal outlays), national defense (20 percent), and international affairs (1.4 percent).[32] I chose education because as a classic example of social policy it demonstrates how family might administer policy in dozens of other social policy expenditures. I also chose two hard cases, places where one would not necessarily expect family to act as an administrator, using practical and theoretical criteria. Starting with the broad list of tax expenditures, I eliminated all categories that are available only to corporate taxpayers. Next, due to the complexity of tax expenditures, I selected categories that had five or less expenditures each so I would be able to conduct an exhaustive search of each of the provisions. Finally, I chose two categories that were not traditionally associated with family. In particular, I selected a category specifically *excluded* by Christopher Howard because it was not about social policy—national defense—and a category generally not considered very family related, international affairs. Finding family in education policy indicates that family works as an administrator in social welfare policies; finding family across all three indicates it is used more broadly as a value in the administration of social policies in the tax code. Though most prominent by far in education, I found family administers policy in all three areas.

First, in the case of higher education tax expenditures, the federal government subsidizes college expenses through provisions in the tax code. Although higher education is subsidized at both the national and state levels, individual students alone are responsible for financing their college education through grants, loans, work-study, and/or family contribution. If higher education tax incentives are available *only* to the student taxpayer, it would indicate a core value of individualism (individual merit, individual achievement). Higher education tax expenditures that are available to taxpayers *other* than the individual student indicate other values, such as family, or corporate responsibility. That is, when focusing on administration in the tax code, tax expenditures that rely on corporations to administer suggests that there is a key link between work and education. However, I found that education tax expenditures were available to family members who acted on behalf of their dependents and relatives. Family is a core value in the administration of the social policy of American tax expenditures.

In 2006, the federal budget outlays for higher education topped $39.8 billion.[33] The same year, tax expenditures for higher education reached $16.2 billion.[34] The money "spent" through tax expenditures allows individual taxpayers to better afford higher education, for example, by permitting them to deduct the interest paid on their student loans. Table 5.2 below lists the ten major tax benefits for higher education in 2006. It succinctly summarizes who qualifies for educational benefits.

The table clearly shows that family members are the overwhelming beneficiaries of education "spending" in the tax code. Of the ten benefits, only two—employer-provided educational assistance and business deductions for work-related education—are limited solely to the taxpayer. Similarly, only one benefit, a Coverdell Savings account, is open to taxpayers regardless of their relationship to the beneficiary. For the other seven major education benefits, the tax code channels education spending through taxpayers to their spouses, children, and extended family relations.

The analysis of education policy in the nation's tax code complicates the notion of the liberal individual. Though there are many aspects of higher education that delineate and give rights to students apart from their parents, guardians, or kin relations more generally, provisions in the tax code reify one's family status.[35] Indeed, the tax code both capitalizes on and reinforces family relationships to accomplish particular goals. What higher education so clearly illustrates is not just that family members (even when they pay no taxes) qualify for educational assistance, but that they qualify when their taxpaying relatives act on their behalf. For millions of Americans, government subsidization of their college education comes without ever filling out a student financial aid form or without the explicit transfer of funds from the public coffers to colleges across the nations. Tax expenditures provide this often unseen and uncounted assistance through the scores of hidden administrators—moms, dads, and grandparents—who must learn the rules (and are held accountable) about what qualifies as a legitimate education expense and how much they are allowed to spend. Families are an essential part of new governance.[36]

Policies that target traditional welfare areas, such as education, intuitively seem to be places where family would act as an administrator, but education may be criticized as being an easy case. Family administration,

TABLE 5-2
2005 Tax Benefits for Higher Education

Tax Benefit	Description	Eligibility		
		Taxpayer	Family Members & Dependents	Others
Scholarships, Fellowships, Grants, and Tuition Reductions	Aid used for educational expenses in pursuit of a higher degree is not taxable.	Yes	Widow/Widower Child Spouse	No
Hope Credit	Up to $1500 credit per eligible student	Yes (if not a dependent)	Spouse Son Daughter Stepchild Foster child Brother Sister Half Brother Half Sister Stepbrother Stepsister Father Mother Grandparent Stepfather Stepmother Son-in-law Daughter-in-law Father-in-law Brother-in-law Sister-in-law Descendant (grandchild or niece) Other dependent	No
Lifetime Learning Credit	Up to $2000 credit per return	Yes (if not a dependent)	Same as for Hope Scholarship (above)	No
Student Loan Interest Deduction	Up to $4000 of interest paid on student loans	Yes	Same as for Hope Scholarship (above)	No
Coverdell Education Savings Accounts (Education IRAs)	Trust for the purpose of assisting with qualified education expenses	Yes	Any	Anyone under the age of 18 or is special needs.
Withdrawls from traditional or Roth IRAs	Early withdrawls for education not subject to 10% surtax	Yes	Spouse Son Children Grandchildren	No

TABLE 5-2 (continued)

Tax Benefit	Description	Eligibility		
		Taxpayer	Family Members & Dependents	Others
Education Savings Bond Program	Exclude interest on savings bonds	Yes	Same as for Hope Scholarship (above)	No
Employer Provided Educational Assistance	Employer provided tax-free benefits for education up to $5250	Yes	No	No
Qualified Tuition Programs	Distribution and transfer of money in qualified tuition programs may be tax free	Yes	Spouse Child Brother Sister Stepbrother Stepsister Father Mother Parental Ancestor Stepfather Stepmother Son Niece Nephew Aunt Uncle Son-in-law Daughter-in-law Father-in-law Mother-in-law Brother-in-law Sister-in-law Spouse of any of the above First Cousin	No
Business Deduction for Work-Related Education	Additional itemized deductions for education expenses required for work	Yes	No	No

SOURCE: Author's analysis of data in: "Tax Benefits for Education," (Washington, D.C.: Department of Treasury, Internal Revenue Service, 2006)

however, is not limited to areas traditionally associated with family and social policy, in fact, it occurs across a broad range of tax expenditures. Looking at two hard cases, national defense and international affairs, shows that many types of individual tax expenditures rely on family as an administrator.

First, under the function of "National Defense" the Joint Committee on Taxation, which determines what qualifies as an expenditure, lists three items: (1) exclusion of benefits and allowances to Armed Forces personnel ($2.8 billion); (2) exclusion of military disability benefits ($100 million); and (3) deduction of overnight-travel expenses of National Guard and Reserve Members.[37] In the first two cases, the IRC reduces taxes by excluding benefits-in-kind, allowances, or reimbursements from income. Although many military benefits are targeted directly to the uniformed serviceperson, such as travel allowances that allow leave between consecutive tours, even these travel allowances can be used for the cost of round-trip travel for dependent students and reassignment costs associated with needs of a dependent.

The exclusion of benefits and allowances to Armed Forces personnel, which amounted to almost $3 billion, includes a category of family allowances that is given to servicemen and servicewomen for benefits targeted directly to their spouses and (dependent) children. Members of the armed services exclude from their taxable income qualified educational, emergency, evacuation, and separation expenses.[38] Though the serviceperson gains indirectly from these benefits, the targeted beneficiaries of these programs are spouses, children, and other relatives. Family acts as a criterion of eligibility, determining who may qualify for the goods and services, but more importantly family members act on behalf of other family members. That is, the member of the armed services—*not her spouse and children*—reduces her taxable income. The IRC provides benefits directly targeted to particular individuals through a taxpaying relative.

Second, the equally unlikely category of international affairs also shows that family is a value in tax policy. For 2006, the Joint Committee on Taxation lists two expenditures that individuals may claim under the international affairs function: (1) exclusion of income earned abroad by U.S. citizens ($3.8 billion) and (2) exclusion of certain allowances for federal employees abroad ($600 million).[39] Although the first category, income earned abroad by U.S. citizens, does not have a family connection because the taxpayer takes such deductions on his or her behalf, the second category, allowances for federal employees abroad, does show the importance of family administration.[40]

Like armed forces personnel, U.S. citizens who earn money abroad or are employed by the U.S. government abroad are able to reduce their taxable income. In fact, this provision of international affairs looks a great deal like the exclusion of benefits for military personnel. U.S. government employees who work in foreign countries are able to reduce their taxable income through provisions directly targeted at providing services for their spouses and dependent children. For example, federal employees abroad may receive allowances for the education of their dependents (in certain circumstances) or for separate maintenance of dependents. These are services that directly benefit dependents that are granted through federal employees. Like members of the armed services, families of civil servants abroad also benefit through indirect subsidies granted to their relatives such as transportation, housing, travel, and medical expenses.[41]

When expenditures may be claimed not only by and for the individual taxpayer but also on behalf of others, the taxpayer acts as a policy administrator. Administration regularly occurs on behalf of individuals who are unable to file their own tax returns, such as young children or dependent adult parents. Major social policy programs through the tax code targeted toward these individuals, such as dependent care, healthcare, and education credits, make the point most clearly: family members are encouraged by the IRC to act in concert with the state to administer social policies.[42] By examining what appeared to be the two most difficult expenditure functions, national defense and international affairs, I found that even in these areas family plays a role. That is, when it comes to individual tax expenditures, beneficiaries are often individuals other than the person taking the expenditure.

Family is an important part of social policy administration in the tax code. Yet, much of what it does remains hidden in the shadows of direct expenditure programs that rely on more traditional administrators. The services that families are encouraged to provide through the tax code seem natural and normal. Indeed, policymakers who import definitions of family may rely on "common sense" or boilerplate law and policy from other areas. Just as policymakers reached back into the common law notions of family status to put family-households at the core of the tax code in the 1940s to solve the income-splitting division between common law and community property states, the use of family—and particular definitions thereof—may have little to do with an agenda that specifically seeks to promote a particular vision of family. Indeed, family may serve as a simple way to execute public policy, and understandings of family may be adopted from other parts of law and society. Fundamentally, this often unconscious adoption may have ramifications for future tax policy. Merely because family is an important value in the code and an important social practice for Americans does not mean that more specific assumptions about family are equally unproblematic. In fact, it is just the opposite. Core assumptions about what makes up a family and who qualifies as a "child" or "mother" in that family are both more specific and more likely to differ from American social practice.

Core Assumptions

Core assumptions break values down into basic categories or ways of thinking about the family. In the case of taxation, core values about family have been based upon the idea that families share resources. I have found that in each of the four major components of taxation—income tax rates, exemptions, deductions, and credits—the assumption that families pool resources is used to aggregate individual taxpayers into larger household units and then determine the rate at which they will be taxed; to encourage family members to administer policy; or to prohibit family members from shirking their tax obligations. There could potentially be significant problems if a gap has developed between the expectations that policymakers had about shared resources and the actual practices of American families. Do American families act in ways that conflict with American tax policy?

To examine the core assumptions in tax policy, I looked in-depth at two tax expenditure areas in further detail: education credits and the EITC. Education credits provide continuity with the previous section on core values; they show how core assumptions work in a typical social service expenditure. The EITC, in contrast, is an atypical expenditure. Not only is it one of the biggest and most costly individual tax expenditures, it actually refunds money to taxpayers beyond the income taxes they have paid. In both, family functions to administer the expenditures. This section evaluates how nearly the assumption that families share resources that lies behind credits, deductions, and exclusions, which collectively make up tax expenditures, matches broader social practices.

The IRC relies heavily on a financial formula for determining which collection of individuals qualifies as a family. Unlike the Immigration and Naturalization Act, which relies almost exclusively on close kinship to determine family (extended vs. nuclear), the IRC has a far more expansive list of relatives (ranging from in-laws to foster children) that often hinges as much on financial dependency as on explicit kin relationship.

The dependency exemption, which determines qualification for many tax expenditure programs, illustrates the balancing act that takes place between kin relationship and shared financial resources. Although a taxpayer generally is considered to have a dependent only if the taxpayer provides the majority of the financial support for the person, the closer the kin relationship the less one has to establish additional shared family resources.[43] A mother who financially supports her son, but does not live with him, qualifies for the dependency exemption. Conversely, the more distant the kin relationship the greater the need to show shared resources. A woman who financially supports her cousin must additionally share a household with him for the entire year to qualify for the exemption. Though kinship is an important factor, families are created in the tax code around the assumption that they share resources.

The IRC assumes that with a small incentive, individuals will be motivated to act on behalf of their families. *Because* families share resources, policymakers are able to take advantage of their financial dependency to encourage individual taxpayers to act in particular ways, such as saving money for a college education. In 2005, the average family with one dependent student in college would save $1,500 on their taxes with either a Hope or Lifetime Learning Credit. The average cost, however, of tuition at a four-year public college was $5,038 ($11,441 with room and board) and $18,838 ($26,489) at a private college.[44] As helpful as the credits are, they provide only a fraction of the costs of college education. Still, more than 7.4 million taxpayers claimed them.[45] Tax credits reduce, but do not eliminate, costs associated with policy goals. Family members are assumed to be willing to bear these costs (costs that a stranger, for example, would likely not) because they already share resources.[46] Tax credits act as an incentive for the behavior that relatives would "naturally" exhibit toward one another.

At the same time that policymakers exploit the assumption that families share resources to achieve their policy objectives, they also are wary of ways that families share resources to the benefit of the individual family at the expense of the Treasury. That is, the tax code also uses the assumption that families share resources to *limit* the ability of individual taxpayers to act on behalf of their family as well.[47] In the case of education, the tax code prohibits deducting student loan interest from a related person.[48] Unlike loans from strangers, who would demand interest in exchange for their financial services, the assumption of shared family resources makes a similar action by a family member circumspect. In this case, *because* families share resources, deducting interest on loans is likely to be a strategy of tax avoidance rather than a genuine college expense.

Unlike aid for higher education, which is targeted broadly at the middle classes, the EITC provides assistance for low-income working families. Originally a temporary credit enacted without fanfare in 1975, the EITC has grown into the primary means of providing earnings assistance for working Americans.[49] The EITC is a negative tax, meaning beneficiaries may receive cash assistance from the IRS beyond what they have paid as income taxes into the system.[50] The credit rewards work by supplementing the income of low-wage workers through benefits that are phased in until they reach a specified income level, plateau, and are then phased out until they reach zero. Even though single adults without children are now eligible, the beneficiaries overwhelmingly remain families.[51]

Like education credits, the core assumption for the EITC is that families share resources. Qualification for the EITC is determined based upon family status, and families with children receive substantially more than families without. The EITC specifically privileges *children* as opposed to other dependents because of their relationship to work. Because children are unable to bring in outside income, the assumption underlying the EITC is that money given to parents will trickle down to their children's well-being with financial assistance for food, heat, and clothes. For tax year 2005, single individuals who received the credit had to earn less than $11,750 to qualify. Single parents with one child, however, had to earn less than $31,030 to qualify.[52] The addition of a single child adds nearly $20,000 to the income that an individual will make and still claim credit. Likewise, the credit benefits families with children substantially more than those without. The maximum amount a single person may qualify for is $390 when her income is between $5,500 and $6,500. In contrast, the maximum amount a single person with one child may qualify for is $2,662 when his income is between $7,800 and $14,400.[53] The more generous payment to families is not a "bonus" for having children. The federal government returns money to taxpayers through the EITC in order to help parents *and* children in low-income families meet their needs. Families with two or more children receive a proportional increase in aid. The tiered structure of the EITC suggests that individual taxpayers who are parents get more resources because taxpaying parents share their resources with their children.

Has a policy gap developed in the core assumption that families share resources, or do American families follow this pattern? From debt obligation between spouses to parental financial responsibility for their children, it seems obvious that families share resources. However, there are few readily available statistical data sources to confirm this. In other words, there are no developed measures of intrafamily finances. The U.S. Census Bureau measures the income of individual family members, but does not likewise gauge if or how family members share those financial resources. Similarly, the Federal Reserve System, which measures family net worth, does not specify individual members' access to that worth. The Data Collection Committee of the Federal Interagency Forum on Child and Family Statistics stressed in 2001, "the need for improvements in measures of household, family, and individual income" and in particular recommended that federal agencies "collect data on the frequency of sharing financial resources in families and households and the amounts shared."[54] The 2001–02 National Survey of Family and Households is exceptional in that it asks about intrafamily dynamics. Though the data cannot tell us how precisely resources are distributed within families, they do show that parents and householders overwhelmingly contribute to the expenses of their offspring and, at times, offspring and family members contribute to household expenses.[55]

Though researchers are not yet able to get at financial resources within families, they are aware that groups other than legally recognized families share resources but are nevertheless unable to claim family benefits. This core assumption has been attacked, at least on paper, by supporters of alternative households ranging from unwed couples to roommates. The Congressional Budget Office summed up the controversy as follows:

> The federal income tax code assumes that married couples combine their incomes and other resources to support themselves and their dependents, and therefore imposes taxes on the joint incomes of spouses. The code stops short of defining all tax units on the basis of shared incomes. On the one hand, married couples are presumed to combine resources and thus must file jointly. On the other hand, people in relationships not based on legal marriage or other family relationships must pay taxes on their separate incomes, even if they consume together. Unmarried couples or two members of the same family sharing a home are taxed as individuals.[56]

Thus, the core assumption that lies behind much of American taxation—families share resources—may be an accurate depiction of family life. However, as more and more households that are not considered by the tax code to be families share resources, the assumption that requires only particular families to be counted has become subject to greater controversy. The core assumption that families share has been used by other groups who share to question the special status that particular families receive.

Peripheral Assumptions

Peripheral assumptions operate within the broad category of financial dependency and tell us specifically who qualifies as a family member and what may be expected of them. In other words, core assumptions tell us that families share resources, but peripheral assumptions tell us more concretely *who* is expected to share *what*.

Though there are countless locations where peripheral assumptions are at work in the tax code, in this section I look at assumptions within the EITC about what constitutes a child and also about the nature of contributions to shared family income. The definition of child in the EITC is particularly useful in two regards. First, it provides a contrast to the definition of child in immigration policy (Chapter 4). Whereas the definition of child in immigration policy is strictly limited to clear kin relationships (biological and adopted children), the tax code more explicitly combines not only kin relationships but also financial dependency. Second, when the tax code uses family members to administer goods and services on behalf of legal dependents who cannot act on their own accord, children are the most frequent beneficiaries. Thus, the definition of child in the tax code provides insight into not only who benefits but it also illustrates the implicit policies of which they are the beneficiaries. In addition to the definition of child, this section examines contributions to family income in the EITC. One of the core assumptions of tax policy is that families share resources. Yet the most significant demographic change in the past forty years has been the influx of working women into the paid labor force. This section measures whether gaps have formed in assumptions about women's contribution to shared family income.

Until 2004, when Congress standardized the definition of child, the most striking feature in the tax code was the five separate definitions of child that applied to different parts of the code. In other words, the tax code required taxpayers to reassess their relationship with their children in the dependency exemption, earned income credit, child credit, dependent care credit, and head of household filing status.[57] A single child may or may not have qualified for any number of the above depending upon a combination of the following factors: her kin relationship with the taxpayer, age, financial dependency, residence, and citizenship.[58]

Though the definitions of child have become more closely aligned, I chose to focus on the definition found over time in the EITC because it offers specific insight into the particular assumptions that legislators embed in tax policy. The EITC, originally enacted in 1975, did not have its own definition of child and instead relied on the definition used for the dependency exemption, a common practice for tax expenditures more generally. As the EITC became a larger and more generous program targeted to a particular subset of the population, the peripheral assumptions underlying the definition of child that had sufficed for the rest of the tax code were not adequate. More concretely, because the EITC operates under the core assumption that "families share" and it distributes *family* subsidies to *individual* taxpayers, policymakers have devoted the first twenty-five years of the EITC to narrowing the definition of child to make it more restrictive and the past five to making the definition better fit the social practice of families. Since its inception in 1975, the definition has been amended on seven separate occasions, and in every case, until 1999, the definition has become more stringent.[59]

Between 1975 and 1999, "child" was amended five times. In each of these cases, it was to create stricter requirements. In 1978 and 1984, policymakers added explicit residency requirements. In order to claim the credit, the child had to reside with the taxpayer for at least half of the taxable year and had to reside in the United States. In 1990, when the EITC was further expanded, Congress decided that the EITC needed a separate definition of child to meet the demands of the target population. The definition they created had a four-pronged test: relationship, residency, age, and identification. Amendments in 1994 and 1998 strengthened the identity requirements.

The peripheral assumptions about clear-cut family relationships embedded in the EITC definition of child had become outdated. Changes in family practices, illustrated in Chapter 2, Figures 2.5 and 2.6, show that traditional families are on the decline, and alternative family arrangements are increasingly likely. In practice, American children are less likely to live with two parents who are married to each other and increasingly in homes where one or both guardians are not biological parents. By 1999, policymakers switched course and responded to changing demographic trends by creating a broader relationship test. Policymakers allowed, for the first time, extended family members to qualify as "child," provided they were placed with the taxpayer by a qualified placement agency. In 2001, these requirements were relaxed so that extended family members qualified if they were a member of the recipient's household (for at least half of the year), and they were treated as a child of the recipient. Janet Holtzblatt and Janet McCubbin, both economists at the Treasury Department, note that families in the United States have "complicated lives." The EITC in the late 1990s aimed to address the complicated lives families lead.

However, even though the definition of child in the EITC was amended to better meet the needs of recipients, the increasingly complicated rules made it difficult for parents and guardians to act as administrators. Taxpayers incorrectly claim larger credits than they are qualified to receive. The Joint Committee on Taxation notes that the EITC is "one of the most complex provisions of the Code" and the IRS estimates that taxpayer mistakes (intentional or otherwise) for this expenditure run in the billions of dollars.[60] Further, one quarter of the overpayments alone was due to taxpayers misidentifying children under their care as a qualified "child" under the definition given by the EITC. Parents and guardians who claimed a child in one part of the code (such as the dependency exemption) could not necessarily assume that the same individual would be considered a child under the EITC. Rather, they had to run through the four tests discussed above. Congress acted in 2004 to standardize the definitions of child precisely so that administrators would be better able to do their jobs.

Family practices have changed in many ways, but the demographic practice that has most vexed American tax policy has been the large influx of middle-class wives and mothers into the paid labor force. To be sure,

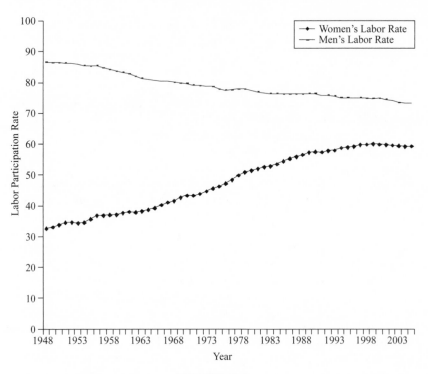

FIGURE 5-3
Labor Force Participation Rates for Men and Women 1948-2005
SOURCE: Author's analysis of data drawn from the Bureau of Labor Statistics.

women have always been a part of the workforce. Following World War II, women's labor force participation rate—which measures the percent of women in the labor force out of the total number of eligible women—was nearly 33 percent. Over time, the percentage continued to increase.

As Figure 5.3 shows, women's labor force participation has been increasing steadily even as men's participation rates have fallen slightly. Identifying women's workforce participation generally, however, masks the broader trend about which particular women are now going to work. What has been a truly remarkable shift since the 1970s has been the large influx of mothers into the workforce.

Figure 5.4 illustrates the labor participation rates of mothers (with children under 18 years of age) by marital status. Though married women with children have been counted by the Bureau of Labor Statistics since 1948, divorced and separated women (with children) have only been counted since 1970 and single mothers since 1980. The picture painted in the past three decades portrays a large influx of working moms. The labor force par-

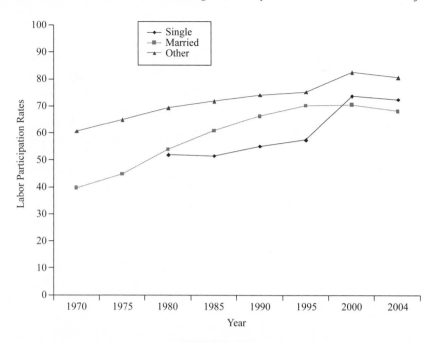

FIGURE 5-4

Mothers' Labor Force Participation Rates by Marital Status, 1970–2004

SOURCE: Author's analysis of data drawn from the Bureau of Labor Statistics and the "Statistical Abstract of the United States: 2006," (Washington, D.C.: U.S. Census Bureau, 2005).

NOTE: "Other" includes women who are divorced, widowed, and married but without a husband present.

ticipation rate of married women with children during this time has risen from 39.7 to 70.6, an increase of 78 percent. As "individuals" (free from relationships) the trend presents little problem for taxation, but as wives and mothers it has ramifications that ripple throughout the tax code.

The tax code generally seeks to assess family income and then tax it both equitably and progressively. Assumptions about how much women contribute to family income were used to structure tax rates and tax expenditures when tax code allowed for joint filing in 1948. The rate structures put in place at that time were for traditional nuclear families with a primary breadwinner. Women's increasing labor force participation has created the so-called marriage tax penalty, which taxes married couples at higher rates than if they were singles. The marriage tax penalty is part and parcel of many parts of the tax code (filing rates, standard deduction, tax credits). It was also a major part of the EITC originally created in 1975, which made no distinctions between single-parent and dual-parent families.

For dual-earner couples, the burden was striking. The marriage penalty for low-income couples hovered between $1,000 and $3,000, a significant percent of total income. Because the EITC did not differentiate between single and married parents, a single working parent with two children who married a working spouse would face stiff penalties. For example, in the extreme case, if a full-time minimum-wage-earning mother with two children married a full-time minimum-wage-earning father with two children, their combined EITC penalty would have been $5,600.[61] In this case, the full-time minimum-wage-earning parents each get the maximum benefit per dollar earned when they are single. By marrying, their total income increases but the credit per dollar earned is reduced significantly. Thus, even though the couple may have the same expenses, their assistance would be severely curtailed. The penalty effectively punished dual-earner families. The ever-popular credit that was supposed to encourage work and marriage punished mothers for doing both. The influx of working women, and especially mothers, into the paid labor force created a policy gap between social practice and the objectives of the credit.

FAMILY, TAX, AND CHANGE OVER TIME

The EITC is helpful for understanding how policies that rely on family to administer their goals adapt to changing family practices. Using parents to administer the credit has been a double-edged sword. On the one hand, the creation and expansion of the EITC reflects the perceived efficiency (economic and political) that family administration garners in the tax code. On the other hand, changing demographic practices that took mothers out of the home and placed them into the workforce has put pressure on the tax code for change. Like the tax code more generally, the EITC had severe marriage penalties that taxed dual-earner married couples at much higher rates than if they remained single. The penalty, which is viewed as unfair in the general tax code, is especially problematic in the EITC for two reasons. First, as a percentage of income, the penalty in the EITC is more significant than the penalty for any other group. Second, because the EITC has developed into an antidote for the problems associated with traditional welfare programs (AFDC), the EITC must promote *both* work and family. This section examines how the EITC has adapted to changing practices of mothers in the workforce, especially the growth of the EITC and the corresponding marriage tax penalty.

The EITC passes muster with liberals and conservatives alike for many of the same reasons that tax expenditures more generally are favored. While liberals appreciate the ends of the credits (helping out needy families) conservatives appreciate the means (tax credits). Further, the EITC is perceived as good fiscal and administrative policy. The IRS already processes over a hundred million tax returns annually, adding one additional credit adds only small marginal costs to their overall administrative burden. Unlike programs that require the creation of new agencies and bureaucracies, the administrative structure to implement the EITC is already in place.[62] Janet Holtzblatt of the Treasury Department explains: "When you compare the EITC to a government program like food stamps you can see the difference. There is $4 billion in administrative costs for food stamps and food stamp recipients are only a fraction of what is served by the EITC. The entire budget of the IRS is only $10 billion."[63] In 2005, the IRS spent a meager $164 million to administer the EITC, a program in which 21.9 million taxpayers claimed $39.7 billion.[64]

The administration of the EITC wins support for being less intrusive and burdensome to recipients than traditional social welfare programs. If EITC recipients are already filling out a tax return, the additional burden of the credit is far less than registration requirements for a program like AFDC or food stamps. Even when the IRS audits a return and asks for supplemental documentation, only a small fraction of EITC recipients are likely to receive an inquiry, and for most the exchange is in the mail. Holtzblatt notes, "again, compare food stamps where applicants have to fill out an application, attach documentation, go to an office, stand in line, wait in line, get interviewed—and everyone has to do it."[65] In 2003, Congress enacted a controversial precertification program, which requires EITC applicants to submit additional paperwork in advance. Even still, the human costs of compliance are lower than traditional social welfare programs.

The rapid growth of the EITC since its origins in the 1970s is due in part to the political and administrative benefits attached to tax expenditures. The rise of the EITC, however, is also due to a change in social practices surrounding the family. As the core of traditional welfare programs, which sought to aid poor children by paying their mothers to be full-time caretakers, grew more distant from the social practice of American families, a gap grew between the policy and practice. As more and more mothers entered the workforce, setting a good example as a mother increasingly meant participation in the paid workforce over welfare state payments. The EITC emerged as a program with an alternative model that promoted family and work.[66] The EITC aided poor children by encouraging and making it possible for their mothers to work, just like middle-class families more generally. As the coalition supporting the age-old AFDC slowly unraveled, defectors turned to the EITC as a viable alternative.[67]

Testifying before the Senate Finance Committee in 2001, Harvard political economist David Ellwood explained the support the credit garners: "Ronald Reagan called the EITC the best antipoverty, the best pro-family,

best job creation plan ever created. He was right. It's been wildly successful."[68] Yet as the program has grown and become more generous, it has
also increased the size of the marriage tax penalty. As much as the EITC has
been painted as the answer to misguided welfare policies that discourage
family, it was originally enacted without distinctions for family size including the number of children in a family as well as parental marital status.
Legislation passed in 1990 amended the EITC so that benefits phased in
and phased out depending on the number of children in the family.[69] The
definition of family still did not take into account the presence of a single
parent or married adults.

Work patterns of American women have changed in ways that policymakers years ago could not or did not envision. A 1997 Congressional
Budget Office report points to changing demographic practices as driving
the creation of the marriage tax penalty. It finds: "If the demographic characteristics of married couples had not changed between 1969 and 1996,
more couples would have received bonuses under 1996 tax law and fewer
would have incurred penalties."[70] The report goes on to state: "simula-
tions indicate that without the demographic change of the last quarter
century, two-thirds of couples would get bonuses and less than one-third
would pay penalties." The marriage tax penalty is a function of outdated
assumptions about women's contribution to family income. The U.S. tax
code, which is fundamentally concerned with income, has had to adapt
to women's increased workforce participation in many ways: adjusting
marginal tax rates, adding credits for childcare, and eliminating—if not
reducing—the disincentive to work and marriage in the "marriage tax
penalty."

Republican policymakers coupled tax policy with concern for American
families in three specific areas: the estate tax (or "death tax" that hurt family farms and businesses), reduction in tax rates (or "relief for American
families"), and the marriage tax penalty.[71] In 2001 Congress passed, and
President George W. Bush signed, a comprehensive tax bill (the Economic
Growth and Tax Relief Recovery Act) that accomplished those three goals.
Though the administration wanted politically popular marriage tax penalty relief for middle-class families, it found that it could not divorce the
discussion of marriage penalty relief for the middle class from marriage
penalty relief for the working poor who received the EITC. Policymakers
in Congress on the left and right would not budge unless *all* married couples would be better off, and they made provisions specifically to bolster
the EITC. Advocates for the poor and advocates for family values were
able to pass tax reform and generous EITC provisions far beyond what
the president had proposed. The historical assumptions embedded in tax
policy along with shifts in broader social practices set the stage for political

actors to overhaul the marriage tax penalty in the Internal Revenue Code generally and specifically in the EITC.

Fulfilling his campaign promise to reduce taxes from their historically high levels, President Bush made it a priority in his first year in office to reform what he had viewed as the misguided fiscal policy of the Clinton Administration. By the time that Bush took office in 2001, taxes as a percentage of Gross Domestic Product (GDP) had reached 20.8 percent—the highest level since World War II. The Bush Administration estimated that cumulative budget surpluses for the next decade would top $5.6 trillion and was determined to reverse the trend of high taxation and enact a tax cut.[72]

As a part of the tax cut, President Bush proposed to reduce the marriage tax penalty in the general tax code. The president's original $112.8 billion plan was targeted specifically at dual-earner households and allowed the lower-earning partner to deduct 10 percent of his or her earnings up to $3,000 from their taxable income. Though President Bush's proposal would reduce penalties for many dual-earner couples making $50,000 or more, it would not offer relief for Americans who received the EITC.[73] Because the EITC is a credit, and many recipients already pay no income tax or pay reduced income tax (they do pay regressive payroll taxes), this solution would not help them.

Early in 2001, as economic forecasters predicted a potential slowdown in the economy, members of Congress on both sides of the aisle agreed that that tax cuts were necessary. Even though the House, with a Republican majority, could give the president much of what he asked, members were not willing to follow his proposals for marriage penalty relief. In fact, of all the provisions of the tax plan, Congress's blueprint for marriage penalty relief deviated furthest from the president's plan. Ways and Means Chair William Thomas (R-CA) crafted HR 6, The Marriage Penalty and Family Tax Relief Recovery Act, which doubled the 15 percent bracket and standard deductions for married couples subject to conventional tax rates to twice that of single persons. The EITC was also amended. Low-income married couples could make more money and still qualify for the EITC through more generous phase-out rates for married couples and by defining earned income as gross income. Thomas's bill did alleviate the penalty for a broad spectrum of Americans. But it also came with a hefty price tag—$223 billion—twice the amount President Bush had proposed.

Thomas's bill reduced the marriage tax penalty, but it also increased the marriage tax bonuses to those American families with one breadwinner already paying lower taxes as a married couple than as two single individuals. Unlike the president's targeted plan, Congress supported a measure that made *all* married people better off whether they were penalized before or not. The congressional plan was the only one that social conservatives would support. Social conservatives realized the difficult situation they were in—on the one hand the tax code penalized marriage because more and more wives and mothers were in the workforce, but on the other hand they did not want to favor dual-earner couples over traditional families. As a measure of how important this particular solution was, Senator Chuck Grassley (R-IA) started off the Senate hearings in the Finance Committee, which he chaired, by stating: "I'm confident that we can find common ground in this area [marriage tax penalty] and that we'll report legislation that promotes and strengthens marriage providing income tax relief to married couples, marriages with a stay-at-home parents and marriage where both husband and wife work."[74]

With a Republican majority large enough to pass HR 6—with or without Democratic support—the Republicans in the House crafted a bill that many Democrats would like, but had no input in creating. House Republicans deviated from the president's proposals, increasing aid for the working poor (EITC) and decreasing benefits for wealthier parents. Even with some lingering hard feelings, 64 Democrats voted for the Republican proposal. This is not surprising as 48 Democrats had defected from the party line in 2000, voting for a Republican tax cut plan with similar marriage penalty relief that was eventually vetoed by President Clinton.[75]

The situation in the Senate was very different. Evenly split, Senators approached tax legislation far more carefully and with more willingness to compromise on the president's priorities than their House counterparts. Because passage was not a foregone conclusion and consensus had to be built, the Senate gave the specific proposals a great deal of careful consideration. The Senate agreed to the overall direction of the House solution to the marriage tax penalty, but they increased the amount of income married couples could earn and still qualify for the EITC by $3,000. Senate moderates worked to ensure the tax benefits would not stop with the middle class. Olympia Snowe (R-ME) noted the Senate crafted a "thoughtful proposal" that ensured "marriage penalty relief for all couples."[76] After conference, the final legislation matched the Senate's version, except it included a phase-in of the provisions over five years.

Although 2001 was not the first time that Congress had attempted to eliminate the marriage tax penalty in the EITC, it was the first time it was successful. In this case, the policy was able to adapt to changing family practices because it made it to the agenda when problem, policy, and politics streams were joined and further political will was behind helping American families. First, policymakers had recognized the problem as one in which social practices had changed, in particular that (married) mothers were entering the workforce, and they agreed the problem needed to be fixed. Middle-class families brought the issue to the attention of Congressperson Jerry Weller (R-IL) who, over the course of several years, displayed Shad and Michelle Hallinan's wedding photo and told their compelling story often.[77] In hearings and floor debates, members of Congress identified the gap between policy assumptions and social practice as the problem that needed to be addressed. Senator Max Baucus (D-MT), the ranking member of Senate Finance Committee, which held hearings on the penalty, noted that the marriage tax penalty results in difficult trade-offs that members of Congress make when determining rates and structures in the code. He explains, "And partly it's because our work force is changing. We have many more two-earner couples. People, as couples, are much more likely to face the marriage penalty. Clearly, it's something we should address."[78] During the House floor debate, Representative Jennifer Dunn (R-WA) explained that the penalty is an attack on working women, and it is a big problem for the tax code to address. "This is not a problem for couples with a single breadwinner so much, but in today's society, where both the husband and wife work in most households, it is a huge problem."[79]

Second, policymakers proposed solutions that fostered their broader ideological goals. Over and over again, policymakers pointed to defects in the tax code and the need to take action like Illinois Republican Philip Crane, who remarked, "The marriage tax penalty should never have been allowed to creep into the Tax Code in the first place. It violates sound tax policy and runs counter to bedrock American traditions." He continued, "It is urgent that we move quickly to convince taxpayers that we mean business."[80] However, they looked to ready-made solutions that worked with their overall agenda. The proposed policy solutions were only *partially* about the demographic changes that lead to the marriage tax penalty. In large part, reforming the penalty was a contest over political ideology and political solutions each party would have chosen anyway.

Republicans argued that because government is less competent than individual Americans to manage money, any tax cut is a good tax cut. For example, Representative Deborah Pryce (R-OH) summed it up as follows: "If one is paying taxes today, one is paying too much; and if one is married, one is unfairly singled out to pay even more"[81] Democrats generally countered that tax cuts need to be carefully targeted to the needy population. Representative Martin Frost (D-TX) explained: "Democrats want tax relief, and we want tax relief in the context of fairness and in the context of real numbers. We want to provide real relief from the unfair marriage penalty for those couples who pay more taxes just because they are married, but we do not want to provide relief for those who already get a marriage bonus under the code, as the Republicans would do."[82] Though both parties agreed that the tax code needed to be amended, each party formed its solutions to fit its broader ideology.

Third, and finally, policymakers had the right political circumstances to address this policy gap. The ability to amend the EITC and provide more generous benefits for working families was due in large part to the favorable political situation for tax cuts more generally: projected budget surpluses, Republican leadership in the House and the executive, and the political importance of being "pro-family." "Fixing" the marriage tax penalty throughout the tax code has always meant *reducing* rates for those harmed. However, even if there is a disparity—as was clearly the case with the marriage tax penalty—adjusting the tax code even marginally results in significant fluctuations in revenue. The (originally projected) large budget surpluses gave Congress the opportunity to "fix" part of the tax code that was not only unfair but politically unpopular. Representative Dave Weldon (R-FL) made the case on the floor of the House: "Mr. Speaker, I ask you, if we cannot afford to fix problems such as this when we are enjoying surpluses, when can we do it? When can we take the necessary steps to make our tax code fairer, to do away with the unintended consequences of past actions? I say that we can do it now."[83] Republicans in the House and Senate were eager to cut taxes, and especially the politically unpopular marriage tax penalty. Large budget surpluses gave them the opportunity to do so, even if by increasing expenditures in the tax code. The budget gave policy actors the opportunity to enact change, but change in the administration finally allowed them to enact them. Marriage penalty relief had been proposed—and vetoed—by President Clinton. With the executive branch on their side, Republicans in Congress were guaranteed to have better results.

Policymakers were able to successfully amend the IRC because they could mobilize a coalition broad enough to support their proposed change. Marriage tax penalty relief was politically popular because both parties battled to be pro-family. Social conservatives pressed for favoritism for married couples while more socially moderate or liberal members favored eliminating discrimination against working wives and mothers. There was not a single policymaker willing to stand up and defend the marriage tax penalty as good policy. Representative Mike Pence (R-OH) reached to the heights of moral authority when he stated, "families should be encouraged today. I stand in strong support of this rule. I stand in strong support of this bill. It is time to end the illogical, immoral and unfair marriage penalty; and I believe in my heart Congress will do so today."[84] Representative James Traficant (D-OH) reached in a different direction as he somewhat crudely explained, "It is time to treat married couples at least as well as we treat casual sex participants in the United States of America."[85] Even Members of Congress opposed to the specifics of the legislation supported the spirit of marriage penalty relief and the notion that federal law should help American families. Representative Tammy Baldwin, Wisconsin's openly gay legislator, explained: "The marriage penalty is an unfair burden on many working families and I strongly support legislation to eliminate it. However, the Republican bill that is on the House floor today costs far too much and does far too little for Wisconsin families."[86]

Because the issue on the table was about *family* and with the EITC the potentially most vulnerable families, the coalition in favor of amending the EITC included members across party and ideology. Democrats and Republicans favored generous allowances for the EITC; they disagreed, however, on provisions for the marriage penalty in *other* parts of the tax code. Even the conservative Heritage Foundation pushed Congress for more generous (and more expensive) relief for the EITC because it would promote *family* for those who were most vulnerable.[87] The liberal Center for Budget and Policy Priorities supported changes in the EITC because the credit would better meet the needs of low-income Americans.

By the time the marriage tax penalty made it to the agenda in 2001, it seemed as though it was unstoppable. Everyone supported a policy change, and balancing the EITC with upper- and middle-class tax cuts seemed to be a bipartisan solution. Marriage tax penalty relief, importantly, distributed benefits widely—both to the middle class and to EITC recipients. Thus, many married Americans could benefit from the changes in tax law. Further, though the marriage tax penalty was only one piece of a much broader tax bill, policymakers chose to emphasize this particular aspect. By playing up family, they were able to portray the benefits to American society—helping or aiding American families—as even more widely distributed than any particular analysis of the numbers would allow. Though policymakers touted the changes to the tax code as vitally important, marriage tax penalty relief was not a major change to tax policy more generally. Indeed, it left the basic structure of taxation firmly in place.

CONCLUSION

Originally enacted to promote work by relieving regressive payroll taxes, the EITC nevertheless has blossomed into an alternative to welfare that promotes both family and work. However, even though the credit is hailed as an answer to the failing welfare program, it was not originally designed for that purpose. The influx of mothers into the paid labor force made the EITC a better alternative to traditional social welfare programs that paid women to stay home with their children. Politically and administratively popular with policymakers, the EITC also encourages work. At the same time that the tax credit has become more popular—increasing in size and benefits—it has also had to adapt significantly to its family-based constituency. The EITC has been amended to take account of the number of children in a family in 1990 and the marital status of parents with the reforms in 2001 in order to reduce penalties for dual-earner families.

The case of marriage tax penalty reform in the tax code generally was successful because changes would expand the program, distributing costs and increasing beneficiaries in the tax code as a whole. Middle-class Americans who were deeply affected by the marriage tax penalty lobbied for change. They found supporters both in the administration, which wished to cut taxes more generally, and with liberals and moderates who wanted to expand the EITC to better meet the needs of the target population. A marriage-tax penalty coalition became effective only when the EITC was included so that conservatives, moderates, and liberals not only supported reform but actively worked to bring it about. The resulting change was peripheral to the tax code—important to those families who benefited, but not a significant change in the way that taxation works in America. The marriage tax penalty helped push the flagging issue of cutting taxes back on the national agenda after "the taxpaying public ... seems to have lost its lust for the prize."[88] Tax cuts, the darling of fiscal conservatives, now had a family face enabling Congress and the president to pass the largest cuts since Ronald Reagan did so.

Alternative theories of change and the tax code suggest that the tax code changes incrementally or alternatively that it expands considerably after major events (like wars).[89] In part, both cases are true. The history of the development of the tax code from the Civil War until today shows that major wars have been the catalyst for expanding the administrative capacity of the tax code. Often, though not always, the tax code makes incremental adjustments as seen with legislation to change the definition of child and to fix the marriage tax penalty in the EITC. The analysis provided here adds depth to both of these theories of change by showing how particular components of policy are likely to come under fire and the ways in which supporters and opponents organize around both the means and ends to achieve their goals. It also shows that even though marriage tax penalty relief was politically popular, altering the code to alleviate the burdens on dual-earner households was peripheral to how the code works, and hence a smaller change for policy.

Looking closely at family as a means in the tax code suggests the future challenge for tax expenditures in general, and the EITC in particular, may be less about adapting to changing family practices than to a new set of administrators. Paradoxically, though "welfare" and Nixon's "guaranteed minimum income" remain politically forbidden words, the EITC—which seemingly combines both—has become extremely popular and looks to continue to do so in the future. Yet, tax expenditures in general, and the EITC in particular, have an Achilles' heel. The low administrative costs associated with expenditures means that the burden of compliance shifts from federal bureaucrats to parents who act as administrators. Based on data from filings in 1999, the IRS estimates that EITC overpayment rates are as high as 27 percent to 32 percent, in dollar figures between $8.5 and $9.9 billion.[90] By passing the responsibility of implementing the program from government bureaucrats to parents acting as administrators, federal policymakers have shifted the costs from traditional administration to taxpayer compliance. Parents and family members are expected to know and correctly utilize the credit but are unprepared for the complexity of the tax code. Tax code simplification, proposed by President Bush and passed by Congress, may be less about making taxpaying more convenient and increasingly about better preparing the shadow bureaucracy to do its job.

CHAPTER SIX

Rhetoric and Reality: The Family Farm

Author Marty Strange seems merely to sum up conventional wisdom about the normative power of the family farm when he notes on page one of his book, *Family Farming*: "Defending [the family farm] has long been the common rhetorical fare of politicians and opinion makers. You can't get a farm bill through Congress without invoking the image of the family farm."[1] Symbols, images, and language used to represent them are an important part of American politics and policymaking even as their use waxes and wanes over time. The self-sufficient farmer has been an especially potent symbol invoked by Thomas Jefferson as the backbone of American democracy. Though modern policymakers call on the ideal of the yeoman farmer working his field of wheat, corn, or soy to sell policies to an increasingly urban/suburban America, the words *family farm* often attached to it have been the common rhetorical fare of politicians beginning only in the 1940s. Prior to World War II, politicians and opinion makers passed the two most significant prewar agriculture policies (the 1862 Homestead Act and the 1933 Agricultural Adjustment Act) without reference to the "family farm." Although the symbol of the independent yeoman farm family has a long tradition, the political phrase *family farm* associated with American agriculture policy is a modern invention.

To be sure, families who live on farms have been a part of American society since its colonial origins. These farm families have populated small northeastern dairy farms, large southern cotton plantations, grain-producing homesteads in the Midwest, and large fruit farms in the West. Looking back, observers today might select criteria to determine which of these farms (likely the northeastern and midwestern) qualify as "family farms." To Americans prior to World War II, however, the phrase *family farm* would not bring to mind the same Jeffersonian image of the self-sufficient farmer, it would not exclude large farms worked by slaves, and it would not have a powerful normative draw. The words *family farm*, which evoke a distinct type of farm today, are a product of twentieth-century policy and discourse.

This chapter examines the rhetorical use of the family farm and the effect that invoking this phrase has for support for American agriculture policy. Unlike the chapters on family as a criterion of immigration policy (Chapter 4) or as an administrator in tax policy (Chapter 5), where I examined the policies in depth, in this chapter I focus on family as a normative ideal and concentrate on the language used to talk about policy rather than the intricacies of policy itself. The first part of the chapter lays out the values and assumptions behind the symbol of the family farm in contemporary America. It contrasts the symbol of the family farm (and the popular support it garners) with the social practice of farming as defined by the United States Department of Agriculture (USDA) statistics on family farming. There is a clear gap between the way that American agriculture is talked about (as a battle between nameless, faceless corporate-farms/agribusiness and the all-American family farmer) and the actual practice of farming. The second part of the chapter offers a historical explanation for why the Jeffersonian ideal has come to be associated with the phrase *family farm* and American agriculture policy by looking at the use of the phrase by politicians, policymakers, and the media. Even though the words *family farm* have been used in different ways throughout American history, during World War II the phrase began to signify a type of farm—categorically distinct from and superior to other (nonfamily) farms. The third and final part of the chapter looks at how the policy gap between the rhetoric of family farms and the social practice of family farming is exploited for political gain.

THE FAMILY FARM AS A NORMATIVE IDEAL

Symbols are an important part of the policymaking process. Murray Edelman explains that symbols have the capacity both to "serve as powerful means of expression" as well as "convey benefits to particular groups."[2] Individuals respond to symbols, such as the Jeffersonian ideal of the yeoman farm family, because it allows them to imbue politics with individual meaning. In other words, citizens' understanding of and participation in politics is conditioned through symbols. Edelman treats language as a symbolic part of politics. For the purposes of this chapter, however, I make a distinction between the symbol—the image or ideal that Americans hold about farms—and the language used to reinforce it—the phrase *family farm*. By keeping the symbolic image and the rhetorical practice distinct, one can see how the Jeffersonian ideal, which has been used to greater or lesser extent throughout American history, has been coupled with the phrase *family farm* in postwar America to produce broad and lasting support for American agriculture policy.

The power of language to "sanctify action is exactly what makes politics different from other methods of allocating values. Through language a group cannot only achieve an immediate result but also win the acquiescence of those whose lasting support is needed."[3] The rhetorical use of the family farm has leant incredible staying power for American agriculture policy that may do little to help those farmers Americans associate with it. Indeed, in contemporary politics the family farm is not analyzed, discussed, or debated. Rather, the term "masquerades as description" bolstering its powerful emotional appeal.[4] The rhetorical use of the words *family farm* in the post–World War II era has created a distinct type of farm category in the American mind, which draws on the Jeffersonian legacy but is a wholly contemporary phenomenon.

The family farm is more than just one way to frame an issue; it acts as what I call a normative ideal. That is, the family farm is not simply part of a utilitarian calculation—a means to provide agriculture products to Americans—but it is an end in and of itself. Americans revere the family farm because it embodies important American values, and it is a connection to their cultural past. For policymakers, using the words *family farm* lends credibility to their policy position at the same time it reinforces a cultural understanding. As this chapter will show, when policymakers invoke the image of the family farm they are tapping a core American value, a way of life that must be protected and promoted because it is good in and of itself. This image of the family farm is built on core assumptions about the size and operation of farming that do not match social practice. This section examines the values and assumptions behind strong public opinion favoring the family farm. It shows the gap between the cultural image of the family farm, cultivated by rhetoric, and the social practice of family farming, as defined by the USDA. This policy gap grows wider with the tacit consent of American policymakers.

Values

When legislators make policy, they use American values to set the scope of policymaking. When they talk about policy, they also rely on appeals to values to justify policy positions. The language they use indicates the values that they find important. Policymakers invoke the family farm as a simple phrase that embodies culturally rich core American values. When they speak about family farms and taxes or the economy or the environment, they tie their policy positions to commonly held values like self-sufficiency, independence, and a respect for the land.

The image of the family farm looms large in American culture, portrayed in stories of foreclosure on the national evening news, in Hollywood blockbusters like *Field of Dreams*, and in political speech. It is an image that most Americans have seen or heard about: "a lone tractor in a distant field, its trailing plume of dust marking the furrow as the farmer breaks the soil."[5] Though he has more modern machinery, this farmer works the land from dusk to dawn much like his father and grandfather before him. While he is plowing the field, the farmer's wife and daughters are busy with the livestock and tending to the gardens.[6] The family farmer is honest, exemplifying the best American values of "self-sufficiency, self-determination, rugged individualism, [and] independence."[7]

Policy images generally are in part empirical and in part emotive, but the family farm draws heavily from the latter.[8] Even if they are unwilling to give up an urban lifestyle for the farm, Americans value those who work on the family farm. Journalist Gregg Easterbrook sums up the power of the family farm image:

Few economic endeavors have any aura of romance and tradition. We don't get misty at the sight of a chain store framed against a prairie landscape or take comfort in knowing that each morning thousands of lawyers head out into the predawn darkness to tend to their lawsuits. Farming, though, occupies an honored place in our culture. Even big-city sophisticates who would sooner die than attend a Grange Hall dance find it reassuring to know that somewhere out there honest folk are working the earth much as it has been worked for centuries.[9]

The family farm is more than an economic enterprise, more than a way to produce food, it is an institution imbued with shared cultural values.

The family farm also produces better citizens. Even though he never used the phrase *family farm*, Thomas Jefferson praised the agrarian lifestyle as the only means of promoting true democracy. Jefferson paints farmers as superior: "those who labour in the earth are the chosen people of God, if ever he had a chosen people, whose breasts he has made his peculiar deposit for substantial and genuine virtue."[10] Jefferson contrasts the virtue of rural life for promoting a democratic society with the cancer of urban centers: "The mobs of great cities add just so much to the support of pure government, as sores do to the strength of the human body. It is the manners and the spirit of a people which preserve a republic in vigour. A degeneracy in these is a canker which soon eats to the heart of its laws and constitution."[11] The family farm is the link between the present and the past, a line connecting an American heritage of Thomas Jefferson's democratic-agrarian vision, the agricultural roots of many American families, and the quintessential American values ascribed to family farmers.[12]

Popular support for agriculture policies designed to help the family farm today rely on the connection between the rhetoric of "family farms" and American heritage. Americans support family farms as a way of life, a value in and of themselves. Public opinion data reveal that Americans support family farms and approve of policies targeted for family farms even when they do not generally approve of the policy for other types of agricultural arrangements or businesses. A 2004, PIPA/Knowledge Networks Poll found that while Americans are steadfastly opposed to subsidies for large or corporate farms, they overwhelmingly support subsidies for family farmers.[13] A similar Zogby poll in 1999 found that 69 percent of Americans believe that family farms are *better* than large corporate farms, which provide low-cost products and stable jobs, because family farms are a "fundamental part of our culture and an important connection to our past."[14]

American support for the family farm extends beyond the domain of agriculture policies. In 2000, Republicans in Congress framed the debate over the estate tax as putting an undue and unfair burden on family farms and small businesses. To make their point, they sent a tax bill to President Bill Clinton via a courier not usually found on the streets of Washington, DC—a bright red tractor driven by a Montana farmer.[15] The Republicans hammered home a politically effective (albeit not entirely accurate) point: the estate tax harms American family farmers. Though Americans generally favor taxing the wealthy, they wished to exempt family farms. A 2002 survey found that 56 percent of Americans approved of reforming the estate tax to exempt family farms and small businesses as opposed to 39 percent who wished to eliminate it.[16] In a 2003 survey, when asked why they favored eliminating the estate tax, 74 percent responded that forcing the sale of small businesses and family farms was a reason.[17]

Policymakers in Congress invoke the family farm in policy debates—like the estate tax—building on the popular support the family farm garners at the same time that their words reinforce and legitimize the importance of the family farm. Although they can frame farm debates in a number of different ways, policymakers often choose to talk about farming in the language of family. By all measures, policymakers disproportionately invoke this normative ideal in their speech. Between 1988 and 2005 when members of Congress talked about farms, 14 percent of these debates and discussions specifically mentioned family farms. To put this in perspective, only 2 percent of the sections on farming in the *U.S Code*—the statutory laws these same policymakers create—also reference the family farm.

Further, policymakers draw on the symbol of the family farm more than American newspapers do. Figure 6.1 compares family farm mentions in the *Congressional Record*, the *New York Times*, a national urban news

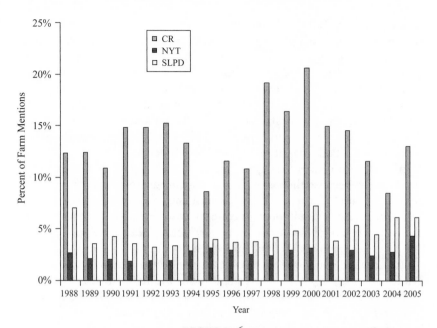

FIGURE 6-1

Family Farm Mentions as a Percent of All Farm Mentions in the *Congressional Record*, *New York Times*, and the *St. Louis Post Dispatch*, 1988–2005

SOURCE: Author's analysis of the *Congressional Record*, *New York Times*, and *St. Louis Post Dispatch*.

source, and the *St. Louis Post Dispatch*, a midwestern newspaper more hospitable to agricultural interests.[18] Using the percent of entries that mention family farm out of the total number of entries that include the word farm as the unit of analysis shows a disparity between the language of farm discussion in the newspapers compared to policymakers in the *Congressional Record*. In any given year the *Congressional Record* uses the family farm, at a minimum, twice as often as the newspapers, and at a maximum, eight times as much. Policymakers invoke the family farm in their debates far more often than in the statutes they write, far more often than the national urban-focused *New York Times*, and even far more often than the midwestern-centered *St. Louis Post Dispatch*.

Assumptions

When policymakers and pollsters invoke the image of the family farm, they rely on core assumptions, which take the general concept of family farm and break it down into more specific categories. Core assumptions tell us what a family farm is—and, in this case, equally importantly what it is not. A family farm is family owned, small, and a significant part of American culture and heritage. Perhaps more importantly, the family farm is painted over and over again as the opposite of a large and impersonal corporate farm/agribusiness. Whereas corporate farms are large and generic, family farms are small and personal. The image of the family farm pits the culturally rich mom-and-pop operation (David) versus the nameless, faceless corporation (Goliath). Survey question wording, used to record public opinion, illustrates this dichotomy. According to Zogby's Real America Poll, mentioned above, respondents were able to choose from two positions: either (a) "Large corporations farms [*sic*] are better for America because they provide low cost products and stable jobs," or (b) "Small family farms are better because they are a fundamental part of our culture and are an important connection to our past." The wording of the survey responses serves to underscore Murray Edelman's point about the power of language to build support and maintain the status quo.

To see whether policymakers' core assumptions about family farms also reinforce a dichotomy between small farms intimately tied to American culture and large corporate farms, I conducted a search of electronically available issues of the *Congressional Record* (1985–2004). If the core assumptions in policymakers' rhetoric about farms dichotomize farms into family farms, on the one hand, and large corporate farms on the other, I would expect to find language about corporate farms in the same passages as family farms. If they do not, language about corporate farms will occur

TABLE 6-1
Terms Present in Family Farm vs. Non-Family Farm Debates in the
Congressional Record, 1985–2004

Term	Family Farm (n=108)	Farm (n=434)
Family-owned	39%	2%
Small farm	47%	8%
Culture	29%	10%
Heritage	43%	8%
Agribusiness	47%	21%
Corporate Farm	35%	3%
Megafarm	6%	0
Large farm	30%	2%

SOURCE: Author's analysis of the *Congressional Record.*

equally in family and nonfamily farm debates. Looking only at entries that talked in-depth about family farms, I found that when policymakers talk about family farms, they contrast the traditional family farm image with corporate farms/agribusiness.[19] Table 6.1 shows the result of this search.

When they talk about family farms, policymakers not only use words traditionally associated with the family farm image like family-owned (39 percent), small farm (47 percent), culture (31 percent), and heritage (46 percent), they likewise contrast that image with corporate agriculture, mentioning agribusiness (47 percent), corporate farm (35 percent) and large farms (28 percent) frequently. Table 6.1 shows that these words are particular to *family* farm debates. A similar search of the *Congressional Record* for in-depth farm debates that do not mention family farms produces quite different results. Neither the words associated with family farms nor the words associated with corporate farms appear with the regularity they do in family farm debates.[20]

The core assumptions in policymakers' rhetoric about family farms reinforces the image of family farms as small and a part of American culture and heritage at the same time that it differentiates them from corporate farms/agribusiness. Family farms are defined in opposition to this alternative model. Unlike policy, which must use peripheral assumptions that further break down these categories and specify exactly who qualifies, the language supporting farms does not need to be as specific. In fact, the benefit of invoking the family farm is precisely in its ambiguity. When pressed to define the family farm, Senator Byron Dorgan (D-ND) summed it up best: "I do not have a simple definition. I guess a yard light. I mean a family living out there on the farm, human beings living out there, that is a family farm, I guess I could define it."[21] This definition (or rather lack thereof) underscores the cultural importance of the family farm and taps into the idea that family farms are somehow different than corporate farms because they keep the yard lights burning. At the same time, Senator Dorgan's definition allows each and every American to hold his or her own ideas about what exactly constitutes a family farm.

Policy Gaps

Even though the image of family farms as small, family owned, and part of American culture or heritage is reinforced by policymakers' rhetoric, the practice of farming in America is very different. There is a gap between the rhetorical image of family farms and the social practice of American agriculture. Contrary to the image, family farms, as defined in practice by the USDA, vary extensively in their size, scope, and business arrangement. In fact, according to the USDA (whose definition of family farms is intentionally broad) family farms do not stand in opposition to corporate farms; 90 percent of all "corporate" farms are *family* operated.[22]

The USDA collects data on the family farm, which it defines as "any farm organized as a sole proprietorship, partnership, or family corporation."[23] Essentially, family farms are self-operated, they do not have hired managers. As one can see, the USDA uses an entirely different set of assumptions to delineate family farms. The department does not define a family farm by its size, its heritage (how many generations worked the land), or what the farm may contribute to American culture. Instead, the USDA relies on labor statistics for family presence in the organization and management of the farm. Family farms are essentially a labor model.

According to the USDA's definition, 98 percent of American farms are family farms. By defining family farm broadly, the USDA overstates the number of family farms compared to most academic estimates, and severely overstates the number of family farms compared to the image of a family farm that most Americans hold. In part, the deviation between the cultural image of a family farm and the department's definition is practical. It is difficult, if not impossible, to actually measure the cultural stereotype. Even defining the family farm as small, for example, begs the question of what constitutes a small farm in an age when technological advancements have increased exponentially the amount of land a single family can operate. However, in part, the deviation between the image and the department's definition is a calculated strategy to include as many part-time and retirement farms as possible. In the 1950s and early 1960s, part-time and retirement farms were on the rise whereas full-time commercially productive family farms—as then defined—were on the decline. USDA historian David Brewster explains the political importance of the change in social practice: "It was only a matter of time, under these circumstances, until family operations began falling not only numerically but also as a percentage of the total. If the Government continued to use the postwar criteria, [Secretary of Agriculture Ezra Taft] Benson or one of his successors would be convicted by the USDA's own statistics of presiding over the demise of the American family farm."[24] Needless to say, the definition was amended. The new USDA definition included farms of all sizes and for all purposes, and the number of family farms jumped from a little more than half to well over 90 percent.[25]

The practice of farming, as defined by the official department that monitors it, looks very different than the family farm image. Breaking down the monolithic "family farm" group shows great diversity in this large category of agriculture. According to the USDA, small family farms, which have annual sales less than $250,000 and come the closest to the assumptions behind the cultural image of the family farmer, make up only 24 percent of all "family farms." Although less than a quarter of all farms are small family farms, this is the largest category of commercially productive agriculture. Large family farms (with annual sales between $250,000 and $500,000), very large family farms (with annual sales over $500,000), and nonfamily farms each account for less than 5 percent of all American farms. Because of the way that family farms are now defined, two-thirds of so-called family farms are not commercially productive and frequently include retired farmers or an increasing suburbanization of rural towns. Noncommercially productive farms include limited-resource farms (11 percent of all farms), retirement (15 percent), and lifestyle/residential (42 percent).

Figure 6.2 presents these data graphically. It shows the percent of each type of farm and its commercial productivity. Clearly, very large family farms in the United States provide the bulk of farm products and they receive the lion's share of government commodity supports, in proportion to their productivity but disproportionate to their number. Medium-sales and large-scale family farms account for less than 14 percent of all farms, yet they account for over 71 percent of farm production and receive approximately three-quarters of federal commodity payments. Of those commercially productive family farms, very large farms alone account for nearly 45 percent of production and a third of commodity subsidies. Smaller noncommercially productive farms, such as retirement, residential/lifestyle, and low-sales, make up 85 percent of all farms but only 15 percent of production. They receive far more government assistance in the form of conservation program payments (64 percent of all Conservation Reserve and Wetlands Reserve program payments).

The image of the family farm is very different from the practice of farming in America as defined by the USDA. Americans express a deep cultural connection with farming as a value and a link to the past. They show support for policies designed to help the family farmer, especially when it gives him a leg up against corporate farming or agribusiness. But the reality of farming in America strays far from the image of family farmers and the faith that Americans place in them. The USDA defines family farmers as a very diverse lot—from noncommercially productive subsistence farmers to multimillion dollar operations. Contrary to the David and Goliath assumption, family farms are not fighting off corporate farms that seek to take their land. Family farms are often corporate farms. As the productive capacity of individual farmers has continued to improve over the years, the greatest threat to family farmers has been *other* family farms.[26]

THE MAKING OF A NORMATIVE IDEAL

The image of the family farm evokes strong support from the American public because the family farm is a cultural institution, a central part of

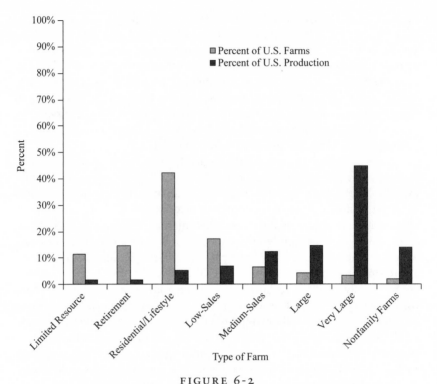

FIGURE 6-2

PRODUCTIVITY OF U.S. FARMS, BY CATEGORY OF FARM

SOURCE: Robert A Hoppe and David E. Banker, "Structure and Finances of U.S. Farms: 2005 Family Farm Report," (United States Department of Agriculture, Economic Research Service, 2006).

NOTE: All categories of family farms except for "nonfamily" farms. Limited Resource, Retirement, and Residential farms are generally not commercially productive. Low and medium sales family farms have sales between $10,000 and $250,000, large family farms have sales $250,000 to $499,999, very large family farms have sales $500,000 or more.

the American fabric since its colonial origins. Even though the family farm (according to either its cultural image or formal definition by the USDA) may have been a part of American society since the beginning, the phrase *family farm* and its normative use in politics appeared relatively recently. It was entirely possible—in fact it was the norm—to pass agriculture legislation prior to World War II without a single mention of the family farm. So when did the language of the family farm enter into politics, and what meaning did it hold? This section seeks to answer these questions by looking at the history of the phrase *family farm*. I trace the concept's development over time through party platforms, the *U.S. Code*, and the *New York Times*. I find that during World War II, the phrase *family farm* takes on new meaning. During the rapid mechanization of agriculture that takes place at this time, the family farm becomes a specific type or category of farm distinct from (and superior to) other types of agricultural arrangements. Ultimately, the normative weight of the family farm justified continued postwar agriculture policies to protect and promote this American institution.

This section relies heavily on specific language and the way in which the language is used in politics. A note on terms and their significance is a necessary precursor to the historical analysis that follows. To find evidence of the family farm in political speech and public policy I searched for the phrases *family farm*, *family-size farm*, and *family-type farm*. I found that the phrases *family-size farm* and *family-type farm* served as a bridge during the 1930s and 1940s when policymakers were trying to come up with the language to describe a small owner-operated farm, what later would become known as the *family farm*. Although it may seem to be splitting hairs, the family farm (as a concept) is different and distinct from families on farms and farm families. As demonstrated in the previous section, the two simple words *family farm* have a strong emotive component that distinguish this type of farm (a *family* farm) from other agricultural enterprises.

This chapter began with a quote from Marty Strange who says that the family farm "has long been the common rhetorical fare of politicians and opinion makers," and further, bills pass Congress only when they invoke its image. This quote intuitively strikes a chord. The family farm seems as though it has been around forever. In actuality, however, the phrase *family farm* would have been a stranger in political discussions throughout much of the nation's history. A survey of party platforms and stories in the *New York Times* since the mid-nineteenth century shows the growth of the family farm as political concept only after 1940.

Party platforms provide a consistent indicator of important political issues in the United States. To get a sense of the importance of the family farm over time, I coded the Republican and Democratic platforms from 1856–2004 for mentions of family farms. Figure 6.3 shows family farm mentions as a percent of all farm mentions in party platforms.[27] Republicans first mention family farms in 1936 and Democrats shortly thereafter in 1940. Family farms drop from the Republican platform after several years, but they never permanently exit either party's political agenda.

In addition to party platforms, news analysis provides an additional indicator of important political issues. Figure 6.4 presents stories about family farms as a percent of all stories that include the word *farm*. It shows how often family farms are mentioned in the *New York Times*

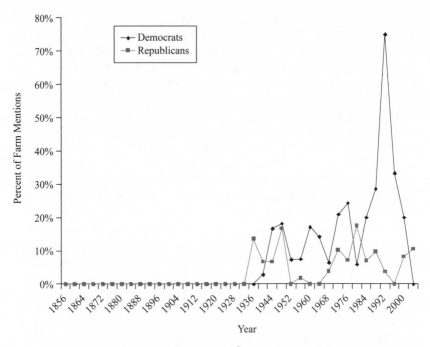

FIGURE 6-3

Family Farm Mentions as a Percent of Total Farm Mentions in Party
Platforms, 1856–2004

SOURCE: Author's analysis of Republican and Democratic party platforms, (accessed http://janda.
org/politxts/PartyPlatforms/listing.html).

from 1851–2005. The pattern is similar to the party platforms. The family
farm is rarely mentioned in the nineteenth and early twentieth centuries,
suggesting that it has little resonance politically at this time. It is not until
the 1940s that it begins to become a common phrase.

Even as Americans today read the "family farm" tradition into their
nation's history, the evidence from party platforms and *New York Times*
stories suggests that the phrase *family farm* was not a widely recogniz-
able political concept prior to the 1940s. Nineteenth and early-twentieth-
century policymakers used the language of farms and farmers, without
distinguishing the family farm as a particular type or category of farm.
According to USDA historian David Brewster: "the phrase 'family farm'
does not seem to have been part of the 19th century's vocabulary." He
goes on to say "Thomas Jefferson, sometimes considered the philosophical
spokesman of the American family farm idea, apparently never referred
to the institution by name. Nor did the expression appear in the 1862

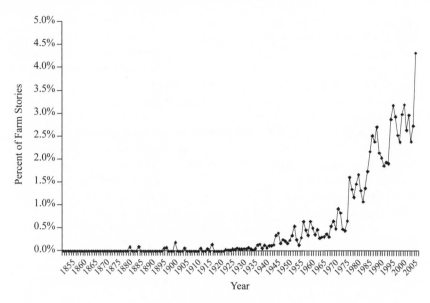

FIGURE 6-4

Family Farm Stories as a Percent of *New York Times* Farm Stories, 1851–2005

SOURCE: Author's analysis of the *New York Times* accessed via Proquest (1851–2000) and Lexis-Nexis (2001–2005).

NOTE: All stories (including book reviews), but not including advertisements/classified or otherwise.

debates on the Homestead Act."[28] Even though they were often intimately familiar with the workings of small owner-operated farms (having been raised on them or currently representing large numbers of Americans living on them) policymakers lacked the political language to talk about these farms as categorically distinct from other farm types such as tenant farms, cooperatives, and corporate farms with shareholders.

Nowhere is this more evident than the Agricultural Adjustment Act of 1933, the federal government's most significant foray into agriculture policy at the time it was enacted and the precursor to contemporary subsidy programs. Passed during the Great Depression, the Agricultural Adjustment Act levied urban manufacturers to subsidize farmers hard hit by debt and foreclosures. Yet, even though the act increased state involvement in agriculture policy and put the financial burden on urbanites, policymakers did not frame the bill as aid to "family farms" or as following a duty to a shared American culture. In fact, like the Homestead Act, policymakers did not mention the family farm at all. The political debates on the floor of Congress, official committee testimony, and the radio addresses by FDR are all free of family farm language. The state's largest venture into American agriculture was not accompanied by language of the family farm. Instead, the hundreds of pages of debate pull few—if any—emotive strings. The debate over the 1933 Agriculture Act was steadfastly about the national economic crisis, and policymakers chose to frame their legislation as a national economic solution.

The architects of the New Deal agriculture programs portrayed programs designed to help farmers as bettering the position of urban producers and consumers rather than as shoring up farms as "the foundation of democracy."[29] In other words, they stressed economic over political benefits. The often spirited exchange in testimony before the Senate Agriculture and Forestry Committee on March 27, 1933, of Mrs. Nell Q. Donnelly, a dress manufacturer, and committee member Senator Louis Murphy (D-IA) offers insight into how the act was framed. Mrs. Donnelly was steadfastly opposed to taxes paid by urbanites that would be given to rural farmers, while the Iowa Senator was determined to pass this bill.

> Senator Murphy: If we give him [the farmer] a bigger purchasing power, it is possible there will be an increased demand for the things you produce in your factory. Do you think that this is probable?
>
> Mrs. Donnelly: Probably; yes.
>
> Senator Murphy: Of course that is the theory on which this whole thing rests. You think that is possible?
>
> Mrs. Donnelly: It would be possible of course. If there were more people wanting to buy my merchandise, if I wanted to increase my business, I could increase it.
>
> Senator Murphy: Suppose we could start that process. Things are about as bad as they could be, aren't they?[30]

Ultimately, Mrs. Donnelly sums up the dissatisfaction of many urbanites, "I don't think you should increase the farmers' purchasing power out of the wage-earner's pockets."[31] At the time of the state's largest foray into agriculture, national policymakers did not invoke the family farm either as criteria of eligibility so that family farms would be the only ones receiving state aid or as a normative ideal so that the nation *ought* to help family farms. Instead, they talked about the national economic benefits of farm subsidies.

Though evidence suggests there are practical political reasons why family farms were not singled out, such as Secretary of Agriculture Henry Wallace wanted to ensure the support of large farms,[32] or that policymakers implicitly thought of family farms when they spoke in the generic terms of farms and farmers,[33] by far the most glaring reason is that policymakers at this time lacked an established language for talking about the family farm as a distinct type or category of farm. When politicians and opinion leaders talked about "family farms" prior to World War II, it served largely as background—the location for events or the place where one was raised—it was not a category of farms distinct from corporate farms and hence could not need or deserve state intervention.

To get a sense of the meaning behind family farm—and not just its prevalence—I coded the first 100 years of electronically available stories in the *New York Times* (1851–1950) for family farm mentions.[34] In particular I looked at the meaning that the words *family farm* held in each story. The years I looked at provide a rich history of the development of the family farm as a political concept. In this 100-year period, there are three discourses surrounding the family farm. In the first, the family farm is a locale, the place where events occur. As such, "family" fills in for a proper name and "farm" serves as another word for estate. For example, in 1896 the *New York Times* wrote that Boston Mayor Josiah Quincy had spent time on the "old family farm or estate in the town of Quincy, near Boston."[35] In the second, the family farm is a background characteristic, often one highlighted to show how far a businessman has come in the world or how down to earth a prominent politician really is. In the obituary of Edward Scripps, the newspaper magnate, the *New York Times* reported that at eighteen, "Scripps left the family farm in Winchester, Ohio, and joined the *Detroit Evening News* as a newsboy."[36] The third discourse is of the family farm as a distinct category of agriculture. Overwhelmingly, stories of the third discourse stress the potential threat to this type of agriculture and the need to protect or preserve it. A 1944 story describes the necessary work of Congress to shift from a wartime to a peacetime economy, arguing that how they do their job "may determine whether...the future trend in American agriculture will be towards large 'factory farms' or the small family farm."[37]

In the first two categories, family is a private enterprise or background characteristic and there is no political story, no reason why federal policymakers should talk about family farms. In the third category, the family farm becomes a distinct type of farm and one on which policymakers have a clear effect. The creation of the family farm as distinct category of agriculture suggests important political consequences for American agriculture policies. Figure 6.5 shows the number of stories per year that use the family farm as a distinct type of category versus the other two (locale and background) together.

Prior to 1925, all family farm entries were about location or an individual's background. After 1925, and expanding in the 1930s and 1940s, the family farm is used increasingly both as a category or type of farm as well as the more mundane location and background. Importantly, the figure shows that family farm as a category does not usurp other ways of discussing it. They both grow significantly during the late 1930s and early

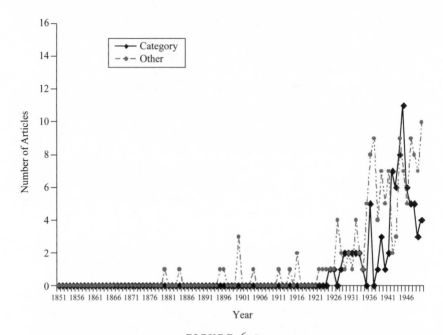

FIGURE 6-5
New York Times Stories That Reference the Family Farm, 1851–1950
SOURCE: Author's analysis of the *New York Times* accesses via Proquest.
NOTE: All stories (including book reviews) but not including advertisements/classified or otherwise.
"Category" refers to family farm as a distinct type of agriculture, "other" refers to family as a location
or background characteristic.

1940s. These three ways of talking about family farms coexist at the same time in the *New York Times*.

World War II opened the door for comprehensive discussions about where American agriculture policy ought to go in the future.[38] War preparations, production, and postwar anxiety about how to return to "normalcy" stressed continued state involvement with agriculture policy and a normative commitment to the family farm. This domestic policy response to the war not only changed agriculture, it also changed the way that Americans *talked* about agriculture. That is, during World War II American agriculture became political rather than just economic. Historical evidence points to two key reasons why the family farm as a concept came to take the more political meaning as a distinct type of agriculture during this time.

First and foremost, federal intervention in agriculture, ironically, pushed many farmers off their land, endangering the "family farm" through New Deal and wartime policies. Depression-era policies drove marginal farmers—disproportionately poor, sharecroppers, and African Americans—from their land and to city life and day labor.[39] Federal subsidies that paid farmers *not* to produce farm goods gave incentives to unscrupulous landlords in cotton-producing southern states to evict longtime sharecroppers. According to David Conrad: "there was no place for dispossessed tenants to go but to the road or to the towns and cities to try and get on relief . . . They were without homes, food, or work, half-clothed and sick of body and soul—the 'grapes of wrath' of a government which had not intended to harm them."[40] Likewise, those marginal farmers in the Dustbowl states were the first to leave their homesteads for paid labor in the West. As many as 500,000 farmers left the Great Plains during the drought.[41] The shift from working small plots, either as sharecroppers or independent farmers, to working in large industrial farms in the South and West changed American agriculture models from one where laborers had a stake in the land to one in which they received daily wages and were easily replaced by mechanization on ever-growing farms. Day laborers allowed southern and western farms to maintain their size or even to grow, increasing reliance on outside (and inexpensive) labor rather than the independent family model.[42] The shift in labor practices that accompanied the Great Depression was an important source of change in American agriculture, but because it affected those farmers at the margins, it was not closely associated with middle-class and often midwestern family farms.

Whereas massive changes in agriculture during the Great Depression served to quietly push families from their farms, war preparations and full-scale mobilization revolutionized American agricultural production and popularized the notion that the family farm was endangered by technology that would produce factory farms. Increased demand for agricultural products by domestic and foreign consumers led the federal government to prod farmers to likewise increase their wartime production. Old labor-intensive farming practices were quickly modernized to use more advanced equipment when young men left the farms for service abroad or better paying jobs in urban factories.[43] The new way of farming, which produced agricultural surpluses even during the height of war demand, threatened the traditional family farm.[44] The House Committee on Postwar Economic Policy and Planning spelled out the problem in a 1946 report: "In order to permit farm income to be maintained at lower prices the family-sized farm, particularly in the South, needs to be enlarged; this means that fewer people will be needed in agriculture if the benefits of low-cost mechanized production are to be passed on to consumers without depressing farm-family income."[45] The mechanization of agriculture that took place during the war made American farms that employed this technology the most efficient in the world.[46] Family farmers who were not commercially profitable were encouraged to leave or enlarge their operations. Public policy during the New Deal and World War II pushed farmers off their land. Though the trends were significant in both, during the war the "family farm problem" received national attention as Americans saw a new domestic threat—corporate farms and agrifactories—to a traditional staple of American life.

Second, family farming was easily and favorably contrasted with collective farming in communist states. Political leaders could reward attentive farmers and at the same time please the broader public by imbuing family farms with democratic ideals. With an end to the crises caused by the Great Depression and World War II, expensive farm subsidies lacked political justification. Farm programs were neither necessary to feed the country nor to fuel demand for urban producers. Rural legislators and farm interests, however, were not about to give up lucrative payments. If subsidy programs could not be portrayed as a national economic necessity, they could be justified as a national cultural necessity. In other words, American farm programs promoted a uniquely American way of life. In a time where the failings of democracy led to the Third Reich and with the impending specter of communism around the globe, the family farm took on additional normative weight. It was a "cornerstone of our national strength" and "one of the most effective bulwarks any nation can have against communism."[47] Jefferson, whose democratic-agrarian vision never mentioned the family farm by name, became a proponent of the American family farm posthumously.[48] According to historian Virgil W. Dean, by 1948 "the president and a large majority of Americans who were not farmers retained a strong emotional bond with the nation's farm families—the backbone of a democratic society and the nation's basic industry, according to Jefferson's agrarian philosophy."[49] Though economists then (and still today) argued that the small-scale family farm is potentially inefficient, they lost out to the normative weight that it carried. Interest groups and supporters of agriculture subsidies, loans, and other government payments rallied around the family farm.

The transformation of the family farm from a location or background characteristic of a self-made man to a full-scale category of agriculture did not take place overnight. The *New York Times* shows that family farms were described as a category sporadically since 1925. The "temporary" state interference in agriculture during the Great Depression and through World War II laid the permanent structural foundations for a postwar agricultural policy. The language of postwar agriculture policy created the family farm tradition that justified continued state intervention. Mrs. Donnelly's 1933 testimony before the Senate Agriculture Committee reminds us that American subsidy programs were argued for as a part of a nonaffective economic theory, but by 1946 the House Special Committee on Postwar Economic Policy and Planning had rewritten American agricultural history to place agriculture not only at the center of the nation's economy but also its moral and political development.

> Agriculture is the cornerstone of our economy. The independence of the Nation was won by the stubborn resistance of the subsistence farmers who made up the greater part of the population in the early years. American agriculture, throughout its development was characterized by individual family sized owner-operated farms. This contributed greatly to the independent spirit and moral character of the entire population, and was the backbone of our political and economic democracy as they developed in America.[50]

The stated purpose of the report, "to determine what national policies will best contribute to its welfare and future progress," not surprisingly cast the family farm as a key player in the nation's future well-being. The transformation of the farm—and the threat that mechanization engendered—along with a new world order created the necessary political justification for helping, aiding, and especially protecting the family farm that would carry through in the decades following World War II.

The justification and appeal to the family farm have been crucial for continued success of agriculture programs. The family farm has become a dominant symbol that American citizens identify with agriculture programs. Even as American agriculture continued to change—the average farm size grew dramatically—the rhetoric of the family farm remained the same. It continued to play up the dire straits of small family farmers. In truth, the diversity of so-called family farms meant that what was good for one family farmer may have hurt another. Variation in size, crop, and geographical location has been glossed over by a common rhetoric and image.

The importance of family farms to American agriculture programs should not be overstated. Clearly interest groups, institutional overrepresentation of rural interests, and path dependence have kept agriculture programs in place. However, as Frank Baumgartner and Bryan Jones have explained, policies that have a strong image are able to maintain institutional support. The powerful supporting idea underlying American agriculture policy to this day—at least the face shown to the American public—remains the family farm.

THE FAMILY FARM AND POLICY CHANGE

The normatively charged rhetoric of the family farm has continued to be a part of congressional policymaking well into the 1990s. Policymakers regularly invoke the image of the family farm in debates about agricultural subsidies and loans as well as for a host of other programs. The extensive use of the family farm in policy debates leads to the important question: why do policymakers continue to rely on this particular image when agriculture is so diverse? More importantly, does the rhetorical use of this family ideal promote their policy objectives when it comes to policy stasis and change?

The literature on American agriculture policy is dominated by the study of interest groups and the coalitions they forge to achieve their policy objectives.[51] The evidence points to the strong position of well-organized interests and the benefits of geographic representation. It would be naive to suggest that the way that policymakers talk about an issue can trump very real constituency, party, and interest group pressures. But as Baumgartner and Jones argue, policy image is central for maintaining policy monopolies or the structural arrangements in any policy area. Policy images simplify complex problems and give policymakers and the public a common language and understanding. Baumgartner and Jones note, "every public policy problem is usually understood, even by the politically sophisticated, in simplified and symbolic terms."[52] The family farm as the embodiment of American culture continues to be a powerful policy image for U.S. agriculture, even as the percent of Americans engaged in farming has declined dramatically since World War II.

In this section I examine policy discourse in 1996 when Congress passed, and the president signed, the most significant overhaul of agriculture policy since the Great Depression, the Federal Agriculture Improvement and Reform Act (FAIR Act, but commonly referred to as the Freedom to Farm Act). Though overhaul of the nation's agriculture subsidy program would seem to show that family farm language was not terribly important, the following discussion reveals just the opposite. Because agriculture subsidy opponents did not take on the powerful symbol of the family farm (indeed they tiptoed around it and left it perfectly intact) the 1996 "overhaul" was only a partial policy change. When the market turned down, the family farm returned, and opponents of subsidies reversed their votes and restored agriculture programs. Careful attention to the language of the policy debate shows that the symbol of the family farm, which needs to be protected and promoted, underlies support for expensive subsidy programs.

In 1996, when legislators tried to reform the decades-old system of subsidies, it looked as though agriculture policy would jettison the core value of family and put a new core value in its place—economic efficiency. Legislators stressed the importance of getting the state out of farmers' fields and allowing them to enter into the global free market. Even though the free-market rhetoric was central to the new policy debate, legislators did not take on the old family farm value. Instead, it was left in there to justify programs that benefit particular state constituencies. Free marketers stressed free-market procedures (letting the market determine planting decisions) *not* outcomes (inefficient farms would be eliminated). They were unwilling and unable to condemn the family farm. As markets turned down, the family farm surfaced again to justify additional emergency expenditures and eventually the return of even bigger subsidy programs.

To understand how policymakers talked about policy reform, I studied the debate that took place before approval of the conference committee report on March 28, 1996. I looked specifically at the language that was used to justify the elimination of farm subsidies in favor of the free market and the place that family farm rhetoric played in the debate. To present a well-ordered study of the interactive debate, the analysis presented in the body of the chapter is from the U.S. Senate; remarks from the House are included in the notes.[53]

The FAIR Act promised to eliminate traditional subsidy payments, planting requirements, and acreage restrictions for American farmers. Farmers would receive fixed guaranteed payments—regardless of what crop or how much of it they produced—from the federal government for seven years as a way to transition to the free market.[54] FAIR was heralded as a step in the right direction by many economists and free-market conservatives who long viewed traditional agriculture programs as inefficient and invasive. These critics argued that rather than letting the market determine what farmers planted, there was an archaic system of price guarantees and land idling where the USDA dictated to farmers what they could plant and where Americans were charged twice for their food (in their tax dollars and in the price they paid at the local supermarket). After Republican victories in the 1994 congressional elections, the newly elected leadership, especially in the House, prioritized cutting back what they deemed bloated federal expenditures. Agriculture policy was due for a substantial trim.

Policymakers tried, unsuccessfully, to get legislation enacted in 1995 as the 1990 farm bill was set to expire. However, the 1995 farm bill got caught up with a broader Republican push to cut federal spending and hence the deficit. At the time, farm subsidies came with a seven-year price tag of $56.6 billion, a substantial chunk of money that budget hawks targeted. House Agriculture Committee Chairman Pat Roberts (R-KS) proposed the Freedom to Farm Act, an earlier version of the legislation that eventually passed in 1996, but the bill faced stiff opposition. Rural interests—both Democratic and Republican—disliked the sizeable changes in agriculture policy, and interest groups representing specific commodities lobbied hard to defeat the measure.

In the Agriculture Committee, Republican lawmakers put the needs of their constituents first and were unable to pass reform measures. When a frustrated Chairman Roberts could not gain enough support in committee to pass the Freedom to Farm Act, he made good on his threats to take the bill out of the hands of the agriculture committee and turn it over directly to the House leadership. The Freedom to Farm Act was folded into the omnibus budget reconciliation legislation. Members of Congress had no opportunity to debate or amend the most significant changes to American agriculture programs in sixty years. Although the omnibus bill passed both Houses, President Bill Clinton vetoed the legislation citing among other things the elimination of a farm safety net. The agriculture provisions "would provide windfall payments to producers when prices are high, but not protect family farm income when prices are low."[55]

With Republicans insisting that Congress would not reauthorize current agriculture programs for another year and Clinton's veto of their proposed measure, the countdown clock for agriculture programs started ticking. Unless Congress passed a new reauthorization, policy would revert back to permanent law, the Agricultural Act of 1949, wreaking havoc in commodities markets by increasing the subsidies for some crops by as much as 300 percent and eliminating others entirely.[56] Policymakers had until April 1996, when farmers harvested the last of the winter wheat, to come to an agreement.

Under the gun, members of Congress sat down early in 1996 to craft a farm bill that could muster broad political support. Pressure to reduce federal agriculture spending by billions of dollars had fractured long-term coalitions within party, region, and commodities. In a fight for scarce resources, a gain for one program would be a loss for another. Expensive nutrition programs would be paid for by lower crop subsidies and vice versa. Even as fiscal conservatives, urban liberals, and environmentalists favored the Freedom to Farm legislation—rural Republican and Democratic legislators fought for the subsidy programs that would benefit their particular districts. Forging a broad enough coalition to get the measure through both houses and signed by the president all within 90 days seemed to be a particularly daunting task.

To accomplish their goals, House Agriculture Chairman Roberts and his counterpart in the Senate, Richard Lugar (R-IN), took very different approaches. While Roberts fought hard for the Federal Agriculture Improvement and Reform Act with a series of procedural moves in order to reduce dissention and block amendments, Lugar compromised early with his Senate colleagues.[57] With Senator Patrick Leahy (D-VT), Lugar championed a bipartisan alternative that retained the heart of the Federal Agriculture Improvement and Reform bill—decoupling subsidy payments and crop production—but also included money for conservation, nutrition, and rural development.

To sustain coalitions strong enough to pass stand-alone agriculture reform, both chairmen had to balance the interests of free-market conservatives who wanted government out of agriculture totally and constituencies that benefited from programs. Lugar had to sweeten the Senate legislation (increasing the price) by continuing programs for the urban poor and environmental conservation. Food stamps stayed under the purview of Agriculture and off the chopping block. Further, both chairmen acquiesced to the demands of particular commodities like tobacco, sugar, rice, and cotton. Not only were commodity interest groups well organized (and persistent) but a strong coalition required the backing of southerners who would not support legislation that would disadvantage their districts. Though these commodity programs were particularly offensive to free-market advocates, their cost was largely borne by consumers, not by federal coffers.[58]

Lugar and Roberts were aided substantially in their coalition-building efforts because strong markets for agriculture products in 1996 meant that farmers would actually gain more (at least in the short term) by the FAIR Act than they would through traditional subsidy programs. When farmers "did the math" they found they benefited by the new Act. According to one farm lobbyist, "I think what finally happened is those old boys in the commodity groups said, 'That's just too much money to leave on the table.' " He continued, "I call this the 'Freedom to Buy a New Pickup' bill."[59] By mid-March, the House and Senate had passed their respective versions of agriculture reform. The more moderate Senate version contained provisions not in the House bill. Most importantly, the Senate version kept the 1949 Agricultural Act (permanent law) intact, leaving the door open for traditional subsidies to return after 2002. With a price tag of $50 billion, the Senate version cost $3 billion more than the House bill. Tough compromises would now face the Conference Committee.

As southern farmers began their spring planting, House and Senate conferees worked out their differences in late night committee hearings. The pressure to pass an agriculture bill was acute. Though the White House still disapproved of replacing subsidies with fixed payments, Secretary of Agriculture Dan Glickman no longer reminded policymakers of President Clinton's earlier veto and opposition to fixed payments. Glickman noted, "The hour is late, and further delay only hurts the people this department is here to serve."[60] When it was over, conferees agreed to replace traditional subsidy programs with seven-year fixed payments to transition to market-based agriculture. Several contentious issues threatened to sink the farm bill—notably whether to retain the 1949 Agricultural Act as permanent law (as in the Senate version), peanut subsidies, and a northeastern dairy compact—but midnight compromises kept all three in the final package cleared by the Senate on March 28 and the House a few hours later. President Clinton signed the bill into law on April 4, 1996. After sixty years, Congress dismantled the heart of "temporary" programs put into place during the Great Depression to buoy American farmers' income.

Though the final legislation is not limited to family farms and in fact fails to mention the family farm in a single one of its ten titles, the symbol and rhetoric of the family farm ideal played an important part in congressional debate.[61] As this section will demonstrate, defenders of subsidy programs pointed to the elimination of a safety net for family farmers that would let an important way of life—an American cultural institution—fall through. Free-market advocates, however, shifted the discussion away from domestic home towns and toward international markets. Importantly, free marketers argued that the market was the proper mechanism for determining crop production, *not* that it brought about the most desirable ends. That is, opponents of subsidies refused to attack the family farm as outdated or the elimination of unproductive and inefficient (family) farms as desirable. They left intact the powerful policy image associated with American agriculture since World War II.

Defenders of subsidy programs and government aid in agricultural production contended that family farms were endangered by the Federal Agriculture Improvement and Reform Act. For these advocates, mostly Democratic members from rural areas who benefited by the current system of agriculture subsidies, the objective of American farm policy is more than just efficient agricultural production, but agricultural production by family farms.[62] The cultural importance of the family farm—not economic or agricultural concerns—justifies a national farm policy. Senator Byron Dorgan (D-ND) articulated this position both most eloquently and most passionately. Dorgan identifies family farmers in America by the light in their yard that shines every night, illuminating America's rural heartland after a hard day's work.

For Dorgan, the only purpose of American agriculture policy is to keep the yard lights burning. He states explicitly that farm policy should not be about the production of agriculture products, but *family farm* production.

There are some people who say it does not matter whether there are any lights out there in the prairie. They do not care whether the lights dot the prairie at night; that land will be farmed. We do not have to have people living out there to have people farming. We can have corporate agrifactories farm this country from California to Maine. . . . We do not have to worry about the little guy. We do not have to worry about the family.[63]

Dorgan consciously and repeatedly associates the Federal Agriculture Improvement and Reform Bill with agribusiness, factory farms, and an end to a particularly important American tradition. Further, he argues the state has no business in farming if it is not to help preserve a particular way of life. The business of the state is not to open up free markets, as proponents of the 1996 farm bill claim, but to protect family farmers from it. He says, "if we in Congress are not interested in who farms, if we are neutral on the question of whether there are family farms out there with yard lights burning and people living on the farms, if we are neutral on that, if we do not care. . . . Get rid of it altogether." Dorgan continues, "we do not need a USDA, in my judgment, if the purpose of the farm program here in Congress is not to try to nurture and maintain and help and strengthen family farms."[64]

Dorgan draws extensively on the family farm ideal and makes explicit that the role of agriculture policy is to preserve a particularly American way of life. The family farm—not economic or agricultural concerns—justifies government involvement. His arguments are part and parcel of the family farm discourse of World War II. However, unlike the past fifty years of agriculture legislation, in 1996 these sentiments would not carry the day. The value of the family farm was subsumed to the free market.

Unlike Dorgan, with his heavy reliance on the cultural importance of the family farm ideal, proponents of the 1996 farm bill pushed agriculture debate away from home towns and toward the free market. Speaking next after Senator Dorgan, Senator and Agriculture Committee member Larry Craig (R-ID), sought to diffuse the weight of the family farm by stressing the business aspect of family farms. He says:

The young farmers of Idaho—and, yes, they are family farmers—but they have millions of dollars invested. I find it interesting, when we worry about farmers, we always fall back on the word "family," "family." Farming is a big business in my State today. It is family-run, in many instances, but those families have assets in the millions of dollars, and they work daily as astute, well-trained businessmen and women trying to operate their agribusiness.[65]

Craig, unlike his fellow supporters of the bill, makes both explicit and lengthy comments about what family farms look like. The argument he employs, however, about the role of government in agriculture, is typical for supporters of the 1996 bill.[66] Craig stresses the importance of free markets and the role of government to protect access to markets, *not* farmers. He concludes, "Government, does, in my opinion, have a legitimate role in agriculture, and it is as a cooperator, to cooperate in the area of trade, to knock down the political barriers that might artificially be established that disallow production agriculture from getting into world markets."[67] The farm bill, for free-market advocates like Craig, is the answer to unwieldy state intervention. Government "does not have a responsibility to dictate the market or to micromanage the family farm or the agricultural production unit."[68]

For free-market advocates, the old system of state subsidized agriculture is not only inefficient but also outdated. Senator Lauch Faircloth (R-NC), who described himself as "one of only a few working farmers in Congress," explains that the nature of agriculture production and marketing has changed and the United States needs to keep pace. "The world has changed dramatically since I first took over the farm from my father. Whether we like it or not, NAFTA and GATT are now the law of the land." Free-market advocates framed agriculture debates as reducing the interference of government in the daily lives of farmers and instead looked to economic markets on a global scale.

In the end, after all the debate the Senate agreed to the conference report by a vote of 74 to 26, the House 389 to 318. The lopsided votes suggested that Congress was pursuing a new value in agriculture policy—the free market—at the expense of the family farm. The normative commitment to the family farm since World War II seemed to have reached its end. Looking only at the strong opponents and strong proponents of the bill, however, leaves out the important middle ground. Members in the middle whose support was necessary were granted compromises and concessions that broke the original budget constraints. Looking at those members of Congress who compromised and supported particular farm programs at the same time they generally approved of the bill shows that the language of the family farm was used to justify subsidies that benefited particular constituencies *regardless* of one's position on the overall bill. That is, in the vast middle ground, members of Congress both advocated for free-market principles and the protection of family farmers. The inclusion of the Northeast Dairy compact illustrates how the policymakers could keep two contradictory values in the final 1996 legislation.

Out of all of the debates surrounding the farm bill, three commodity programs were targeted and discussed at length: peanuts, sugar, and dairy.[69] Dairy remained especially contentious all the way to the end. In particular, the Northeast Dairy Compact—which would allow only northeastern states to set minimum milk prices above USDA levels—was distressing not only to free-market advocates but also to members from dairy states in the Midwest.[70] Senator Patrick Leahy (D-VT), an agriculture committee member and coauthor of the farm bill under discussion in the Senate, fought for the legislation on the grounds that it was good for producers and consumers and justified the dairy compact in particular this way: "They [dairy farmers] dot the New England countryside. They are a beautiful part of our heritage." The compact will "provide family farmers throughout the region with a decent living, so that they will be able to pass on their farms to their children and their children's children."[71] For Leahy, and the other representatives of northeastern interests, the broader adoption of free-market principles coincides with family farm "milk cartels."

Democratic Senator Russ Feingold, representing the dairy-producing state of Wisconsin, was incensed with the compact: "It is the antithesis of market orientation."[72] Feingold points out the hypocrisy of the farm bill language. He says: "In fact, this compact flies in the face of the rhetoric associated with this very farm bill. I've heard so many Senators claim this bill allows farmers to make decisions based on the market, not on Government payments. But the compact attempts to insulate a small group of farmers from the very market conditions this bill embraces so tightly."[73] Though it is far from surprising that midwestern senators were opposed to a dairy compact that would put farmers in their states at a competitive disadvantage, the language that supporters and opponents of this one piece of the farm bill employed is telling. It is not merely the case that Democrats from rural states employed family farm rhetoric and Republicans and nonrural senators employed rhetoric of the free market. Senators fell back on family farm rhetoric to justify government intervention in agriculture policy for particular constituencies and free-market language to oppose them—no matter what their overall position on the farm bill. That is, to justify programs that benefited their constituents, senators drew on the language of family farm as a national cultural symbol.

Though free-market values seemingly won the battle that late night in March, the policy image of the family farm remained firm. Notably, even when they were strongly advocating a free-market philosophy, policymakers talked only about procedure and not outcome. In other words they extolled the virtue of opening up markets, but no senators and only one member of Congress was willing to state that market outcomes were efficient, just, or appropriate. Representative Stephen Buyer (R-IN) came the closest to endorsing free-market outcomes when he stated: "the weaning of farmers off government subsidies is important to our country's financial health. Government should not be in the business of subsidizing inefficient operations." Not one other senator or representative—even those representing urban districts—promoted the end to inefficient (often family) farms. Most telling in the debate over the 1996 farm bill is the dog that did not bark: though the majority did not rely on the family farm in their rhetoric, neither were they willing to condemn it.

What was heralded in 1996 as a new era of agriculture lasted only six years when major subsidy programs returned as part and parcel of American agriculture policy. Between 1998 and 2001, as prices for agricultural products slumped, Congress passed a series of emergency farm bailouts totaling $30.5 billion.[74] In 1998, *The New Republic* voiced concern about the backpeddling in American agriculture policy: "it's a little worrisome to see that even free-market conservatives shy away from articulating the principles of Freedom to Farm" in the face of "sorrowful meditations on the plight of . . . hearty yeoman, rising at dawn to begin their back-breaking labor, in danger of losing land their families have tilled for generations."[75] In 2002, much to the dismay of free-market advocates who thought they had won a permanent victory in 1996, American agriculture policy reverted to subsidy programs. Congress passed, and President Bush signed, a six-year $440.8 billion farm bill that included farm subsidies that had been eliminated in 1996 as well as new subsidy programs to help protect American farmers.[76] Senator Byron Dorgan, who had vowed in 1996 that "we will have another day," finally made good on his promise.

Why, when legislators seemed to embrace free-market values, was policy change so short-lived? I argue that policy change in 1996 was only partial. The dominant policy image, the idea that agriculture is there to help family farms, remained firmly embedded in American public policy in a number of ways. Though subsidies were being phased out, free-market principles did little to displace the entrenched interest groups, agricultural advocates, and the powerful symbol of the family farm. Indeed as the market turned down, support for family farms increased. Farms made it back on the agenda and policy change was enacted that reinstated expensive subsidy programs. In 1996, the problem was defined as international market behavior, not domestic farm demographics. The new legislative solution only temporarily superceded the value of the family farm. Although they focused policy around the market, they did not remove the family farm ideal from agriculture policy.

First, in 1996 policymakers defined the problem to be fixed as one of government intervention—not changing farm demographics. Though small commercially producing family farms have been on the decline since the beginning of the twentieth century, policymakers distinctly avoided discussing it, focusing instead on international markets. Senator Charles Grassley (R-IA) explains that the 1996 farm bill provides a "glidepath" to transition American producers into a "new era of agriculture." He states further: "This new era will also be influenced by opening of markets in Europe and the Pacific rim when free-trade agreements, such as GATT are allowed a chance to work. Most farmers welcome the opportunity to meet every competitor abroad, compete in every market, and send a clear signal—which this bill does—that we are going to supply that market. We are going to be in the market to stay."[77] Policymakers on both sides of the aisle wanted to "fix" American agriculture policy.

Senator Herb Kohl (D-WI) summed it up as follows: "I think every Member of the Senate would agree that agricultural policy needs reform. The realities of production, markets and budgets change rapidly, and therefore what is demanded is a periodic revamping of agriculture policy."[78] The world had changed, and policymakers wanted American agriculture policy to do the same.

Second, policymakers proposed a solution that would be costly at first but would ultimately simplify the state's role in agriculture production without regard to future consequences. Policymakers who long wanted to get rid of expensive and inefficient farm subsidies proposed eliminating long-term government involvement and transitional payments.

Democrats and Republicans from urban and rural areas all agreed that farm policy required a new solution. Based upon the problem they identified, a gap between market in agriculture policy and market in the global economy, policymakers passed a bill that unhinged sixty years of agriculture policy. They did not, however, talk about the gap in the social practice of farming.

Policymakers failed to discuss the declining number of commercially productive family farms and the need to adapt agriculture policy to better aid larger and larger corporate farms. That is, policymakers were unwilling to commit to the changing face of agriculture production in the United States. The gap that is most significant in American agriculture—the decline of small commercially productive family farms—remains solidly intact because of the normative weight that family farms (and "protecting" family farms) holds with Americans. Even in 1996, the decline of these family farms was not a problem to be solved by further hastening their demise or reforming policy to better meet the needs of large (family or otherwise) farm producers. Instead, policymakers glossed over the diversity of farms and the difficulty of defining family farms because the normative ideal of the family farm still justifies state agriculture programs: the members of Congress who serve on agriculture committees as well as the billions of dollars that farm bills bring home to the districts. And even though agriculture bills continue to upset free-market conservatives, the family farm ideal was used *at the same time* by free-market conservatives to promote the repeal of the estate tax.

In the end, it appeared as if the 1996 compromise that retained permanent law, at the insistence of Senate Minority leader Tom Daschle, sealed the fate of the farm reform. First passed with the Senate version of the farm bill and later kept in conference as a way to assure enough Democratic support for agreement by both houses, the compromise allayed fears that family farmers would be abandoned. It also doomed the reform if the market faltered, as it did in 1998. The FAIR Act ultimately gave farmers an "out" if they chose to take it.

Though this procedural measure was clearly important, Congress (in all likelihood) would not have allowed American farms to fail even without it. Without dismantling the old policy image, and the powerful monopoly it supports, change is not likely to be enduring. Policymakers sold the bill at a time when many farmers—and family farmers—would benefit by large cash payments as the market was strong. The *National Journal* reported in 1996 that permanent law "will act as a hammer forcing Congress to pass a new farm bill by 2002. But if farmers are unhappy, Congress won't wait that long."[79] Indeed, Congress readily abandoned the reform measures and passed emergency supplemental money when the market turned down.

Ultimately, policymakers were committed to market procedure but not market outcomes. The coalition of free-market conservatives, environmentalists, and even farm supporters that worked to pass FAIR quickly unraveled in the face of potential long-term consequences. Though farm subsidies are concentrated within the shrinking agricultural sector, proponents are able to portray them effectively as having diffuse benefits. Farm subsidies not only aid individual producers, they also promote a particularly important American way of life. In 2002, an election year when control of the Senate was at stake, there was little doubt that a farm bill would be passed to keep agriculture interests appeased and human interest farm foreclosures off the national news.

The gap between the social practice of farming and the rhetoric of a family farm is wide and growing every day. Though Senator Craig was willing to point out the fuzzy distinction between family farms and large agribusiness, most policymakers use the language of family farm to exploit the distinction: to bring home sugar subsidies or milk programs that benefit an industry over a particular way of farming. Though they may not agree with Senator Byron Dorgan's political position, most legislators would welcome his definition of the family farm as a "yard light." This definition is intentionally vague, pulling at emotional strings rather than empirical evidence. It is precisely the ambiguity of the family farm ideal, the gap between rhetoric and social practice, that gives it political weight.

CONCLUSION

The family farm has come to be important in the language of farm policy in the United States. Policymakers invoke family farms in their political speech more often than in the policies they write or the newspaper stories that report on them. By invoking the family farm, a special American tradition, policymakers reinforce the agriculture policy monopoly. The language of the family farm that they use makes it seem as though the

family farm has forever occupied this role. This is not the case. The contemporary family farm, which is a distinct (and superior) type of agriculture, is a by-product of World War II. After the war, American agriculture
policy—which had previously been justified by national economic need
and the war—found a new cause.

However, all too often critics of American farm policy overlook the importance of family farm language in the justification and continuation of
"inefficient" farm subsidies. For example, Orden, Paarlberg, and Roe, in
a well-documented history of American agriculture policy reform, argue
repeatedly that "the central policy reform problem in American agriculture
endures: the problem of removing programs and entitlements that have lost
their original justification."[80] The authors correctly point to the New Deal
as the institutional foundation of American agriculture policy, but they miss
the way that the original 1933 justification—the betterment of the national
economy—had been replaced after World War II by the need to protect
and preserve an American democratic cultural institution. The family farm
rhetoric in the 1990s is a direct reflection on the *postwar* justification, not
that of the New Deal. To overhaul agriculture policy and truly eliminate the
subsidy programs, policymakers and free-market advocates need to dismantle the powerful policy monopoly that promotes the status quo in American
agriculture: the agriculture committees, the farm lobbies, and the powerful
idea of the family farm around which they are organized.

Orden, Paarlberg, and Roe are not alone in neglecting symbols and
agriculture: most of the literature on agriculture policy and policy change
focuses not on symbols, but rather on the power of interest groups.[81]
Agriculture policy is seen as a primary illustration of the "iron triangle"
of policymaking, where congressional committees, executive agencies, and
interest groups have a common goal of protecting American agriculture
interests. However, as Baumgartner and Jones clearly demonstrate, powerful institutions and interest groups remain powerful as long as they have
a compelling policy image. I have argued throughout this chapter that
behind the very real actors and institutions that keep agriculture policy in
place lies the influential normative draw of the family farm.

Americans are not ready to give up on family farms and neither are
politicians who invoke the language in policy debates (like the estate tax)
to rousing political success. The policy gap between the practice of larger
and larger business-oriented (family) farms and the normative ideal of the
family farm—with the yard light burning—continues to grow. The overwhelming support the family farm garners for agriculture (and especially
federal dollars for individual districts) and other policies (like the estate
tax) means that the gap has been, and continues to be, exploited by those
who benefit most.

CHAPTER SEVEN

Conclusion

I set out in this research project with two central aims: to more closely examine the role of family in the policy process and to understand the consequences of embedding family throughout public policy. To achieve these goals, I conducted research into the way that family is used in public policy in three areas—immigration, taxation, and agriculture—over time. Although I have addressed both how family is embedded in each of the three policy areas and the consequence this has for the policy, I have not yet addressed a key question: what are the consequences for everyday Americans? That is, just as embedded family assumptions have an impact on politics, so they may also have an impact upon Americans whose lives are directly affected by these policies. In this conclusion I look across the case studies, first reviewing my conclusions about the role of family in the policy process and speculating on its relationship to the state more generally. I next turn to generalizations about the policy process and, in particular, features of the 1990s that made change more or less successful. Having addressed two of the aims of this research project—examining both policy and politics—I explore the consequences of embedded family assumptions for American residents and citizens.

FAMILY IN THE POLICY PROCESS

Throughout this research project, I found that family plays an important role in the policy process. That is, family acts as the means to achieve a wide variety of public policy ends in three ways. First, family is a criterion of eligibility to determine who may receive goods and services. As demonstrated with U.S. immigration policy, approximately 80 percent of all immigration to the United States is due to family connection. Second, family also acts as an administrator that distributes goods to other family members. An important component of the federal income tax is tax expenditures, which encourage taxpayers to act in particular ways on *behalf* of other persons. Families have become a shadow bureaucracy, administering many social welfare policies, like education credits or the Earned Income Tax Credit (EITC), embedded in the United States tax code. Third, family functions as a normative ideal that provides justification for a particular policy position. Examining the language of federal agriculture policy, I found that Americans are especially supportive of American family farms—even though it is not clear, in practice, what constitutes this particular type of agricultural arrangement. Legislators who claim that a particular policy will help or protect family farms, whether agriculture subsidies or the estate tax repeal, make their positions politically popular.

Family, then, plays an essential part in the creation, execution, and maintenance of American public policy. To remove family from public policy and look to other ways of determining eligibility, administering goods and services, and justifying policy positions would tear down much of the functional capacity the American state now enjoys. Beyond the specific role it plays in any particular public policy, the broader conclusion of my research suggests that we rethink the place of family in relationship to the size, scope, and development of the American state.

Though American political development scholars have looked at the state (either in state building or state capacity) through the lens of more traditional courts, parties, and bureaucracies,[1] American families act functionally as part of the state—even if they are traditionally thought of as part of a private realm. Political scientists have been moving toward an evaluation of the state that looks at the functional processes and outcomes rather than official institutions. Theda Skocpol, for one, argues that "we must examine the relationships between states and political parties, and understand the impact of state and party organizations on the outlooks and capacities of social groups that are still active in the political process."[2] She deliberately chooses the term *polity-centered* to underscore the importance of looking at all three of these together—not merely the state as a site of official action. More recently, scholars have expanded the scope of their examination to take account of the alternative ways that policy goals are accomplished. Christopher Howard examines the "hidden welfare state" or social welfare policy provided in the United States tax code. Though evaluations of welfare provision generally focus on traditional government programs (Medicare, Social Security, Aid to Families with Dependent Children [AFDC]/Temporary Assistance to Needy Families [TANF]), Howard shows how a host of "hidden" welfare policies are a part of the nation's tax code.[3] Likewise, Jacob Hacker investigates the state's capacity to provide health care and pensions through public and private means.[4]

Though these scholars do not invoke family—as part of Skocpol's polity, as part of Howard's hidden welfare state, or as part of Hacker's divided welfare state—American families determine who gets what and how they get it and provide the justification for public provision. The ability of policymakers to harness the resources of the state depends, in part, on their ability to enlist the help of American families. Importantly, the American family does not replace the state but aids in designing and carrying out public policy goals.

Though political actors for much of American history have spoken of family as private and the antithesis of the public state, in fact family has always been part of American governance, from the common law of domestic relations to major public programs like AFDC.[5] Scholarly work by historians suggests a large role for family prior to the twentieth century, though it is unclear how extensive and exactly what role family played.[6] It is beyond the scope of this book to speculate about the similarities and differences between nineteenth- and twentieth-century family-state relationships. Certainly, this is a rich area for future research. In this book, I have focused specifically on twentieth-century policy, defined as government legislative and administrative activities. In the wake of World War II and the expansion of the American state, legislators relied on the American family to aid them in the return to "normalization." Though family was a part of immigration, tax, and agriculture policy to greater or lesser extent before the end of the war, postwar legislation made it a key part of each. To better meet changing international demand, immigration policy in place since 1924 was rewritten in 1952 and ammended in 1965 into one comprehensive act that bolstered family as a criterion of eligibility. The federal income tax, first used during World War I, was expanded to be a mass-based tax during World War II. Though couples could choose to file jointly since the very first day of the tax, the 1948 Revenue Act embedded families into the center of the tax code by requiring joint filing for married couples. Agriculture subsidies, in place since 1933, were revised for the protection of "family farms" in 1949. Though a great deal has changed in the six decades since the end of World War II, the policies of normalization in these three areas and their assumptions about family still remain the law Americans use today.

Amid the dramatic changes in each of the three areas, the role of family went relatively unnoticed. Commentators on immigration policy since the Immigration and Nationality Act of 1952 have focused on racial criteria that came out in 1965 rather than what filled its place—family. Tax analysts have looked at family in the tax code in determining filing statuses, but they have not examined family as the administrators of social policy. For all of the research on new governance and scaling back the visible number of government employees, family as the "shadow bureaucrats" who administer the new social welfare policy in the United States has gone relatively unnoticed. Likewise, critics of agriculture policy who talk about how agriculture has outgrown its original justification fail to see that the postwar desire to save the cultural-democratic family farm rather than economic necessity during the New Deal is an important policy image that justifies continued spending.

Family, often thought of as a personal arrangement, has very public implications. The ability of policymakers to pass legislation, the ability to administer it, and the functional criteria that determine who gets what all involve family. Looking at the functional use of family by policymakers breaks down traditional modes of thinking of family as "private" and the state as "public." Indeed, it shows us how the state relies on so-called private arrangements for public ends.

CONSEQUENCES FOR POLICY

The second aim of this book is to understand the consequences when policy actors rely on family. By looking in depth at the structure of policy, I show that what is in policy and where it is located are important for understanding the politics surrounding policy: how problems get defined, policy communities involved, and coalitions that form around the *means* used to accomplish policy goals and not merely the ends. The three policy areas presented in this book, on immigration, taxation, and agriculture, show that values and assumptions about family are embedded across policy areas. When these values and assumptions become outdated, they create a policy gap that is the site of political contestation.

Within each of the broader policy areas I examined more particular case studies: how activists were able to amend immigration law to allow single persons to adopt abroad; how immigration preference categories for adult brothers and sisters have failed to change despite the presence of a policy gap; how the EITC has adapted to the influx of mothers into the paid labor force; and how the rhetoric of the family farm, attached to major agriculture subsidies, has shaped the debate over eliminating these programs. In three of these cases, large-scale attempts to change these programs occurred in the mid-1990s after Republicans took over control of both houses of Congress for the first time in forty years. With a lame-duck Democratic president after 1996, and a Republican in 2000, Republicans were able to open a window of opportunity that had been closed for decades, though they were not entirely successful in enacting all of the changes they wanted.

Though Republicans in Congress initially had party cohesion and a large enough majority to enact change, they had only mixed success passing reforms to the three policy areas examined in this book. Republicans were able to pass significant tax reform, including reducing the marriage penalty in the income tax, but they were not able to pass immigration reform, and they were not able to permanently eliminate the agriculture subsidy programs in place since the Great Depression. Why, under similar political circumstances and relying on family, were they not equally successful?

Looking at policy structure provides a more nuanced approach that connects what is in public policies to the actors and institutions of the policy process to broader social practices. With family as a means in the policy process in all three areas, political will was defined by coalitions that included supporters of a policy's means (family) as well as ends (immigration, tax, and agriculture). A large part of the variation in Republicans' success had to do with coalition building and the strange bedfellows that prevailed in order to support legislation that would "aid American families" or fight against legislation that would hurt them. In each of the three cases, strict party votes would come undone as regional and ideological coalitions developed. In the case of the outright defeat of plans to re- form legal immigration, conservative Republicans were outmaneuvered as proimmigration groups joined with labor groups, business leaders, re- ligions organizations, and the Christian Coalition. Legislation that sought to limit the number of legal immigrants (adult brothers and sisters) in the United States was labeled antifamily. Republicans lost their traditional supporters as proimmigration groups played up both the economic effects of the legislation (for business) and the social implications of an immigra- tion policy that limited family members (for churches, synagogues, and the religious right).

In their partial victory, agriculture policy, Republican proposals to eliminate the decades-old subsidy programs were initially met with mixed support. Urban and suburban legislators of both parties signed on to the reforms. However, dispersed farm interests across the country made it impossible—especially in the Senate—to disregard agricultural interests. In 1995, the original Freedom to Farm Act drew the support of agribusi- ness, which wanted to eliminate planting restrictions, and only a handful of farm groups. In 1996, with a strong agriculture market more farm groups were enthusiastic about the plan. The conference report passed by large majorities as nonrural Democrats along with Republicans voted in favor of the bill. Though Senate minority leader Tom Daschle insisted on keeping the permanent law in place, whether or not he had it is doubtful, at best, if Congress would let American "family farms" perish. As the markets turned down in the late 1990s, Congress stepped in to appropriate billions of dollars in emergency spending—before the date of reauthorization. The ideological coalition of free marketers and urban/suburban legislators together with farm interests had quickly fallen apart. By 2002, farm subsidy programs returned full force.

In their victory, Republicans were able to pass large tax reforms, reducing the marginal tax rate for Americans and reducing and in some cases eliminating the marriage tax penalty. Although President George W. Bush originally proposed a targeted marriage penalty relief plan that would provide assistance only to taxpaying Americans where *both* couples worked and were penalized under the prereformed tax code, Republicans in Congress broadened the scope considerably. Bearing in mind their Democratic colleagues, Republicans included provisions to reform the marriage penalty in the EITC as well as the tax code more generally. Further, bearing in mind the necessary support of conservative Republicans, the proposals would not be limited to couples harmed by the current tax code. That is, the plan provided bonuses for married couples with a single breadwinner. Congressional Republicans who wished to reform the tax code were able to get both Democrats, who liked the EITC reforms, and Republicans, who were promarriage, on board. The left-leaning Center for Budget and Policy Priorities (CBPP) as well as the right-leaning Heritage Foundation both approved of EITC reform. The CBPP liked traditional Democratic aims of helping out *needy* families while the Heritage Foundation was in favor of supporting needy *families*.

The coalitions that formed around each of these three issues were able to broaden their scope by invoking family. For example, proimmigration groups were able to include the religious right because they painted an image of the family under attack. Although some might argue that the family emphasis is due to the social conservatives who came to office in the 1990s, in fact, family has been part and parcel of the policies under debate for much longer. It has been a part of each of the three policy areas at least since World War II, and in some cases decades earlier. Far from being a Republican issue, family is invoked by both parties in the debates. Robert Rector of the Heritage Foundation summed up the party influence: "I think they use the term family equally, but it's meaning different things to their constituents."[7]

Family changes the politics in American policymaking, but it cannot trump two important factors. First, as political scientists have demonstrated, it is much easier to create or expand a program than it is to contract it. Entrenched interests have an advantage over those who wish to challenge them. Second, it matters what policy actors wish to change. Altering assumptions in the periphery that allows single parents to adopt abroad does not have a large impact on policy. It is much easier to adapt than removing decades-old agriculture subsidies that would fundamentally alter American agriculture. It is less surprising that the subsidies were reinstated than it is that they were temporarily removed to begin with.

THE POLITICS OF FAMILY

Even though family has been an important structural component of policy for decades, the catchphrase "family values" that is so common in American politics today is relatively new. For many readers, the politics of family is closely associated with American conservatives, especially the new right in the Republican party. In this section I address briefly how it is that family can be both a structural component in public policies at least since World War II and a part of the renewed emphasis on "family values" that has cropped up in the past three decades in party politics.[8]

The present focus of *both* political parties couples family with more traditional ideological aims. The Republicans in 1976 asserted, "families—not government programs—are the best way to make sure our children are properly nurtured, our elderly are cared for, our cultural and spiritual heritages are perpetuated, our laws are observed and our values are preserved."[9] Republicans united family values and the promotion of American families with policy positions they already favored.

Because of our concern for family values, we affirm our beliefs, stated elsewhere in this Platform, in many elements that will make our country a more hospitable environment for family life—neighborhood schools; educational systems that include and are responsive to parents' concerns; estate tax changes to establish more realistic exemptions which will minimize disruption of already bereaved families; a position on abortion that values human life; a welfare policy to encourage rather than discourage families to stay together and seek economic independence; a tax system that assists rather than penalizes families with elderly members, children in day care or children in college; economic and employment policies that stop the shrinkage of our dollars and stimulate the creation of jobs so that families can plan for their economic security.[10]

Likewise, Democrats invoked "working families" in their platforms once in 1972 and every year between 1988 and 2004. Democratic concerns about working families take a traditional New Deal cast toward making government programs and services more accessible and available for people in need. For Democrats, state programs alleviate pressure on American families. Thus, in 1976 Democrats explained that problems like unemployment lead to many evils including "strained family relationships."[11] The answer is increased public initiatives: "There are houses to build, urban centers to rebuild, roads and railroads to construct and repair, rivers to clean, and new sources of energy to develop."[12] In contrast to the Republicans, the Democrats propose that additional support for family farms, welfare, and voluntary population control will improve the lives of American families.

The increased emphasis on family for both parties has not meant changing goals and priorities, but it has meant changing the way that goals and priorities are framed.[13] Republicans push for decreased government involvement not merely because government is inefficient, but also because it helps American families. Giving parents choice in public education or reducing taxes means giving them the freedom to make the best decisions for their families. Democrats seek to expand definitions of family already in place, allowing more people to participate in federal programs. Democrats talk of the need to help working families by making more people eligible for immigration or using extra tax dollars to shore up and increase federal programs to which most Americans have access (like Social Security). The inclusion of family in the rhetoric of both parties, as discussed above, has allowed diverse coalitions—who otherwise might be opposed to one another's interests—to form and work together. Though both parties engage family as an important part of politics, a means of accomplishing policy goals, they stress different means. Republicans like family administration in tax expenditures like the EITC because it reduces the size of government while Democrats like helping all families by increasing eligibility for programs like immigration and the EITC.

Party rhetoric takes the current emphasis on family and uses it as a frame for traditional party goals. But current party politics should not take away from the enduring role that family has played in the policy process throughout the twentieth century. Indeed, my research suggests that future scholarship can further examine the relationship between the parties' commitment to family and the success of programs framed in pro-family ways (such as the estate tax).

THE REMAINING QUESTION: CONSEQUENCES FOR AMERICANS

Throughout this book, I have argued that policy gaps together with features of the policy process have an impact on policy. Gaps not only affect public policy, they also impinge on the lives of Americans. Though embedding family in a wide range of public policies may be politically expedient, it makes personal relationships the qualifier for government goods and services. Rather than guaranteeing access to all Americans, certain "individual" benefits are available or distributed only to individuals in particular family units.

What it means to be a family unit in the United States depends on which policy one chooses to examine. Generally, family can be described in the abstract as nuclear and dependent upon one another. I found particular assumptions about the roles that family members take on and the expectations that they have for one another, as well as the state, differ in the three policies examined in this book. For immigrants, a family is determined almost exclusively by blood or legal ties (marriage and adoption). The assumptions in immigration policy favor the emotional proximity of close relations. For taxpayers, however, blood and legal ties are only one part of what it means to be a family. Financial dependence plays a significant part of official designations. For farmers, family relationships are intentionally ambiguous. The familial relationship, however, confers upon these farmers the status of "family farm" and the cultural import that goes along with it. Individuals who do not meet the family criteria for one policy area, such as immigration, still may be a family under other policy areas, like tax or agriculture. American public policy sends mixed signals to Americans.

More important than the mixed messages that public policies send, assumptions embedded in public policy, no matter how accurate they may seem to be, leave out segments of the population that do not conform with those assumptions. I found in each of three areas I investigated that an individual whose social practices do not match the assumptions embedded in policy does not have access to "individual" benefits.

First, immigration laws—which prioritize nuclear kin relationships—have at their center a specific model of family that may be at odds with any particular individual's family as well as cultural practices of family more generally. Nancy Cott explains that the history of American immigration law has tended to punish those whose marital patterns were not like Americans and promote those whose were. "Immigrants inclined toward desirable patterns of love and marriage . . . were seen as voluntarily choosing and contributing to what it means to be free Americans."[14] For a host of potential Americans, non-Western family practices that differed from traditional American family practices—which prioritized emotional proximity—meant discrimination or outright exclusion. Still today, because immigration law prioritizes emotional proximity of the nuclear family, families who deviate from this model are denied entry. Unlike the Canadian system, for which an individual has wider latitude to bring in aunts, uncles, or other extended family relations, U.S. immigration law remains set by predetermined familial relationships. Miami relatives of Cuban Elian Gonzalez, the young boy whose mother perished in an attempt to reach asylum in Florida, had no standing with the

Immigration and Naturalization Service to petition for asylum on Elian's behalf.[15] Same-sex couples, like American Eric Nelson and his Russian partner Andrei, do not qualify for family-related reunification visas.[16] Gulan Tolani, an immigrant from India who died a month before his immigration papers arrived, left his widow and one of his sons facing deportation. His younger (American-born) son would be left in the care of a foster family.[17] By placing assumptions about family at the core of immigration policy, what appears to be a personal decision or a personal hardship has far-reaching effects.

When family acts as a shadow bureaucracy in the tax code, carrying out the implicit policy in education credits and the EITC, it is politically popular with legislators on both sides of the aisle. But while tax expenditures forge strong bonds in the legislature, they do not guarantee that everyone who qualifies for education assistance will receive it. At times, the assumption that families share resources—so fundamental to the workings of the tax code—does not work in practice as it does in theory. For example, embedding assumptions about shared family resources has far-ranging consequences for students whose families choose not to assist them with college expenses. Parents are not obligated to pay for college expenses even if they can afford the rising cost of tuition. Students, whose parents claim them as dependents on their tax returns, are not eligible to claim either the Hope or Lifetime Learning Credits. Further, students under the age of twenty-three are considered dependents of their parents for federally assisted student loans if their parents can afford to assist them with college expenses—unless the student is working on an advanced degree, is a veteran, orphan, married, or has dependents of his or her own.[18] That is, parental financial data determines the "Expected Family Contribution" and hence eligibility for federally subsidized student aid regardless of how much aid parents are actually willing to provide.

Relying on family members to execute policy goals shifts costs of programs from federal bureaucrats to family members. The EITC, the nation's largest aid program for needy families, is distributed only to taxpayers who claim the credit on their tax form. Though the Internal Revenue Service (IRS) does not collect data on eligible individuals who do not claim the EITC, Joel Wanacheck of the Center for Budget and Policy Priorities estimates that somewhere between 75 percent and 80 percent of eligible individuals claim the credit.[19] The numbers suggest that the EITC does a good job reaching its target population, but there are costs to the claimants. By shifting the administrative burden from state bureaucrats to family members, compliance costs increase, and EITC claimants are more likely to be audited by the IRS. A Consumer Federation of America study estimates that taxpayers spend $994 million annually to file for the EITC, the majority of which goes to paid tax preparers who act on claimants' behalf.[20] Paid tax preparers file 44 percent of paper returns and 82 percent of electronic returns claiming the EITC. But EITC claimants, who may lack the language skills or specialized knowledge to fill out the forms, do not always get more accurate returns for their money. Two-thirds of the EITC tax returns flagged by the IRS for further investigation were submitted by paid preparers.[21] According to Janet Holtzblatt, Deputy Director of Individual Taxation at the Treasury Department, "The EITC imposes the compliance costs directly on the individual taxpayer. The taxpayer, in order to qualify for the EITC, must file a tax return, must understand the tax law, and must deal with the IRS if there are any questions regarding his or her claim."[22]

Finally, the language of "family farm" obscures the fact that larger commercially productive "family farms" squeeze out smaller "family farms." What benefits one, may not benefit (and in fact, may harm) the other. Chuck Hassbrook, program director at the Center for Rural Affairs, wrote a *New York Times* op-ed piece in 1997 against the estate tax repeal. For Hassbrook, though the estate tax repeal would seem to help small to moderate family farms, in fact it would make things worse. Hassbrook explains that estate taxes as they are now help to "level the playing field."[23] However, large exemptions in place combined with the repeal (favored in Congress) "means a wealthy couple engaged in farming could transfer a farm estate of $5.5 million (more than 10 times the assets of the average Nebraska farmer) to their heirs without paying any taxes at all." Hassebrook complains that the image of family farms is used to sell a policy that actually *harms* these same farms. Ultimately, "small farmers are the poster children for the campaign to end estate taxes, but they would not be the beneficiaries."

Embedding assumptions about family into the workings of American public policy means that American citizens and residents are adversely affected if their family life differs from the image that American policymakers hold. Above and beyond the cost borne by any one person, it suggests a system in which individual benefits are contingent on family status *as interpreted* by America's policymakers. That is, the primary lawmaking body, highly criticized for not representing Americans as a whole (members of Congress are more often wealthy, white, heterosexual, and male), decides who qualifies as a family member and what they are eligible to receive. Although including family in public policies may make sense or be politically expedient, it reinforces particular family norms, such as gender roles in immigration policy that dictate distinct criteria for children of American fathers and mothers born abroad. It also reinforces ideas about dependency, the emotional dependency of nuclear family members (in the case of immigration policy) or financial dependency of extended kin (tax policy). Most of all, embedding family under the surface of public policy reinforces the idea that the American state is hands-off when it comes to family when, in fact, the American state depends on the work of American families generally and specific assumptions about the characteristics of those families in particular.

Though political scientists think in terms of individuals, in the eyes of the state individuals are part of family relationships. These relationships are used to achieve public policy goals that may seem to have little to do with family. Though policies that rely on family include assumptions that are inaccurate or outdated, the value of family remains relatively unscathed. The ability to hold an abstract value (like family) at the same time that the assumptions in federal law and nearly every state in the nation deny one's own experience of family is particularly noteworthy. It shows the importance of values (family) for stability and continuity in public programs at the same time that particular assumptions leave open the opportunity, and in some cases sow the seeds, for change.

Family Search Criteria

The following Boolean search was conducted of the *Congressional Record*, *U.S. Code*, and *Federal Register*.

(FAMILY! or SPOUSE! or HUSBAND! or WIFE! or PARENT or GRANDPARENT! or MOTHER! or STEPMOTHER! or MOTHER-IN-LAW! or GRANDMOTHER! or FATHER! or STEPFATHER! or FATHER-IN-LAW! or GRANDFATHER! or GRANDCHILD! or OFFSPRING! or SIBLING! or BROTHER! or STEPBROTHER! or BROTHER-IN-LAW! or SISTER! or STEPSISTER! or SISTER-IN-LAW or DAUGHTER or STEPDAUGHTER or DAUGHTER-IN-LAW! or SON or STEPSON! or SON-IN-LAW! or AUNT! or UNCLE or COUSIN! or NIECE! or NEPHEW! or WIDOW! or WIDOWER or MARRIAGE! or PARENTHOOD or KIN or GUARDIAN) or text (CHILD and (PARENT or GUARDIAN or SPOUSE)).

Congressional Record

The *Congressional Record* records the daily proceedings of the House and Senate and is printed daily by the Government Printing Office. The *Record* provides additional information beyond a verbatim transcript of the days' events. First, even though on the floor congressional members often ask for truncated reading of bills and amendments or make motions in abbreviated form, the *Record* prints bills, amendments, and motions in their entirety. Second, members are able to correct grammatical mistakes and add additional statements to their testimony.

The *Congressional Record* is broken down into four parts.

1. Proceedings of the House: In addition to debate on the floor, the *Record* contains "communications from the president and executive branch, memorials, petitions, and various information (including amendments and cosponsors) on legislation introduced and/or

passed." Bills and resolutions introduced are not printed in the *Record* if they are already printed elsewhere. House and Senate members both may revise their statements.

2. Proceedings of the Senate: Same as proceedings of the House with the exception that senators may insert unfinished remarks in the *Record*.

3. Extensions of Remarks: Used exclusively by House members, the Extensions of Remarks consists of additional legislative statements and extraneous materials such as letters, tributes, or newspaper articles.

4. *Daily Digest*: The *Digest* provides a brief summary of major highlights of the day.

U.S Code

The *U.S. Code* is the general and permanent laws of the United States. Published by the Office of the Law Revision Counsel, House of Representatives, hard copies of the *Code* are available every six years. Electronic versions of the *Code* are updated more frequently. The *Code* is divided into fifty Titles, two of which have been repealed or superceded. Titles are further broken down into Chapters and Sections.

Federal Register

The *Federal Register* is published daily by the Office of the Federal Register, National Archives and Records Administration. The *Register* is the official daily publication for Rules, Proposed Rules, and Notices of federal agencies and organizations, as well as Executive Orders and other Presidential Documents. The *Register* is divided into four sections:

1. Presidential Documents, including executive orders and proclamations

2. Rules and Regulations, including policy statements and interpretations of rules

3. Proposed Rules, including petitions for rulemaking and other advance proposals

4. Notices, including scheduled hearings and meetings open to the public, grant applications, and administrative orders.

SOURCE: Library of Congress (http//thomas.loc.gov/home/abt.cong.rec.html) and the U.S. National Archives and Records Administration (http://www.archives.gov/)

Titles of the U.S. Code

Title	Name	Rank	No. of Chapters Family Words	% Chapters Family Words
1	General Provisions	13	1	33
2	The Congress	14	9	33
3	The President	2	3	60
4	Flag and Seal, Seat of Gov't, and the States	23	1	20
5	Government Organization and Employees	10	20	43
6	Surety Bonds [Repealed]	—	—	—
7	Agriculture	23	22	20
8	Aliens and Nationality	35	2	13
9	Arbitration	44	0	0
10	Armed Forces	28	49	17
11	Bankruptcy	3	5	56
12	Banks and Banking	9	23	47
13	Census	28	1	17
14	Coast Guard	6	7	50
15	Commerce and Trade	23	19	20
16	Conservation	27	16	19
17	Copyrights	15	4	31
18	Crimes and Criminal Procedure	16	36	30
19	Custom Duties	22	5	22
20	Education	17	21	28
21	Food and Drugs	21	6	25
22	Foreign Relations and Intercourse	12	27	34
23	Highways	44	0	0
24	Hospitals and Asylums	23	2	20
25	Indians	4	23	52

Title	Name	Rank	No. of Chapters Family Words	% Chapters Family Words
26	Internal Revenue Code	4	33	52
27	Intoxicating Liquors	44	0	0
28	Judiciary and Judicial Procedures	31	12	16
29	Labor	11	12	39
30	Mineral Lands and Mining	38	3	10
31	Money and Finance	18	7	28
32	National Guard	6	2	50
33	Navigation and Navigable Waters	38	4	10
34	Navy [Replaced by Title 10]	—	—	—
35	Patents	44	0	0
36	Patriotic and National Observances	18	28	28
37	Pay and Allowances of the Uniformed Servs.	20	3	27
38	Veterans' Benefits	1	31	74
39	Postal Service	37	2	11
40	Public Buildings, Property, and Works	31	4	16
41	Public Contracts	44	0	0
42	The Public Health and Welfare	8	70	48
43	Public Lands	38	4	10
44	Public Printing and Documents	43	1	5
45	Railroads	34	3	14
46	Shipping	36	10	12
47	Telegraphs, Telephones, and Radiotelegraphs	38	1	10
48	Territories and Insular Possessions	31	3	16
49	Transportation	42	7	8
50	War and National Defense	28	7	17

Defining "Child" in Immigration Law
1952–2002

1952: "Child defined"
• (b)(1) The term "child" means an unmarried person under twenty-one years of age who is—

(A) a legitimate child; or

(B) a stepchild, provided the child had not reached the age of eighteen years at the time the marriage creating the status of stepchild occurred; or

(C) a child legitimated under the law of the child's residence or domicile, or under the law of the father's residence or domicile, whether in or outside the United States, if such legitimation takes place before the child reaches the age of eighteen years and the child is in the legal custody of the legitimating parent or parents at the time of such legitimation.

1957: Added provisions for out-of-wedlock children and adopted children

1961: Permanent rules for adoption of orphans abroad.

1965: Expands definition of child to include a child under the age of fourteen at the time the petition was filed who is an orphan for adoption.

1975: Provided for adoption of alien children under the age of fourteen by unmarried U.S. citizens.

1981: Child defined as under sixteen (rather than fourteen) when either (E) adopted or (F) an orphan for adoption

1986: Gave illegitimate children status through their *fathers* as well as their mothers but only if they have a "bona fide parent-child relationship" with them.

1988: In the case of illegitimate child, the term *parent* does not include natural father of the child if the father has disappeared.

1989: Extended measure above.

1995: Changed wording from illegitimate to out of wedlock.

1999: Technical/conforming amendment

2000: Altered the definition of child to include international resolutions.

Amendments to Immigration Law
Affecting Criteria of Eligibility
(Sections: 1101, 1151, 1152, 1153)

Year	Public-Law Number	Sections Affected
1957	85-316	1101
1959	86-363	1153
1961	87-301	1101, 1152
1965	89-236	1101, 1151, 1152, 1153
1975	94-115	1101
1976	94-571	1151, 1152, 1153
1978	95-412	1151, 1152
	95-417	1153
1980	96-212	1151, 1152, 1153
1981	97-116	1101, 1151, 1152
1986	99-603	1101, 1152
	99-653	1101
1988	100-459	1101
	100-525	1101, 1152
1989	101-162	1101
1990	101-649	1151, 1152, 1153
1991	102-232	1151, 1152, 1153
1994	103-416	1151, 1153
	103-322	1151
1995	104-51	1101
1996	104-208	1151, 1152
1999	106-139	1101
	106-113	1153
2000	106-279	1101
	106-313	1152
	106-386	1151
	106-536	1153
2002	107-208	1151
	107-273	1153

Notes

CHAPTER 1

1. *Baehr v. Lewin*, 74 Haw. 530, 852 P.2d 44 (1993).

2. 142 Cong. Rec. S 10100.

3. According to the House Judiciary Committee Report on the Defense of Marriage Act (104–664), "Recognition of same sex 'marriages' in Hawaii could also have profound implications for federal law as well. The word 'marriage' appears in more than 800 sections of federal statutes and regulations, and the word 'spouse' appears more than 3100 times. With very limited exceptions, these terms are not defined in federal law" (10).

4. Nancy F. Cott, *Public Vows: A History of Marriage and the Nation* (Cambridge, MA: Harvard University Press, 2000), 152–55.

5. Patricia Strach and Kathleen Sullivan, "Beyond the Welfare State" (paper presented at the Annual Meeting of the Western Political Science Association, Albuquerque, NM, March 16–18, 2006).

6. Theodora Ooms, "Families and Government: Implementing a Family Perspective in Public Policy," *Social Thought* 16, no. 2 (1990): 74; James Q. Wilson, *The Moral Sense* (New York: The Free Press, 1993), 158–62; Joan Aldous and Wilfred Dumon, "Family Policy in the 1980s: Controversy and Consensus," *Journal of Marriage and the Family* 52 (1990): 1137.

7. http://www.census.gov/population/www/cps/cpsdef.html. Accessed 7/16/2006.

8. But see Priscilla Yamin, "Nuptial Nation: Marriage and the Politics of Civic Membership in the US" (Dissertation, New School for Social Research, 2005); Gwynn Thomas, "Ties that Bind and Break: The Uses of Family in the Political Struggles of Chile, 1970–1990" (Dissertation, University of Wisconsin, 2005).

9. Paul Allen Beck and M. Kent Jennings, "Family Traditions, Political Periods, and the Development of Partisan Orientations," *The Journal of Politics* 53, no. 3 (1991); Bruce Campbell, "A Theoretical Approach to Peer Influence in Adolescent Socialization," *American Journal of Political Science* 24 (1980); James W. Clark, "Family Structure and Political Socialization Among Urban Black Children," *American Journal of Political Science* 17, no. 2 (1973); R. W. Connoll, "Political Socialization in the American Family: The Evidence Re-Examined," *Public Opinion*

Quarterly 36, no. 3 (1972); William A. Glaser, "The Family and Voting Turnout," *Public Opinion Quarterly* 23, no. 4 (1959–1960); M. Kent Jennings and Richard G. Niemi, *Generations and Politics: A Panel Study of Young Adults and their Parents* (Princeton, NJ: Princeton University Press, 1981); Richard M. Merelman, "The Family and Political Socialization: Toward a Theory of Exchange," *The Journal of Politics* 42, no. 2 (1980); Richard G. Niemi, *How Family Members Perceive Each Other: Political and Social Attitudes in Two Generations* (New Haven, CT: Yale University Press, 1974); Stanley Allen Renshon, "Personality and Family Dynamics in the Political Socialization Process," *American Journal of Political Science* 19, no. 1 (1975).

10. Virginia Sapiro, "Private Costs of Public Commitment or Public Costs of Private Commitments? Family Roles versus Political Ambition," *American Journal of Political Science* 26, no. 2 (1982); Yvette M. Alex-Assensoh, *Neighborhoods, Family, and Political Behavior in Urban America* (New York: Garland, 1998); Nancy Burns, Kay Lehman Schlozman, and Sidney Verba, "The Public Consequences of Private Inequality: Family Life and Citizen Participation," *American Political Science Review* 91, no. 2 (1997); Eric Plutzer and Michael McBurnett, "Family Life and American Politics: The 'Marriage Gap' Reconsidered," *Public Opinion Quarterly* 55, no. 1 (1991); David C. Barker and James D. Tinnick III, "Competing Visions of Parental Roles and Ideological Constraint," *The American Political Science Review* 100, no. 2 (2006); Nancy Burns, Kay Lehman Schlozman, and Sidney Verba, *The Private Roots of Public Action: Gender, Equality, and Political Participation* (Cambridge, MA: Harvard University Press, 2001).

11. See Jyl J. Josephson, *Gender, Families, and State: Child Support Policies in the United States* (Lanham, MA: Rowman & Littlefield Publishers, Inc., 1997); Steven K. Wisensale, *Family Leave Policy: The Political Economy of Work and Family in America.* (Armonk, NY: M. E. Sharpe, 2001); Christopher Howard, *The Hidden Welfare State* (Princeton, NJ: Princeton University Press, 1997); Theda Skocpol, *Protecting Soldiers and Mothers* (Cambridge, MA: Belknap Press, 1992).

12. Paula Baker, "The Domestication of Politics: Women and American Political Society, 1780–1920," *The American Historical Review* 89, no. 3 (1984); Mary P. Ryan, "Gender and Public Access: Women's Politics in Nineteenth-Century America," in *Feminism: The Public and the Private*, ed. Joan B. Landes (New York: Oxford University Press, 1998).

13. Rebecca Edwards, *Angels in the Machinery: Gender in American Party Politics from the Civil War to the Progressive Era* (New York: Oxford University Press, 1997).

14. Theda Skocpol, *Protecting Soldiers and Mothers* (Cambridge, MA: Belknap Press, 1992).

15. Aileen S. Kraditor, *The Ideas of the Woman Suffrage Movement, 1890–1920* (New York: Columbia University Press, 1965); Rebecca Edwards, *Angels in the Machinery: Gender in American Party Politics from the Civil War to the Progressive Era* (New York: Oxford University Press, 1997); Linda K. Kerber, *No Constitutional Right to be Ladies: Women and the Obligations of Citizenship* (New York: Hill and Wang, 1998); Linda K. Kerber, "The Republican Mother: Women and the Enlightenment—An American Perspective," *American Quarterly* 28, no. 2 (1976).

16. Jacqueline Stevens, *Reproducing the State* (Princeton, NJ: Princeton University Press, 1999); Nancy F. Cott, *Public Vows : A History of Marriage and the Nation* (Cambridge, MA: Harvard University Press, 2000).

17. Paula Baker, "The Domestication of Politics: Women and American Political Society, 1780–1920," *The American Historical Review* 89, no. 3 (1984); Jyl J. Josephson, *Gender, Families, and State: Child Support Policies in the United States* (Lanham, MA: Rowman & Littlefield Publishers, Inc., 1997); Martha Minow and Mary Lyndon Shanley, "Revisioning the Family: Relational Rights and Responsibilities," in *Reconstructing Political Theory: Feminist Perspectives*, ed. Mary Lyndon Shanley and Uma Narayan (University Park: The Pennsylvania State University Press, 1997).

18. Nancy Burns, Kay Lehman Schlozman, and Sidney Verba, *The Private Roots of Public Action: Gender, Equality, and Political Participation* (Cambridge, MA: Harvard University Press, 2001).

19. Irene Diamond, *Families, Politics, and Public Policy: A Feminist Dialogue on Women and the State* (New York: Longman, 1983), 2.

20. Harold L. Wilensky, *The Western State and Equality: Structural and Ideological Roots of Public Expenditures* (Berkeley: University of California Press, 1975); Harold L. Wilensky, *Industrial Society and the Supply and Organization of Social Welfare Service in the United States* (New York: Russell Sage Foundation, 1958); Bruce W. Heady, "Trade Unions and National Wage Policies," *Journal of Politics* 32 (1970); Edward Berkowitz and Kim Mcquaid, "Businessman and Bureaucrat: The Evolution of the American Social Welfare System, 1900–1940," *Journal of Economic History* 38 (1978); Gaston V. Rimlinger, *Welfare Policy and Industrialization in Europe, America, Russia* (New York: Wiley, 1971). Theda Skocpol and Gretchen Ritter, "Gender and the Origins of Modern Social Policies in Britain and the United States," in *Social Policy in the United States*, ed. Theda Skocpol (Princeton, NJ: Princeton University Press, 1995); Jacob S. Hacker, *The Divided Welfare State: The Battle over Public and Private Social Benefits in the United States* (Cambridge, MA: Cambridge University Press, 2002); Christopher Howard, *The Hidden Welfare State* (Princeton, NJ: Princeton University Press, 1997).

21. Michael K. Brown, *Race, Money, and the American Welfare State* (Ithaca, NY: Cornell University Press, 1999); Jacob S. Hacker, *The Divided Welfare State: The Battle over Public and Private Social Benefits in the United States* (Cambridge: Cambridge University Press, 2002).

22. Alice Kessler-Harris, "Designing Women and Old Fools: The Construction of the Social Security Amendments of 1939," in *U.S. History as Women's History*, ed. Linda K. Kerber, Alice Kessler-Harris, and Kathryn Kish Sklar (Chapel Hill: University of North Carolina Press, 1995), 91–92.

23. Stephen Goldsmith and William D. Eggers, *Governing by Network: The New Shape of the Public Sector* (Washington, DC: Brookings Institution Press, 2004), 9–14.

24. Jacob S. Hacker, *The Divided Welfare State: The Battle over Public and Private Social Benefits in the United States* (Cambridge, MA: Cambridge University Press, 2002); Marie Gottschalk, *The Shadow Welfare State: Labor, Business, and the Politics of Health Care in the United States* (Ithaca, NY: Cornell University

Press, 2000); Christopher Howard, *The Hidden Welfare State* (Princeton, NJ: Princeton University Press, 1997); Christopher Howard, "Is the American Welfare State Unusually Small?" *PS: Political Science and Politics* 36, no. 3 (2003).

25. Michael K. Brown, "State Capacity and Political Choice: Interpreting the Failure of the Third New Deal," *Studies in American Political Development* 9 (1995); Daniel P. Carpenter, *The Forging of Bureaucratic Autonomy* (Princeton, NJ: Princeton University Press, 2001); Stephen Skowronek, *Building a New American State: The Expansion of National Administrative Capacities 1877–1920* (Cambridge, MA: Cambridge University Press, 1982).

26. Paul Manna, *School's In: Federalism and the National Education Agenda* (Washington, DC: Georgetown University Press, 2006) chapter 2.

27. Patricia Strach and Kathleen Sullivan, "Beyond the Welfare State" (paper presented at the Annual Meeting of the Western Political Science Association, Albuquerque, NM, March 16–18, 2006).

28. Nancy F. Cott, *Public Vows: A History of Marriage and the Nation* (Cambridge, MA: Harvard University Press, 2000); Jacqueline Stevens, *Reproducing the State* (Princeton, NJ: Princeton University Press, 1999).

29. Aristotle, *Politics* (New York: Oxford University Press, 1995).

30. John Locke, "The Second Treatise of Government," in *Two Treatises of Government*, ed. Mark Goldie (London: Everyman, 1690/1993).

31. James Q. Wilson, *The Moral Sense* (New York: The Free Press, 1993) For criticisms of the naturalness of family, see Nancy F. Cott, *Public Vows: A History of Marriage and the Nation* (Cambridge, MA: Harvard University Press, 2000); Jacqueline Stevens, *Reproducing the State* (Princeton, NJ: Princeton University Press, 1999); Martha Fineman, *The Neutered Mother, the Sexual Family, and Other Twentieth Century Tragedies* (New York: Routledge, 1995).

32. Arland Thornton, "Changing Attitudes toward Family Issues in the United States," *Journal of Marriage and the Family* 51, no. 4 (1989): 873.

33. Kathleen Sullivan, *Constitutional Context: Women and Rights Discourse in Nineteenth-Century America* (Baltimore, MD: Johns Hopkins University Press, 2007).

34. A search of journal titles in the top 28 political science journals between 1907 and 2002 reveals that "family" appears in article titles only seventy-two times. Only twenty-two are in the field of American politics; and nearly half (ten) of these are about political socialization. [Journals were searched via the JSTOR as of 7/11/2006. The political science journals include: *American Journal of International Law* (1907–2005), *American Journal of Political Science* (1957–2004), *American Political Science Review* (1906–2002), *Asian Survey* (1932–2002), *British Journal of Political Science* (1971–2000), *Canadian Journal of Political Science* (1928–2000), *Comparative Politics* (1968–2000), *International Affairs* (1922–2000), *International Organization* (1947–2002), *International Security* (1976–2001), *International Studies Quarterly* (1957–2000), *International Studies Review* (1999–2000), *Journal of Conflict Resolution* (1957–2002), *Journal of Palestine Studies* (1971–2002), *Journal of Peace Research* (1964–2002), *Journal of Politics* (1939–2002), *Journal of Southern African Studies* (1974–2002), *Legislative Studies Quarterly* (1976–2000), *Mershon International Studies Review* (1994–

1998), *Middle East Report* (1971–2000), *Political Behavior* (1979–2002), *Political Research Quarterly* (1948–2004), *Political Science Quarterly* (1886–2001), *Political Theory* (1973–2002), Proceedings *of the American Political Science Association* (1904–1913), *PS: Political Science and Politics* (1968–2002), *Public Opinion Quarterly* (1937–2000), and *World Politics* (1948–2004).]

35. Gary S. Becker, *A Treatise on the Family* (Cambridge, MA: Harvard University Press, 1981).

36. Keith Krehbiel, *Pivotal Politics: A Theory of U.S. Lawmaking* (Chicago: University of Chicago Press, 1998); Gary W. Cox and Matthew D. McCubbins, *Legislative Leviathan: Party Government in House* (Berkeley: University of California Press, 1993); Gary W. Cox and Matthew D. McCubbins, "Bonding, Structure, and the Stability of Political Parties: Party Government in the House," in *Positive Theories of Congressional Institutions*, ed. Kenneth A. Shepsle and Barry R. Weingast (Ann Arbor: University of Michigan Press, 1995); David W. Rohde, "Parties and Committees in the House: Member Motivations, Issues, and Institutional Arrangements," in *Positive Theories of Congressional Institutions*, ed. Kenneth A. Shepsle and Barry R. Weingast (Ann Arbor: University of Michigan, 1995); Daniel P. Carpenter, *The Forging of Bureaucratic Autonomy* (Princeton: Princeton University Press, 2001); Kenneth Mayer, *With the Stroke of a Pen: Executive Orders and Presidential Power* (Princeton, NJ: Princeton University Press, 2002); Jeffrey Segal and Harold J. Spaeth, *The Supreme Court and the Attitudinal Model Revisited* (Cambridge, MA: Cambridge University Press, 2002); Robert Dahl, "Decision-Making in a Democracy: The Supreme Court as a National Policy-Maker," *The Journal of Public Law* 6 (1957); Lee Epstein, Jack Knight, and Andrew Martin, "The Supreme Court as a *Strategic* National Policymaker," *Emory Law Journal* 50 (2001); Gerald N. Rosenberg, "The Road Taken: Robert A. Dahl's *Decision-Making in a Democracy: The Supreme Court as a National Policy-Maker*," *Emory Law Journal* 50 (2001); Paul J. Quirk and Bruce Nesmith, "Divided Government and Policy Making: Negotiating the Laws," in *The Presidency and the Political System*, ed. Michael Nelson (Washington, DC: CQ Press, 1995); Mark Schneider, Paul Eric Teske, and Michael Mintrom, *Public Entrepreneurs: Agents for Change in American Government* (Princeton, NJ: Princeton University Press, 1995); Mark Schneider and Paul Eric Teske, "Toward a Theory of the Political Entrepreneur: Evidence from Local Government," *The American Political Science Review* 86, no. 3 (1995); Adam D. Sheingate, "Political Entrepreneurship, Institutional Change, and American Political Development," *Studies in American Political Development* 17 (2003); John Kingdon, *Agendas, Alternatives, and Public Policies* (Boston: Little, Brown, 1984); Frank R. Baumgartner and Bryan D. Jones, *Agendas and Instability in American Politics* (Chicago: University of Chicago Press, 1993); Nelson Polsby, *Political Innovation in America: The Politics of Policy Innovation* (New Haven, CT: Yale University Press, 1984); Steven J. Balla and John R. Wright, "Interest Groups, Advisory Committees, and Congressional Control of the Bureaucracy," *American Journal of Political Science* 45, no. 4 (2001); Frank R. Baumgartner and Beth L. Leach, "Interest Niches and Policy Bandwagons: Patterns of Interest Group Involvement in National Politics," *The Journal of Politics* 63, no. 4 (2001); William P. Browne, *Cultivating Congress: Constituents, Issues, and Interests in Agricultural*

Policymaking (Lawrence: University Press of Kansas, 1995); Richard L. Hall and Frank W. Wayman, "Buying Time: Moneyed Interests and the Mobilization of Bias in Congressional Committees," *The American Political Science Review* 84, no. 3 (1990); John Mark Hansen, *Gaining Access: Congress and the Farm Lobby, 1919–1981* (Chicago: The University of Chicago Press, 1991); Mancur Olson, Jr., *The Logic of Collective Action: Public Goods and the Theory of Groups* (Cambridge, MA: Harvard University Press, 1965); Kay Lehman Schlozman and John T. Tierney, *Organized Interests and American Democracy* (New York: Harper and Row, 1986); Graham K. Wilson, *Special Interests and Policymaking: Agricultural Policies and Politics in Britain and the United States of America, 1956–70* (New York: John Wiley & Sons, 1977); Kenneth M. Goldstein, *Interest Groups, Lobbying, and Participation in America* (Cambridge, MA: Cambridge University Press, 1999); Frank R. Baumgartner and Bryan D. Jones, *Agendas and Instability in American Politics* (Chicago: University of Chicago Press, 1993); John Kingdon, *Agendas, Alternatives, and Public Policies* (Boston: Little, Brown, 1984); Deborah Stone, "Causal Stories and the Formation of Policy Agendas," *Political Science Quarterly* 104 (1989); Deborah A. Stone, *Policy Paradox: The Art of Political Decision Making*, Rev. ed. (New York: Norton, 2002). Samuel P. Huntington, *American Politics: The Promise of Disharmony* (Cambridge, MA: Belknap Press, 1981); Rogers Smith, "Beyond Tocqueville, Myrdal, and Hartz: The Multiple Traditions in America," *American Political Science Review* 87, no. 3 (1993).

37. E. E. Schattschneider, *Politics, Pressures and the Tariff: A Study of Free Private Enterprise in Pressure Politics, as Shown in the 1929–1930 Revision of the Tariff* (New York: Prentice Hall, 1935); Theodore J. Lowi, "Four Systems of Policy, Politics, and Choice," *Public Administration Review* 32, no. 4 (1972); Theodore J. Lowi, "Decision Making vs. Policy Making: Toward an Antidote for Technocracy," *Public Administration Review* 30, no. 3 (1970). But see Jacob S. Hacker, *The Divided Welfare State: The Battle over Public and Private Social Benefits in the United States* (Cambridge, MA: Cambridge University Press, 2002); Jacob S. Hacker, "Privatizing Risk without Privatizing the Welfare State: The Hidden Politics of Social Policy Retrenchment in the United States," *American Political Science Review* 98, no. 2 (2004); Paul Pierson, *Dismantling the Welfare State? Reagan, Thatcher and the Politics of Retrenchment* (Cambridge, MA: Cambridge University Press, 1994).

38. Christopher Hood, *The Tools of Government* (London: MacMillan, 1984); Evert Vedung, "Policy Instruments: Typologies and Theories," in *Carrots, Sticks, and Sermons: Policy Instruments and Their Evaluation*, ed. Marie Louise Memelmans-Videc, Ray C. Rist, and Evert Vedung (New Brunswick, NJ: Transaction Publishers, 1998); Michael Howlett and M. Ramesh, *Studying Public Policy: Policy Cycles and Policy Subsystems* (New York: Oxford University Press, 1995); Anne Schneider and Helen Ingram, "Behavioral Assumptions of Policy Tools," *Journal of Politics* 52, no. 2 (1990); Lester M. Salamon, "The New Governance and the Tools of Public Action: An Introduction," in *The Tools of Government: A Guide to New Governance*, ed. Lester M. Salamon (New York: Oxford University Press, 2002); Michael Howlett, "Policy Instruments, Policy Styles, and Policy Implementation: National Approaches to Theories of Instrument Choice," *Policy Studies Journal* 19, no. 2 (1991).

39. Christopher Hood, *The Tools of Government* (London: MacMillan, 1984), 8.

40. This is especially true in environmental policy. See Arild Vatn, "Rationality, Institutions, and Environmental Policy," *Ecological Economics* 55 (2005); Lovell S. Jarvis, "The Rise and Decline of Rent-Seeking Activity in the Brazilian Coffee Sector: Lessons from the Imposition and Removal of Coffee Export Quotas," *World Development* 33, no. 11 (2005); Till Requate, "Dynamic Incentives by Environmental Policy Instruments—A Survey," *Ecological Economics* 54 (2005); Petrus Kautto and Jukka Simila, "Recently Introduced Policy Instruments and Intervention Theories," *Evaluation* 11, no. 1 (2005); Heather Campbell, "Prices, Devices, People or Rules: The Relative Effectiveness of Policy Instruments in Water Conservation," *Review of Policy Research* 21, no. 5 (2004); Florentina Astleithner and Alexander Hamedinger, "The Analysis of Sustainability Indicators as Socially Constructed Policy Instruments: Benefits and Challenges of 'Interactive Research,'" *Local Environment* 8, no. 6 (2003); Carolyn Fischer, Ian W. H. Parry, and William A. Pizer, "Instrument Choice for Environmental Protection when Technological Innovation is Endogenous," *Journal of Environmental Economics and Management* 45, no. 3 (2003); Sangeeta Bansal and Shubhashis Gangopadhyay, "Tax/Subsidy Policies in the Presence of Environmentally Aware Consumers," *Journal of Environmental Economics and Management* 45, no. 2 (2003); Rauno Sairinen, "The Politics of Regulatory Reform: 'New' Environmental Policy Instruments in Finland," *Environmental Politics* 12, no. 1 (2003); Dolf J. Gielen and Yuichi Moriguchi, "Materials Policy Design," *Environmental Economics and Policy Studies* 5, no. 1 (2002); Chilik Yu and Laurence J. Jr. O'Toole, "Policy Instruments for Reducing Toxic Releases," *Evaluation Review* 22, no. 5 (1998). For other policy areas see: Roger L. Mackett et al., "A Methodology for Evaluating Walking Buses as an Instrument of Urban Transport Policy," *Transport Policy* 10, no. 3 (2003); Joe Dewbre and Cameron Short, "Alternative Policy Instruments for Agriculture Support: Consequences for Trade, Farm Income, and Competitiveness," *Canadian Journal of Agricultural Economics* 50, no. 4 (2002); Susan Giaimo and Philip Manow, "Adapting the Welfare State," *Comparative Political Science* 32, no. 8 (1999); Robin Boadway, "Redistributing Smarter: Self-Selection, Targeting, and Non-Conventional Policy Instruments," *Canadian Public Policy* 24, no. 3 (1998); Charlotte Halpern, "Institutional Change through Innovation: The URBAN Community Initiative in Berlin, 1994–1999," *Environment and Planning C: Government and Policy* 23 (2005).

41. Karen Orren and Stephen Skowronek, *The Search for American Political Development* (2004).

42. Joe Soss, "Lessons of Welfare: Policy Design, Political Learning, and Political Action," *The American Political Science Review* 93, no. 2 (1999).

43. Suzanne Mettler, *Soldiers to Citizens: The GI Bill and the Making of the Greatest Generation* (New York: Oxford University Press, 2005), 144.

44. Giandomenico Majone, *Evidence, Argument, and Persuasion in the Policy Process* (New Haven, CT: Yale University Press, 1989), 150.

45. Michael K. Brown, *Race, Money, and the American Welfare State* (Ithaca, NY: Cornell University Press, 1999); Alice Kessler-Harris, "Designing Women and

Old Fools: The Construction of the Social Security Amendments of 1939," in *U.S. History as Women's History*, ed. Linda K. Kerber, Alice Kessler-Harris, and Kathryn Kish Sklar (Chapel Hill: University of North Carolina Press, 1995); Linda K. Kerber, *No Constitutional Right to be Ladies: Women and the Obligations of Citizenship* (New York: Hill and Wang, 1998).

46. Giandomenico Majone, *Evidence, Argument, and Persuasion in the Policy Process* (New Haven: Yale University Press, 1989), 150.

47. Disjunctures, or gaps, have been used in a variety of theories of change to explain why political change occurs. See Samuel P Huntington, *American Politics: The Promise of Disharmony* (Cambridge, MA: Belknap Press, 1981); Robert C. Lieberman, "Ideas, Institutions, and Political Order: Explaining Political Change," *American Political Science Review* 96, no. 4 (2002); Lawrence M. Mead, *The New Politics of Poverty: The Nonworking Poor in America* (New York: Basic Books, 1992); Jill Quadagno, *The Color of Welfare: How Racism Undermined the War on Poverty* (New York: Oxford University Press, 1994).

48. John Kingdon, *Agendas, Alternatives, and Public Policies* (Boston: Little, Brown, 1984).

49. Samuel P Huntington, *American Politics: The Promise of Disharmony* (Cambridge, MA: Belknap Press, 1981), 64–75.

50. Karen Orren and Stephen Skowronek, *The Search for American Political Development* (2004), 14.

51. 142 Cong. Rec. S 10100.

52. B. Guy Peters, *American Public Policy: Promise and Performance* (Chappaqua, NY: Chatham House/Steven Rivers, 1999).

CHAPTER 2

1. For a critical analysis of the public/private distinction see Aileen S. Kraditor, *The Ideas of the Woman Suffrage Movement, 1890–1920* (New York: Columbia University Press, 1965); Joan B. Landes, "Introduction," in *Feminism: The Public and the Private*, ed. Joan B. Landes (New York: Oxford University Press, 1998); Martha Minow and Mary Lyndon Shanley, "Revisioning the Family: Relational Rights and Responsibilities," in *Reconstructing Political Theory: Feminist Perspectives*, ed. Mary Lyndon Shanley and Uma Narayan (University Park: The Pennsylvania State University Press, 1997); Mary P. Ryan, "Gender and Public Access: Women's Politics in Nineteenth-Century America," in *Feminism: The Public and the Private*, ed. Joan B. Landes (New York: Oxford University Press, 1998); Paula Baker, "The Domestication of Politics: Women and American Political Society, 1780–1920," *The American Historical Review* 89, no. 3 (1984).

2. Robert Dahl, *Who Governs? Democracy and Power in an American City* (New Haven, CT: Yale University Press, 1961), 225.

3. Stephen Goldsmith and William D. Eggers, *Governing by Network: The New Shape of the Public Sector* (Washington, DC: Brookings Institution Press, 2004); Lester M. Salamon, "The New Governance and the Tools of Public Action: An Introduction," in *The Tools of Government: A Guide to New Governance*, ed. Lester M. Salamon (New York: Oxford University Press, 2002); Michael Howlett, "Policy Instruments, Policy Styles, and Policy Implementation: National

Approaches to Theories of Instrument Choice," *Policy Studies Journal* 19, no. 2 (1991); Daniel P. Aldrich, "Controversial Project Siting: State Policy Instruments and Flexibility," *Comparative Politics* 38, no. 1 (2005); Stephen H. Linder and B. Guy Peters, "Instruments of Government: Perceptions and Contexts," *Journal of Public Policy* 9, no. 1 (1989); Evert Vedung, "Policy Instruments: Typologies and Theories," in *Carrots, Sticks, and Sermons: Policy Instruments and Their Evaluation*, ed. Marie Louise Memelmans-Videc, Ray C. Rist, and Evert Vedung (New Brunswick, NJ: Transaction Publishers, 1998).

4. Nancy F. Cott, *Public Vows: A History of Marriage and the Nation* (Cambridge, MA: Harvard University Press, 2000); Steven K. Wisensale, *Family Leave Policy: The Political Economy of Work and Family in America.* (Armonk, NY: M. E. Sharpe, 2001); Martha Minow and Mary Lyndon Shanley, "Revisioning the Family: Relational Rights and Responsibilities," in *Reconstructing Political Theory: Feminist Perspectives*, ed. Mary Lyndon Shanley and Uma Narayan (University Park: The Pennsylvania State University Press, 1997).

5. Department of Veteran's Affairs, www1.va.gov/visns/visn02/vet/services/family.html

6. United States Senate, Committee on Veteran's Affairs, *Hearing on Benefits for Survivors: Is America Fulfilling Lincoln's Charge to Care for the Families of Those Killed in the Line of Duty?* February 3, 2005.

7. "2004 Green Book: Background Material and Data on the Programs within the Jurisdiction of the Committee on Ways and Means," (Washington, DC: U.S. House of Representatives, Committee on Ways and Means, 2004).

8. "Annual Statistical Supplement to the Social Security Bulletin, 2005," (Washington, DC: Social Security Administration, 2006).

9. Lester M. Salamon, "The New Governance and the Tools of Public Action: An Introduction," in *The Tools of Government: A Guide to New Governance*, ed. Lester M. Salamon (New York: Oxford University Press, 2002); Stephen Goldsmith and William D. Eggers, *Governing by Network: The New Shape of the Public Sector* (Washington, DC: Brookings Institution Press, 2004).

10. Paul C. Light, *The True Size of Government* (Washington, DC: The Brookings Institution, 1999).

11. For discussions of the requirements and gendered nature of care, see Nancy Folbre, *The Invisible Heart: Economics and Family Values* (New York: The New Press, 2001); Carol Gilligan, *In a Different Voice: Psychological Theory and Women's Development* (Cambridge, MA: Harvard University Press, 1982); Nel Noddings, *Caring: A Feminine Approach to Ethics and Moral Education* (Berkeley: University of California Press, 1984); Joan C. Tronto, "Women and Caring: What Can Feminists Learn about Morality from Caring?," in *Gender/Body/Knowledge: Feminist Reconstructions of Being and Knowing*, ed. Alison M. Jaggar and Susan Bordo (New Brunswick, NJ: Rutgers University Press, 1989).

12. See also Frank R. Baumgartner and Bryan D. Jones, *Agendas and Instability in American Politics* (Chicago: University of Chicago Press, 1993); and Deborah A. Stone, *Policy Paradox: The Art of Political Decision Making*, rev. ed. (New York: Norton, 2002) for a discussion of how policy stories and images change political debates.

13. Deborah Stone, "Causal Stories and the Formation of Policy Agendas," *Political Science Quarterly* 104 (1989): 2812 (emphasis in original). See Paul Burnstein, R. Marie Bricher, and Rachel L. Einwohner, "Policy Alternatives and Political Change: Work, Family, and Gender on the Congressional Agenda, 1945–1990," *American Sociological Review* 60, no. 1 (1995) for one discussion of family in policy framing.

14. Murray J. Edelman, "Political Language and Political Reality," *PS: Political Science* Winter (1985): 11.

15. For a more detailed description of search terms and coding decision rules, see Appendix A.

16. Murray Edelman refers to language that aims at convincing audiences to support a particular policy as hortatory. Hortatory language seeks to gain support by using abstract terms like democracy and justice. Murray J. Edelman, *The Symbolic Uses of Politics* (Urbana: University of Illinois Press, 1964), 134.

17. "In session" for a given week is defined as broadly as possible. If either house is scheduled to meet in any week for at least one day, that week is counted as in session.

18. The first exception occurs in the first week of January 1997 (105th Congress). Here, quite simply, though Congress is scheduled to be in session there are no entries—family-related or otherwise—in the Congressional Record. In the second case, the second week of January 2001 (107th Congress), there are only eighteen total entries in the Record as the Senate is only in Session one day. The House did not convene at all.

19. The *Congressional Quarterly Weekly Report* 55, no. 28 (1997) lists major legislative action on the floor as Defense Appropriations (S 1005); Energy-Water Appropriations (S 1004); Foreign Appropriations (HR 2159; S 955); Interior Appropriations (HR 2107); Juvenile Justice Block Grants (HR 1818); Legislative Branch Appropriations (S 1019); Treasury-General Government Appropriations; VA-HUD Appropriations (HR 2158); Vocational Education and Training Reauthorization (HR 1853).

20. During July 1997, lawmakers in both the House and Senate struggled over the budget. By far the most difficult and contentious part of the negotiations was the tax bill (HR 2014). In addition to wrangling over a proposed tobacco tax, legislators disagreed about the scope and amount of tax cuts and a child tax credit. Alissa J. Rubin, "Tax Issues Divide Parties, Chambers," *Congressional Quarterly Weekly Report* 55, no. 29 (1997): 1682.

21. R. Kent Weaver, "The Politics of Blame Avoidance," *Journal of Public Policy* 6, no. 4 (1986); Paul Pierson, *Dismantling the Welfare State? Reagan, Thatcher and the Politics of Retrenchment* (Cambridge, MA: Cambridge University Press, 1994).

22. Of course it is entirely possible to disagree with Stevens's justification by appealing to a very different family norm. Senator Paul Wellstone (D-MN) counters: "I don't see how, if we are going to make the argument that people feel an economic squeeze at $133,000 a year, while most of the cuts we make in discretionary programs hurt low and moderate income families and their children in the name of sacrifice and in the name of deficit reduction, that this is the right time for us to go forward with a cost-of-living increase."

23. According to Robert Rector of the conservative Heritage Foundation, "I think they [Republicans and Democrats] use the term 'family' equally. But it's meaning different things to their constituents. When Democrats are using the term, I read that as playing to the middle of the road voters they want to convince. Republicans are playing to their base" (Interview with Robert Rector, November 13, 2003).

24. Though fifty-seven women served in the U.S. House in the 105th Congress, only fifty-three were in office in July 1997. Four entered office through special election later (Mary Bono, Lois Capps, Barbara Lee, and Heather Wilson).

25. The four titles where family words do not appear are Arbitration (Title 9), Intoxicating Liquors (Title 27), Patents (Title 35), or Public Contracts (Title 41).

26. The forty-eight titles break the Code into major topic areas, such as Congress, Transportation, and War and National Defense. Each of these titles is further broken down into chapters that comprise broad policies within each area. For example, under Title 7, Agriculture, Food Stamps is one chapter. There is neither a standard length for chapters nor a standard number of chapters in a title. Nevertheless, chapters remain the best unit of analysis as they measure breadth and not merely volume.

27. Other agencies not listed in the text but with family references during this week are Department of Commerce, Department of Labor, as well as Office of Personnel Management, Federal Trade Commission, National Archive and Records Administration, Federal Deposit Insurance Corporation, and Department of Veterans' Affairs.

28. See Nancy Fraser and Linda Gordon, "Decoding 'Dependency': Inscriptions of Power in a Keyword of the U.S. Welfare State," in *Reconstructing Political Theory: Feminist Perspectives*, ed. Mary Lyndon Shanley and Uma Narayan (University Park: Pennsylvania State University Press, 1995).

29. Given the way that relationships and defined by the U.S. Census, it is impossible to have a definitive count of adopted and stepchildren. By U.S. Census estimates, the data presented here may understate the actual amount by as much as a third. See "Adopted Children and Stepchildren: 2000," (Washington, DC: U.S. Census Bureau, 2003). Householders with adopted children have a higher median income ($56,138 compared to $48,200), more education (33.4 percent with bachelors degree compared to 25.9 percent), and greater home ownership (77.8 percent compared to 66.8 percent) than householders with biological children, "Statistical Abstract of the United States: 2006," (Washington, DC: U.S. Census Bureau, 2005).

30. Susan B. Carter, ed., *Labor Force*, vol. II, *Historical Statistics of the United States: Earliest Times to the Present* (Cambridge, MA: Cambridge University Press, 2006).

31. "Statistical Abstract of the United States: 2006," (Washington, DC: U.S. Census Bureau, 2005).

32. The U.S. Census Bureau defines fertility rate as "number of births that 1,000 women would have in their lifetime at each age if they experienced birthrates occurring in the specified year." "Statistical Abstract of the United States: 2006," (Washington, DC: U.S. Census Bureau, 2005), Table 75.

33. Susan B. Carter et al., ed., *Historical Statistics of the United States: Earliest Times to the Present* (Cambridge, MA: Cambridge University Press, 2006), "Statistical Abstract of the United States: 2006," (Washington, DC: U.S. Census Bureau, 2005).

34. "Statistical Abstract of the United States: 2006," (Washington, DC: U.S. Census Bureau, 2005).

35. Susan B. Carter et al., eds., *Historical Statistics of the United States: Earliest Times to the Present* (Cambridge, MA: Cambridge University Press, 2006), "Statistical Abstract of the United States: 2006," (Washington, DC: U.S. Census Bureau, 2005).

36. Arland Thornton, "Changing Attitudes toward Family Issues in the United States," *Journal of Marriage and the Family* 51, no. 4 (1989): 873. Arland Thornton, "Four Decades of Trends in Attitudes Toward Family Issues in the United States: The 1960s Through the 1990s," *Journal of Marriage and the Family* 63, no. 4 (2001).

37. Family member is defined broadly to include any kin relation.

38. Interview with Chris Labonte, Human Rights Campaign, November 17, 2003.

39. Federal policymakers and agencies recognize that families have changed, even if they cannot always identify precisely in what way. Traditional sources of data do not provide specific enough information on the new types of families in America. The Data Collection Committee of the Federal Interagency on Child and Family Statistics explains the problem this way: "Family composition and union formation processes have changed dramatically over the past several decades. The extent to which effective policies can be developed to address the changing needs of American families depends, in large part, on the identification and measurement of different family characteristics." "Counting Couples: Improving Marriage, Remarriage, and Cohabitation Data in the Federal Statistical System" (Bethesda, MD: The Data Collection Committee of the Federal Interagency Forum on Child and Family Statistics, 2001), 19.

CHAPTER 3

1. Frank R. Baumgartner and Bryan D. Jones, *Agendas and Instability in American Politics* (Chicago: University of Chicago Press, 1993); John Kingdon, *Agendas, Alternatives, and Public Policies* (Boston: Little, Brown, 1984); Keith Krehbiel, *Pivotal Politics: A Theory of U.S. Lawmaking* (Chicago: University of Chicago Press, 1998); John Mark Hansen, *Gaining Access: Congress and the Farm Lobby, 1919–1981* (Chicago: The University of Chicago Press, 1991); Daniel P. Carpenter, *The Forging of Bureaucratic Autonomy* (Princeton, NJ: Princeton University Press, 2001).

2. John Kingdon, *Agendas, Alternatives, and Public Policies* (Boston: Little, Brown, 1984); Frank R. Baumgartner and Bryan D. Jones, *Agendas and Instability in American Politics* (Chicago: University of Chicago Press, 1993).

3. Robert C. Lieberman, "Ideas, Institutions, and Political Order: Explaining Political Change," *American Political Science Review* 96, no. 4 (2002): 704.

4. Keith Krehbiel, *Pivotal Politics: A Theory of U.S. Lawmaking* (Chicago: University of Chicago Press, 1998), 47.

5. Gary W. Cox and Matthew D. McCubbins, *Legislative Leviathan: Party Government in House* (Berkeley: University of California Press, 1993); Gary W. Cox and Matthew D. McCubbins, "Bonding, Structure, and the Stability of Political Parties: Party Government in the House," in *Positive Theories of Congressional Institutions*, ed. Kenneth A. Shepsle and Barry R. Weingast (Ann Arbor: University of Michigan Press, 1995); John Londregan and James M. Snyder Jr, "Comparing Committee and Floor Preferences," in *Positive Theories of Congressional Institutions*, ed. Kenneth A. Shepsle and Barry R. Weingast (Ann Arbor: University of Michigan Press, 1995); David W. Rohde, "Parties and Committees in the House: Member Motivations, Issues, and Institutional Arrangements," in *Positive Theories of Congressional Institutions*, ed. Kenneth A. Shepsle and Barry R. Weingast (Ann Arbor: University of Michigan, 1995).

6. Daniel P. Carpenter, *The Forging of Bureaucratic Autonomy* (Princeton, NJ: Princeton University Press, 2001); Kenneth Mayer, *With the Stroke of a Pen: Executive Orders and Presidential Power* (Princeton, NJ: Princeton University Press, 2002); Jeffrey Segal and Harold J. Spaeth, *The Supreme Court and the Attitudinal Model Revisited* (Cambridge, MA: Cambridge University Press, 2002); Jonathan Casper, "The Supreme Court and National Policy Making," *American Political Science Review* 70 (1976); Robert Dahl, "Decision-Making in a Democracy: The Supreme Court as a National Policy-Maker," *The Journal of Public Law* 6 (1957); Lee Epstein, Jack Knight, and Andrew Martin, "The Supreme Court as a *Strategic* National Policymaker," *Emory Law Journal* 50 (2001); Gerald N. Rosenberg, "The Road Taken: Robert A. Dahl's *Decision-Making in a Democracy: The Supreme Court as a National Policy-Maker*," *Emory Law Journal* 50 (2001); Paul J. Quirk and Bruce Nesmith, "Divided Government and Policy Making: Negotiating the Laws," in *The Presidency and the Political System*, ed. Michael Nelson (Washington, DC: CQ Press, 1995).

7. Mark Schneider, Paul Eric Teske, and Michael Mintrom, *Public Entrepreneurs: Agents for Change in American Government* (Princeton, NJ: Princeton University Press, 1995); Mark Schneider and Paul Eric Teske, "Toward a Theory of the Political Entrepreneur: Evidence from Local Government," *The American Political Science Review* 86, no. 3 (1995); Adam D. Sheingate, "Political Entrepreneurship, Institutional Change, and American Political Development," *Studies in American Political Development* 17 (2003); John Kingdon, *Agendas, Alternatives, and Public Policies* (Boston: Little, Brown, 1984); Frank R. Baumgartner and Bryan D. Jones, *Agendas and Instability in American Politics* (Chicago: University of Chicago Press, 1993); Nelson Polsby, *Political Innovation in America: The Politics of Policy Innovation* (New Haven, CT: Yale University Press, 1984).

8. For a discussion on the role of interest groups, see Steven J. Balla and John R. Wright, "Interest Groups, Advisory Committees, and Congressional Control of the Bureaucracy," *American Journal of Political Science* 45, no. 4 (2001); Frank R. Baumgartner and Beth L. Leach, "Interest Niches and Policy Bandwagons: Patterns of Interest Group Involvement in National Politics," *The Journal of*

Politics 63, no. 4 (2001); William P. Browne, *Cultivating Congress: Constituents, Issues, and Interests in Agricultural Policymaking* (Lawrence: University Press of Kansas, 1995); Richard L. Hall and Frank W. Wayman, "Buying Time: Moneyed Interests and the Mobilization of Bias in Congressional Committees," *The American Political Science Review* 84, no. 3 (1990); John Mark Hansen, *Gaining Access: Congress and the Farm Lobby, 1919–1981* (Chicago: The University of Chicago Press, 1991); Mancur Olson, Jr, *The Logic of Collective Action: Public Goods and the Theory of Groups* (Cambridge, MA: Harvard University Press, 1965); Kay Lehman Schlozman and John T. Tierney, *Organized Interests and American Democracy* (New York: Harper and Row, 1986); Graham K. Wilson, *Special Interests and Policymaking: Agricultural Policies and Politics in Britain and the United States of America, 1956–70* (New York: John Wiley & Sons, 1977); Kenneth M. Goldstein, *Interest Groups, Lobbying, and Participation in America* (Cambridge, MA: Cambridge University Press, 1999).

9. For example, Nelson Polsby explains policy innovation in terms of two processes: "The first, the process of invention, causes policy options to come into existence. This is the domain of interest groups and their interests, of persons who specialize in acquiring and deploying knowledge about policies and their intellectual convictions, of persons who are aware of contextually applicable experiences of foreign nations, and of policy entrepreneurs, whose careers and ambitions are focused on the employment of their expertise and on the elaboration and adaptation of knowledge to problems. The second process is a process of systematic search, a process that senses and responds to problems, that harvests policy options and turns them into purposes, both public and career-related, of politicians and public officials" (Nelson Polsby, *Political Innovation in America: The Politics of Policy Innovation* (New Haven, CT: Yale University Press, 1984), 173. See also Robert C. Lieberman, "Ideas, Institutions, and Political Order: Explaining Political Change," *American Political Science Review* 96, no. 4 (2002).

10. Frank R. Baumgartner and Bryan D. Jones, *Agendas and Instability in American Politics* (Chicago: University of Chicago Press, 1993); John Kingdon, *Agendas, Alternatives, and Public Policies* (Boston: Little, Brown, 1984); Deborah Stone, "Causal Stories and the Formation of Policy Agendas," *Political Science Quarterly* 104 (1989); Deborah A. Stone, *Policy Paradox: The Art of Political Decision Making*, rev. ed. (New York: Norton, 2002).

11. Samuel P. Huntington, *American Politics: The Promise of Disharmony* (Cambridge, MA: Belknap Press, 1981); Rogers Smith, "Beyond Tocqueville, Myrdal, and Hartz: The Multiple Traditions in America," *American Political Science Review* 87, no. 3 (1993).

12. Theodore J. Lowi, "Four Systems of Policy, Politics, and Choice," *Public Administration Review* 32, no. 4 (1972); Theodore J. Lowi, "Decision Making vs. Policy Making: Toward an Antidote for Technocracy," *Public Administration Review* 30, no. 3 (1970).

13. But see Anne Larson Schneider and Helen Ingram, *Policy Design for Democracy* (Lawrence: University Press of Kansas, 1997).

14. Paul Pierson, *Dismantling the Welfare State? Reagan, Thatcher and the Politics of Retrenchment* (Cambridge, England: Cambridge University Press,

1994), 39. See also Paul Pierson. *Politics in Time: History, Institutions, and Social Analysis* (Princeton, NJ: Princeton University Press, 2004); Robert C. Lieberman, "Ideas, Institutions, and Political Order: Explaining Political Change," *American Political Science Review* 96, no. 4 (2002); Jacob S. Hacker, *The Divided Welfare State: The Battle over Public and Private Social Benefits in the United States* (Cambridge, England: Cambridge University Press, 2002).

15. Keith Krehbiel, *Pivotal Politics: A Theory of U.S. Lawmaking* (Chicago: University of Chicago Press, 1998).

16. David Braybrooke and Charles Lindblom, *A Strategy of Decision: Policy Evaluation as a Social Process* (New York: Free Press of Glencoe, 1963); Charles Lindblom, "The Science of Muddling Through," *Public Administration Review* 19, no. 2 (1959); Charles Lindblom, "Still Muddling, Not Yet Through," *Public Administration Review* 39, no. 6 (1979); Charles Lindblom and Robert Dahl, *Politics, Economics and Welfare: Planning and Politico-Economic Systems Resolved into Basic Social Processes* (New York: Harper, 1957).

17. John Witte points out that incrementalism is an approach to the policy process, not the outcome of policy. Though the vast majority of policy change may result in very marginal outcomes, large effects can come from relatively small adjustments, John F. Witte, *The Politics and Development of the Federal Income Tax* (Madison: University of Wisconsin Press, 1985).

18. Theodore J. Lowi, "Decision Making vs. Policy Making: Toward an Antidote for Technocracy," *Public Administration Review* 30, no. 3 (1970); Giandomenico Majone, *Evidence, Argument, and Persuasion in the Policy Process* (New Haven, CT: Yale University Press, 1989), 150.

19. Theodore J. Lowi, "Four Systems of Policy, Politics, and Choice," *Public Administration Review* 32, no. 4 (1972); Theodore J. Lowi, "Decision Making vs. Policy Making: Toward an Antidote for Technocracy," *Public Administration Review* 30, no. 3 (1970); Evert Vedung, "Policy Instruments: Typologies and Theories," in *Carrots, Sticks, and Sermons: Policy Instruments and Their Evaluation*, ed. Marie Louise Memelmans-Videc, Ray C. Rist, and Evert Vedung (New Brunswick, NJ: Transaction Publishers, 1998); G. Bruce Doern and V. Seymour Wilson, *Issues in Canadian Public Policy* (Toronto: MacMillan, 1974); Michael Howlett and M. Ramesh, *Studying Public Policy: Policy Cycles and Policy Subsystems* (New York: Oxford University Press, 1995); Christopher Hood, *The Tools of Government* (London: Macmillan, 1984).

20. Samuel P. Huntington, *American Politics: The Promise of Disharmony* (Cambridge, MA: Belknap Press, 1981). Rogers Smith, "Beyond Tocqueville, Myrdal, and Hartz: The Multiple Traditions in America," *American Political Science* 87, no. 3 (1993).

21. Robert C. Lieberman, "Ideas, Institutions, and Political Order: Explaining Political Change," *American Political Science Review* 96, no. 4 (2002): 702.

22. Donald John Devine, *The Political Culture of the United States: The Influence of Member Values on Regime Maintenance* (Boston: Little, Brown, 1972); Charles D. Elder and Roger W. Cobb, *The Political Uses of Symbols* (New York: Longman, 1983); Louis Hartz, *The Liberal Tradition in America: An Interpretation of Political Thought Since the Revolution* (New York: Harcourt,

Brace, 1955); Seymour Martin Lipset, *The First New Nation: The United States in Historical and Comparative Perspective* (New York: Basic Books, 1963).

23. Donald John Devine, *The Political Culture of the United States: The Influence of Member Values on Regime Maintenance* (Boston: Little, Brown, 1972), 227. In addition to the standard values enshrined in the founding documents, observers since Tocqueville have commented on other social/political values that Americans seem to cherish. Political scientists Charles Elder and Roger Cobb, e.g., expand the usual list to include an obligation for Americans to "love their country" and "defend it against all enemies" but little other social obligation; a respect for "common sense" and distrust of elites and intellectuals; and just distribution by the principles of "hard work," "competition," and "individual achievement." Charles D. Elder and Roger W. Cobb, *The Political Uses of Symbols* (New York: Longman, 1983), 91–95.

24. In practice this means that the source of generally agreed upon American values is not liberal ideology alone. Republicanism, for example, has played a part in forming American culture. See Joyce Appleby, "Republicanism in Old and New Contexts," *William and Mary Quarterly* 43 (1986); Lance Banning, "Jeffersonian Ideology Revisited: Liberal and Classical Ideas in the New American Republic," *William and Mary Quarterly* 43 (1986); James T. Kloppenberg, "The Virtues of Liberalism: Christianity, Republicanism, and Ethics in Early American Political Discourse," *Journal of American History* 74 (1987); Gordon Wood, *The Creation of the American Republic, 1776–1787* (Chapel Hill: University of North Carolina Press, 1969).

25. Literature on legislative choice in Congress assumes that policymakers have fixed values. See Keith T. Poole and Howard Rosenthal, *Congress: A Political-Economic History of Roll Call Voting* (New York: Oxford University Press, 1997) for an oft-cited example of measurement of ideological preferences.

26. Lieberman explains: "political ideas and cultural traditions—institutionalized, taken-for-granted understandings of political and social arrangements—...constrain and enable policymaking, both by limiting the range of policies that are considered rational and by giving policymakers a repertoire of legitimating tactics for their favored policies." Robert C. Lieberman, "Ideas, Institutions, and Political Order: Explaining Political Change," *American Political Science Review* 96, no. 4 (2002): 709.

27. This distinction between making policy ideally—informed with all of the options—or realistically, with limited resources is what fueled early incremental literature. Charles Lindblom paints a more constrained picture of how policymakers accomplish their objectives: "An alternative line of attack would be to set as his principal objective, either explicitly or without conscious thought, the relatively simple goal of keeping prices level. This objective might be compromised or complicated by only a few other goals, such as full employment. He [the administrator] would in fact disregard most other social values as beyond his present interest, and he would for the moment not even attempt to rank the few values that he regarded as immediately relevant. Were he pressed, he would quickly admit that he was ignoring many related values and many possible important consequences of his policies." Charles Lindblom, "The Science of Muddling Through," *Public Administration Review* 19,

no. 2 (1959): 79. Further, scholars of public policy and critics of rational choice have both pointed out that decisions are never made from the full universe of choices, Herbert A. Simon, *Administrative Behavior* (New York: Macmillan Co., 1947).

28. Smith advances a thesis of "multiple traditions" in America that stand alongside the traditional values associated with American culture. He explains: "This multiple traditions thesis holds that American political actors have always promoted civic ideologies that blend liberal, democratic republican and inegalitarian ascriptive elements in various combinations designed to be politically popular." Rogers Smith, *Civic Ideals: Conflicting Visions of Citizenship in U.S. History* (New Haven, CT: Yale University Press, 1997), 6.

29. Rogers Smith, *Civic Ideals: Conflicting Visions of Citizenship in U.S. History* (New Haven, CT: Yale University Press, 1997), 15.

30. Carole Pateman explores how the social contract is based on gendered assumptions about women and family, Carole Pateman, *The Sexual Contract* (Stanford, CA: Stanford University Press, 1988).

31. "For Better or for Worse: Marriage and the Federal Income Tax," (Washington, DC: The Congress of the United States, Congressional Budget Office, 1997).

32. Thomas R. Oliver, Philip R. Lee, and Helene L. Lipton, "A Political History of Medicare and Prescription Drug Coverage," *The Milbank Quarterly* 82, no. 2 (2004).

33. Dawn Nuschler, "Social Security Reform," (Washington, DC: Congressional Research Service, 2005).

34. Sabatier and Jenkins-Smith (1999) have a similar model for coalition belief systems. At the deepest level, coalitions share deep core beliefs (which "includes basic ontological and normative beliefs"), at the next level are policy core beliefs (which include "fundamental value priorities"), and the secondary aspects ("a large set of narrower . . . beliefs"). Sabatier and Jenkins-Smith explain the relationship between the belief system and change: "In general, deep core beliefs are very resistant to change—essentially akin to a religious conversion. A coalition's policy core beliefs are somewhat less rigidly held. . . . Beliefs in the secondary aspects are assumed to be more readily adjusted in light of new data, new experience, or changing strategic considerations" Paul A. Sabatier and Hank C. Jenkins-Smith, "The Advocacy Framework: An Assessment," in *Theories of the Policy Process,* ed. Paul A. Sabatier (Boulder, CO: Westview Press, 1999), 122.

35. Jacob S. Hacker, *The Divided Welfare State: The Battle over Public and Private Social Benefits in the United States* (Cambridge, England: Cambridge University Press, 2002), 105.

36. Giandomenico Majone, *Evidence, Argument, and Persuasion in the Policy Process* (New Haven, CT: Yale University Press, 1989), 150.

37. Michael K. Brown, *Race, Money, and the American Welfare State* (Ithaca, NY: Cornell University Press, 1999) p. 206.

38. Support for Clinton, who ultimately signed the legislation that dismantled AFDC, was in no way unanimous. An August 25, 2002 Gallup poll, taken right after Clinton signed the bill, reports that while 58 percent of respondents approved of what Clinton was doing with welfare, 34 percent disapproved. HR

3734 (Personal Responsibility and Work Opportunity Reconciliation Act of 1996) passed the House 256–170 and the Senate 74–24.

39. "2005 Social Security/SSI Fact Sheet," (Washington, DC: Social Security Administration, 2005).

40. Giandomenico Majone, *Evidence, Argument, and Persuasion in the Policy Process* (New Haven, CT: Yale University Press, 1989), 151.

41. John F. Witte, *The Politics and Development of the Federal Income Tax* (Madison: University of Wisconsin Press, 1985).

42. Giandomenico Majone, *Evidence, Argument, and Persuasion in the Policy Process* (New Haven, CT: Yale University Press, 1989), 150.

43. Paul Pierson, *Politics in Time: History, Institutions, and Social Analysis* (Princeton, NJ: Princeton University Press, 2004), 119.

44. For other theories that rely on gaps or disjunctures, see Samuel P Huntington, *American Politics: The Promise of Disharmony* (Cambridge, MA: Belknap Press, 1981); Robert C. Lieberman, "Ideas, Institutions, and Political Order: Explaining Political Change," *American Political Science Review* 96, no. 4 (2002); Lawrence M. Mead, *The New Politics of Poverty: The Nonworking Poor in America* (New York: BasicBooks, 1992); Jill Quadagno, *The Color of Welfare: How Racism Undermined the War on Poverty* (New York: Oxford University Press, 1994); Paul Pierson, *Politics in Time: History, Institutions, and Social Analysis* (Princeton, NJ: Princeton University Press, 2004).

45. See John Kingdon, *Agendas, Alternatives, and Public Policies* (Boston: Little, Brown, 1984); Frank R. Baumgartner and Bryan D. Jones, *Agendas and Instability in American Politics* (Chicago: University of Chicago Press, 1993) for an explanation of the role of policy entrepreneurs in the policy process.

46. Robert C. Lieberman, "Ideas, Institutions, and Political Order: Explaining Political Change," *American Political Science Review* 96, no. 4 (2002): 702.

47. Baumgartner and Jones, *Agendas and Instability in American Politics* (Chicago: University of Chicago Press, 1993).

48. John Kingdon, *Agendas, Alternatives, and Public Policies* (Boston: Little, Brown, 1984), 92–93.

49. John Kingdon, *Agendas, Alternatives, and Public Policies* (Boston: Little, Brown, 1984).

50. Heritage foundation website <http://www.heritage.org/about/> and the Human Rights Campaign website <http://www.hrc.org/Template.cfm?Section=About_HRC> accessed July 11, 2006.

51. Paul Pierson, *Dismantling the Welfare State? Reagan, Thatcher and the Politics of Retrenchment* (Cambridge, MA: Cambridge University Press, 1994); John Kingdon, *Agendas, Alternatives, and Public Policies* (Boston: Little, Brown, 1984); R. Kent Weaver, "The Politics of Blame Avoidance," *Journal of Public Policy* 6, no. 4 (1986).

52. R. Kent Weaver, "The Politics of Blame Avoidance," *Journal of Public Policy* 6, no. 4 (1986); Keith Krehbiel, *Pivotal Politics: A Theory of U.S. Lawmaking* (Chicago: University of Chicago Press, 1998).

53. E. E. Schattschneider, *The Semi-Sovereign People* (New York: Holt, Rinehart, Winston, 1960).

CHAPTER 4

1. *Congressional Quarterly Almanac*, 1963, p. 973.

2. Ian Haney Lopez, *White by Law: The Legal Construction of Race* (New York: New York University Press, 1997); Jacqueline Stevens, *Reproducing the State* (Princeton, NJ: Princeton University Press, 1999).

3. The first program of numerical restrictions, the 1921 Quota Law, was a three-year temporary program. The 1924 National Origins Act, which revised and replaced the national origins system of the Quota Law, carried the first permanent policy restrictions.

4. 8 USC § 1101(a)(17).

5. The five functions of immigration policy discussed above require an extensive administrative structure falling under the authority of three federal departments: Homeland Security, Justice, and State. After large-scale government reorganization mandated by the Homeland Security Act of 2002, the newly minted Department of Homeland Security (DHS) took over the lion's share of administration for many immigration functions previously located in the Department of Justice. The most significant reorganization involved the abolition of the Immigration and Naturalization Service, whose functions have since been divided among three DHS bureaus: the Bureau of Citizenship and Immigration Services, which grants visas and processes requests for legal immigration, naturalization, and refuge/asylum; the Bureau of Customs and Enforcement, which enforces immigration laws throughout the United States and its territories; and the Bureau of Customs and Border Protection, which enforces immigration and customs laws at U.S. ports of entry. The Department of Justice has retained the capacity to determine the status of individual cases (immigration judges) and review regulations and appeals (Board of Immigration Appeals). The responsibilities of the Department of State are limited to the services provided by U.S. consulates abroad.

6. Federal Court of Appeals judges lamented this complexity in the decision of *Lok v. INS*, 548 F.2d 37, 38 (2d Cir. 1977) "We have had occasion to note the striking resemblance between some of the laws we are called upon to interpret and King Minos's labyrinth in ancient Crete. The Tax Laws and the Immigration and Nationality Acts are examples we have cited of Congress's ingenuity in passing statutes certain to accelerate the aging process of judges."

7. The annual quota for a particular country was one-sixth of 1 percent of the number of inhabitants in the continental United States in 1920. In addition, severe restrictions were placed on the Asian Pacific Triangle, effectively shutting down almost all immigration from this region.

8. Because the annual number of refugee visas is set by the president with consultation from Congress, I have listed them separately in Table 4.1.

9. For the purposes of Figure 4.1, the "family" category includes both the explicit and implicit family categories and the "unstructured" category includes nonpreference visas (everyone other than those explicitly specified through family, work, or diversity preferences) as well as natives of the Western Hemisphere before 1978, when this region had no preference categories.

10. For example, the *Congressional Quarterly Almanac* describes the immigra-

tion amendments as follows: "The net effect of the changes in immigration law made by HR 2580 was to eliminate race and national origin as the major basis of preference for admission to the United States," (1965): 462.

11. The importance of family relative to national needs (job skills and employment visas) is driven at least in part by practical concerns over job competition. The Kennedy and later Johnson administrations' original proposals had given first preference restricted status (50 percent of visas) to skilled employees. The bill as reported out of the House subcommittee on Immigration and Nationality, however, had reversed these preferences, granting substantial weight to family over job skills (20 percent of visas). The shift in top preference priority, from work to family, is likely due to concerns about job market competition. James Gimpel and James Edwards note that the immigration subcommittee chair Michael Feighan (D-OH) who submitted the new priorities that were adopted had a strong alliance with organized labor, which was long opposed to employment-based immigration that would drive down wages for American workers. James G. Gimpel and James R. Edwards Jr., *The Congressional Politics of Immigration Reform* (Boston: Allyn and Bacon, 1999).

12. The principle of family unity holds that immigration policy should serve to reunite families. It is a fundamental part of American immigration policy. See Stephen H. Legomsky, *Immigration Law and Policy* (New York: The Foundation Press, 1992), 141–80.

13. Arland Thornton, "Changing Attitudes toward Family Issues in the United States," *Journal of Marriage and the Family* 51, no. 4 (1989).

14. INS Commissioner Doris Meissner spells out the values as follows: "Legal immigrants come to the United States because our citizens believe family members should be able to live together. Legal immigrants come to the United States because our employers need special skills within their workforce. . . . Legal immigrants come to the United States because American citizens understand the humanitarian obligation we have to reach out and protect those who are persecuted" (Subcommittee on Immigration, Committee of the Judiciary. *Prepared Statement on Legal Immigration Reform*, September 13, 1995.

15. INA § 203(d) or 8 USC § 1153(d).

16. A total of 132,917 employment-based preference visas were granted to spouses and children. Author's calculation of data from "Yearbook of Immigration Statistics: 2005" (Washington, DC: Department of Homeland Security, 2006).

17. "Amending the Immigration and Nationality Act, and for Other Purposes" (Washington, DC: U.S. House of Representatives, Committee on the Judiciary, 1965), 12.

18. American immigration policy favors family relationships with the closest possible connections. Though family is an important part of immigration for many nations, the core assumptions—or way of thinking about family throughout the policy—differ dramatically. For example, in Canada preference extends to grandparents, grandchildren, nieces, and nephews. In some instances, a Canadian citizen or permanent resident may sponsor even distant relatives for immigration to Canada. See Citizenship and Immigration Canada: http://www.cic.gc.ca/english/sponsor/index.html accessed 7/6/03.

19. Mark Krikorian, Executive Director of the Center for Immigration Studies, illustrates the controversial nature of peripheral assumptions in his testimony be-

fore the House Subcommittee on Immigration: "If immediate family members of citizens are still to be admitted without numerical limitation . . . we may have to reexamine what the law considers to be 'immediate family.' There would be little disagreement that spouses and unmarried minor children should be included—but what about parents of adult citizens?" Subcommittee on Immigration and Claims, Committee on the Judiciary, *Prepared Testimony on Proposals for Reform of Legal Immigration Policy*, May 17, 1995.

20. Suzanne M. Bianchi and Lynne M. Casper, "American Families," *Population Bulletin* 55, no. 4 (2000).

21. The 1952 Immigration and Nationality Act or 8 USC section 1101.

22. The implication of USC section 1101 (b)(1)(c), which leaves out any explicit mention of mothers, is that children are in residence with their mother.

23. See *Matter of Pineda*, I.D. 3112 (BIA 1989) and *Matter of Vizcaino*, 19 I.&N. Dec. 644 (BIA 1988) for what factors make up a bona-fide relationship. In convoluted fashion, an illegitimate child could not qualify for citizenship before 1986 through the father, but could immediately qualify if the father married before the child was 21. The child would thus have automatic standing through the mother or stepmother. Current law requires a bona-fide parent-relationship for fathers and their children but still allows automatic standing for mothers or stepmothers and their children.

24. The percentage of premarital births put up for adoption decreased from 8.7 percent to 4.1 percent between the periods 1952–1972 and 1973–1981. This decrease is driven by the behavior of white women whose percentage of premarital births put up for adoption declined even more rapidly from 19.3 percent to 7.6 percent for the same periods. Kathy S. Stolley, "Statistics on Adoption in the United States," *The Future of Children* 3, no. 1 (1993): 37.

25. Harry D. Krause, *Family Law in a Nutshell* (St. Paul, MN: West Publishing, 1977), 157.

26. *Congressional Record*, April 21, 1975.

27. "Adoption Bill Gains," *New York Times*, November 20, 1975.

28. "Alien-Infants-Adoption" (Washington, DC: U.S. Senate, Committee on the Judiciary, 1975); "Granting an Alien Child Adopted by American Unmarried United States Citizen the Same Immigration Status as an Alien Child Adopted by a United States Citizen and His Spouse" (Washington, DC: U.S. House of Representatives, Committee on the Judiciary, 1975).

29. *Congressional Record*, April 21, 1975.

30. *Congressional Record*, April 21, 1975.

31. "Ford News Conference," *Congressional Quarterly Weekly Report* 33, no. 15 (1975): 755.

32. "Humanitarian Aid," *Congressional Quarterly Weekly Report* 33, no. 15 (1975).

33. See James G. Gimpel and James R. Edwards Jr., *The Congressional Politics of Immigration Reform* (Boston: Allyn and Bacon, 1999); Kenneth K. Lee, *Huddled Masses, Muddled Laws* (Westport, CT: Praeger, 1998).

34. Question wording (Gallup, CBS/NYT): Should immigration be kept at its present level, increased or decreased? 1965–1993 from John S. Lapinski et al., "Trends: Immigrants and Immigration," *Public Opinion Quarterly* 61, no. 2

(1997), 1999 (Gallup Poll, March 8, 1999), and 2006 (Gallup Poll/CNN/*USA Today*, April 11, 2006).

35. Susan Martin, the Executive Director of the Commission on Immigration Reform (the Jordan Commission) explained, "any system that requires spouses to wait five years is a broken system" (Interview with Susan Martin, November 13, 2003). Pro-immigration groups want to clear the backlogs through amnesties or increased immigration quotas whereas anti-immigration groups want to clear the backlogs by eliminating the preference category altogether.

36. Subcommittee on Immigration, Senate Judiciary Committee, *U.S. Senator Sam Brownbeck (R-KS) Holds Hearing on Immigration Policy*, April 4, 2001.

37. Because of overall country limits, applicants from the Philippines have even longer waits. In July 2006, Filipino siblings receiving visas to come to the United States had first applied on or before January of 1984.

38. "Visa Bulletin," (Washington, DC: United States State Department, 2006).

39. "Special Immigrant Visas," *Congressional Quarterly Almanac* 30 (1972).

40. "Immigration Expansion," *Congressional Quarterly Almanac* 44 (1988): 113.

41. Gallup poll wording in 1965: "Should immigration be kept at its present level, increased, or decreased?" Thirty-nine percent Present, 7 percent Increased, 33 percent Decreased, 20 percent Don't know. In 1995: "In your view, should immigration be kept at its present level, increased, or decreased?" Twenty-eight percent Present, 8 percent Increased, 62 percent Decreased, 4 percent Don't know." Taken from John S. Lapinski et al., "Trends: Immigrants and Immigration," *Public Opinion Quarterly* 61, no. 2 (1997).

42. The exact question wording is as follows: "For the next few questions, I'd like you to concentrate on those immigrants who are in this country legally—in other words, immigrants who have the permission from the government to live in the United States and who have followed all immigration laws ... Would you favor or oppose changes in federal law to reduce the number of immigrants who enter the country legally?" Sixty-two percent Favor, 33 percent Oppose, 5 percent Not Sure. Taken from John S. Lapinski et al., "Trends: Immigrants and Immigration," *Public Opinion Quarterly* 61, no. 2 (1997).

43. Interview with Susan Martin, November 13, 2003.

44. Interview with Doris Meissner, November 19, 2003.

45. Interview with limited immigration group staffer, November 13, 2003.

46. Subcommittee on Immigration, Committee on the Judiciary, *Prepared Statement on Family Reunification Provisions within the Proposed Simpson Bill*, September 13, 1995.

47. U.S. House of Representatives Subcommittee on Immigration and Claims, U.S. Senate Subcommittee on Immigration, *Testimony on Immigration Report*, June 28, 1995.

48. Interview with limited immigration interest group staffer, November 13, 2003.

49. "Senate Votes to Revise Visa Allocations." *Congretional Quarterly Almanac* 45 (1989).

50. Subcommittee on Immigration, Committee on the Judiciary, *Prepared*

Statement on Family Reunification Provisions within the Proposed Simpson Bill, September 13, 1995.

51. Interview with Doris Meissner, November 19, 2003.

52. Interview with pro-immigration interest group staffer. November 10, 2003.

53. Robert Pear, "Clinton Embraces a Proposal to Cut Immigration by a Third," *New York Times,* June 8, 1995.

54. James G. Gimpel and James R. Edwards Jr, *The Congressional Politics of Immigration Reform* (Boston: Allyn and Bacon, 1999), 262.

55. Interview with pro-immigration interest group staffer. November 18, 2003.

56. Interview with pro-immigration interest group staffer, November 10, 2003.

57. Refugees were given special nonrestricted, nonpreference admissions and were not counted toward immigration limitations.

58. Interview with Susan Martin, November 13, 2003.

59. James G. Gimpel and James R. Edwards Jr, *The Congressional Politics of Immigration Reform* (Boston: Allyn and Bacon, 1999).

60. Daniel Tichenor, *The Politics of Immigration Control in America* (Princeton, NJ: Princeton University Press, 2002).

CHAPTER 5

1. Quote taken from Kevin Diaz, "Singles 'Being Dismissed' in Tax Debate," *Star Tribune,* May 4, 2001.

2. John D. Morris, "Inequities in Tax Cited by Treasury," *New York Times,* June 19, 1947; John D. Morris, "'Community Property' Is Big Tax Bill Item," *New York Times,* February 1, 1948.

3. Interview with Democratic Congressional Staffer, October 13, 2003.

4. Article I, Section 8 of the United States Constitution.

5. Article 1, Section 9. In other words, direct taxes were apportioned among the states on the basis of population. The original article was intended to safeguard farm states from land taxes imposed by the more heavily populated manufacturing states. The Supreme Court, however, ruled in 1895 that federal income taxes—unless apportioned by state population—were also a direct tax. Michael J. Graetz and Deborah H. Schenk, *Federal Income Taxation: Principles and Practices,* 3rd ed. (Westbury, NY: The Foundation Press, 1995), 61.

6. W. Elliot Brownlee, *Federal Taxation in America: A Short History* (Cambridge, MA: Cambridge University Press, 1996).

7. Michael J. Graetz and Deborah H. Schenk, *Federal Income Taxation: Principles and Practices,* 3rd ed. (Westbury, NY: The Foundation Press, 1995).

8. *Pollock v. Farmer's Loan & Trust Co.,* 158 US 601 (1895).

9. John F. Witte, *The Politics and Development of the Federal Income Tax* (Madison: University of Wisconsin Press, 1985), 79.

10. Though taxes were levied on human slaves, their status as "property" holds with the principle of taxing based upon consumption.

11. Author's calculation of data taken from "Historical Statistics of the United States: Colonial Times to 1970," (Washington: DC: United States Bureau of the Census, 1976).

12. Their difficulties were compounded by the 1930 Supreme Court rulings in *Lucas v. Earl* 281 US 111 and *Poe v. Seaborn* 252 U.S. 101, which allowed individuals in community property states, but not common law states, to split their wages. After 1930, several states—led by Oklahoma—attempted to switch from common law to community property. By 1948, six states had changed (Oklahoma, Oregon, Hawaii, Nebraska, Michigan, and Pennsylvania) and two more were having serious discussions about following suit (Massachusetts and New York). See Boris I. Bittker, "Federal Income Taxation and the Family," *Stanford Law Review* 27 (1975): 1454; Randolph E. Paul, *Taxation in the United States* (Boston: Little, Brown, and Company, 1954), 385.

13. The more controversial solution, pushed by some members of Congress along with the Treasury, was to create a mandatory joint income tax return and tax all couples on the basis of their joint income, which would have the effect of *raising* taxes for most couples with dual income (whether from two-wage salaries, or one salary and investment income). The response to this plan was overwhelmingly negative. The mandatory joint return was decried loudly by the public as "Un-American" ("Mandatory Joint Returns," *New York Times*, March 26, 1942) and antiwoman. New York socialite Elizabeth Selden Rogers summed up the opposition to this expensive plan in a letter to the editor of the *New York Times* in 1934: "It revives the old idea that married persons are one person and not two absolutely distinct individuals." She continues, "I love my husband devotedly but I never tell him my income." Elizabeth Selden Rogers, "Letter to the Editor: Against Joint Returns," *New York Times*, January 31, 1934. When Congress instead implemented a mandatory joint taxation plan which *lowered* taxes for most American couples, there was no outcry that the tax was either un-American or antiwoman. In fact, there was little opposition whatsoever.

14. John D. Morris, "'Community Property' Is Big Tax Bill Item," *New York Times*, February 1, 1948.

15. John F. Witte, *The Politics and Development of the Federal Income Tax* (Madison: University of Wisconsin Press, 1985).

16. Stanley S. Surrey, *Pathways to Tax Reform: The Concept of Tax Expenditures* (Cambridge, MA: Harvard University Press, 1973), 6.

17. Stanley S. Surrey, *Pathways to Tax Reform: The Concept of Tax Expenditures* (Cambridge, MA: Harvard University Press, 1973), 6.

18. For a discussion of the hidden, or shadow administration, see Paul C. Light, *The True Size of Government* (Washington, DC: The Brookings Institution, 1999).

19. W. Elliot Brownlee, *Federal Taxation in America: A Short History* (Cambridge, MA: Cambridge University Press, 1996), 111.

20. The concept of "tax expenditure" in some circles has taken on the connotation of tax evasion rather than a policy tool. The Joint Economic Committee, under Republican Jim Saxton, released a report which sought to discount the notion of tax expenditure as "loophole." "The tax expenditure concept relies heavily on a normative notion that shielding certain taxpayer income from taxation deprives government of its rightful revenues. This view is inconsistent with the proposition that income belongs to the taxpayers and that tax liability is determined through the democratic process, not through arbitrary, bureaucratic assumptions." Vice

Chairman Jim Saxton, "Tax Expenditures: A Review and Analysis" (Washington, DC: Joint Economic Committee, 1999).

21. According to one tax interest group advocate, the political opportunities presented by the tax code led President Clinton to determine that two new expenditures (the Hope and Lifetime Learning Credits) would be the best way to aid higher education.

22. These numbers are issued by the Joint Committee on Taxation (JCT). Tax expenditures are somewhat controversial because they require value judgments as to what qualifies. Official estimates of tax expenditures are issued both by the Office of Management and Budget and the JCT. The JCT figures, which are generally more inclusive, are used here.

23. For example, deductions for home mortgage insurance benefit middle-class American homeowners and the EITC benefits the working poor.

24. Indeed a simple change in filing status illustrates how important family status is. In 2001, the average American householder, if single, would be subject to a 28 percent marginal tax rate, but if married 15 percent.

25. Christopher Hood, *The Tools of Government* (London: Macmillan, 1984); Lester M. Salamon, "The New Governance and the Tools of Public Action: An Introduction," in *The Tools of Government: A Guide to New Governance*, ed. Lester M. Salamon (New York: Oxford University Press, 2002); Lester M. Salamon, "Rethinking Public Management: Third-Party Government and the Changing Forms of Government Action," *Public Policy* 29, no. 3 (1981); Stephen Goldsmith and William D. Eggers, *Governing by Network: The New Shape of the Public Sector* (Washington, DC: Brookings Institution Press, 2004).

26. Jacob S. Hacker, *The Divided Welfare State: The Battle over Public and Private Social Benefits in the United States* (Cambridge, MA: Cambridge University Press, 2002).

27. Average tuition for a four-year public school in 2004–05 was $5,038. "Digest of Education Statistics Tables and Figures," (Washington DC: Department of Education, National Center for Education Statistics, 2005). The Hope Scholarship provides 100 percent of the first $1,000 in tuition expenses and 50 percent of the next $1,000.

28. Nancy Folbre, *The Invisible Heart: Economics and Family Values* (New York: The New Press, 2001).

29. Christopher Howard, *The Hidden Welfare State*, (Princeton, NJ: Princeton University Press, 1997), 19.

30. There are two major categories of administrators who provide goods and services in exchange for reduced tax burdens: corporations and families. Not surprisingly, in corporate income taxation corporations act predominantly as administrators, and in individual income taxation family members act as administrators.

31. See Christopher Howard, *The Hidden Welfare State*, (Princeton, NJ: Princeton University Press, 1997).

32. The 2006 federal outlays by budget category include both on and off budget amounts. "Estimates of Federal Tax Expenditures for Fiscal Years 2006–2010," (Washington, DC: Joint Committee on Taxation, 2005).

33. Budget of the United States Government, Fiscal Year 2007, Historical Tables.

34. Author's analysis of data drawn from "Estimates of Federal Tax Expenditures for Fiscal Years 2006–2010," (Washington, DC: Joint Committee on Taxation, 2005).

35. For example, the Family Rights and Educational Privacy Act transfers rights to access student records from parents to students when the latter turns eighteen (20 U.S.C. § 1232g; 34 CFR Part 99).

36. Lester M. Salamon, "The New Governance and the Tools of Public Action: An Introduction," in *The Tools of Government: A Guide to New Governance*, ed. Lester M. Salamon (New York: Oxford University Press, 2002).

37. "Estimates of Federal Tax Expenditures for Fiscal Years 2006–2010," (Washington, DC: Joint Committee on Taxation, 2005).

38. "Armed Forces' Tax Guide," (Washington, DC: Department of the Treasury, Internal Revenue Service, 2005).

39. The Joint Committee on Taxation also lists "exclusion of extraterritorial income" ($100 million) which has been repealed by the American jobs Creation Act of 2004. The JCT does not list the exclusion before or after 2006. "Estimates of Federal Tax Expenditures for Fiscal Years 2006–2010" (Washington, DC: Joint Committee on Taxation, 2005).

40. U.S. citizens who earn $80,000 or less per year from foreign sources are able to exclude the income from their federal income taxes. In this case, taxpayers act as administrators of their own financial estates by reducing the amount that they owe the U.S. Treasury. They do not act on behalf of others.

41. "U.S. Government Civilian Employees Stationed Abroad" (Washington, DC: Department of the Treasury, Internal Revenue Service, 2005).

42. For example, in 2006 the Joint Committee on Taxation estimated the following expenditures: child and dependent care at $3.1 billion, tax exclusion for employer provided healthcare at $90.6 billion, and education at $16.2 billion. "Estimates of Federal Tax Expenditures for Fiscal Years 2006–2010," (Washington, DC: Joint Committee on Taxation, 2005).

43. The code does make provisions for multiple support agreements in which no one person provides 51 percent of the support for the care of a dependent.

44. "Digest of Education Statistics Tables and Figures" (Washington DC: Department of Education, National Center for Education Statistics, 2005).

45. "Statistics of Income" (Washington, DC: Department of Treasury, Internal Revenue Service, 2005–06).

46. Likewise, the expectation of shared resources extends to students who apply for government subsidized student loans. These students must produce their parents' tax returns to determine the "Expected Family Contribution" (EFC). Government aid kicks in only *after* the amount families are determined to contribute.

47. One striking example is the so-called kiddie tax, a levy on the unearned income of dependent youths less than eighteen years old. The IRC taxes the income of children at the marginal tax rate of their parents once it reaches a particular limit ($1,700 in 2006). For example, a 12-year-old with $4,000 in investment income would be taxed at his or her parents' marginal tax rate for $2,300. See "Budget Options" (Washington, DC: Congressional Budget Office, 2003); "Tax Rules for Children and Dependents" (Washington, DC: Department of the Treasury, Internal

Revenue Service, 2005). Though there is nothing to stop any taxpayer from shifting her income to a child unrelated to her, the real risk of not getting one's money back makes such a strategy very costly. The reality of shared family income, however, is that it makes little difference to whom it is formally attributed. Parents who put their assets in the names of their dependent children still retain control. In many taxpayers' eyes, this may be a smart way to manage family income, but in the eyes of the IRC it turns children into tax shelters.

48. Related persons include spouse, brothers, sisters, half brothers, half sisters, ancestors (parents, grandparents), lineal descendents (children, grandchildren), and certain corporations, partnerships, trusts and exempt organizations. See "Tax Benefits for Education" (Washington, DC: Department of Treasury, Internal Revenue Service, 2006).

49. In the early 1990s AFDC, the primary program to aid low-income families, surpassed the size and constituency of the EITC. By 2001, the number of families receiving Temporary Assistance for Needy Families had dropped to 2 million, about 11 percent of the estimated 19 million families claiming the EITC. Saul D. Hoffman and Laurence S. Seidman, *Helping Working Families: The Earned Income Tax Credit* (Kalamazoo, MI: W. E. Upjohn Institute for Employment Research, 2003).

50. Though the EITC returns a large portion of income tax, it also assists working Americans with regressive federal payroll taxes. Rather than a complex system of accounting in which employers compute FICA reductions, the federal government allows individual taxpayers to take the EITC. Single persons were made eligible for the EITC for this reason in 1993.

51. As Senator Chuck Grassley (R-IA) explained, the EITC "is targeted particularly to help working families with children." 147 Cong. Rec. S 8252.

52. "Earned Income Credit" (Washington, DC: Department of the Treasury, Internal Revenue Service, 2005).

53. "Earned Income Credit" (Washington, DC: Department of the Treasury, Internal Revenue Service, 2005).

54. "Counting Couples: Improving Marriage, Remarriage, and Cohabitation Data in the Federal Statistical System" (Bethesda, MD: The Data Collection Committee of the Federal Interagency Forum on Child and Family Statistics, 2001).

55. The National Survey on Families and Households asks about the economic relationship of relatives living together in the same household in the third wave (2002) of their panel study.

56. "For Better or for Worse: Marriage and the Federal Income Tax" (Washington, DC: The Congress of the United States, Congressional Budget Office, 1997), 9.

57. Though there were five definitions of child in the tax code, in reality additional provisions of the code rely on the definition of family in one of these five sections. For example, four of the education credits that rely on family (discussed in relation to core assumptions) all define "child" in terms of the dependency exemption in the IRC.

58. The multiple definitions of child in the tax code add incredible complexity in the code. In the instruction manual for 1040 forms, IRS Publication 17 *Your Federal Income Tax (for Individuals)*, the explanation of who qualifies as a child spans a total of 17 pages. "Study of the Overall State of the Federal Tax System

and Recommendations for Simplification, Pursuant to Section 8022 (3)(B) of the Internal Revenue Code of 1986—Volume II: Recommendations of the Staff of the Joint Committee on Taxation to Simplify the Federal Tax System" (Washington, DC: Joint Committee on Taxation, 2001), 50.

59. The course of the definition of child in the EITC is markedly different from the dependency exemption. After 1975, the dependency exemption was altered significantly just once—in 1984 to account for complex support payments in the case of divorce and multiple custody arrangements. The EITC has charted a different path with seven separate amendments.

60. "Study of the Overall State of the Federal Tax System and Recommendations for Simplification, Pursuant to Section 8022 (3)(B) of the Internal Revenue Code of 1986—Volume II: Recommendations of the Staff of the Joint Committee on Taxation to Simplify the Federal Tax System" (Washington, DC: Joint Committee on Taxation, 2001), 71.

61. Saul D. Hoffman and Laurence S. Seidman, *Helping Working Families: The Earned Income Tax Credit* (Kalamazoo, MI: W. E. Upjohn Institute for Employment Research, 2003).

62. Though critics point to out that the IRS may not necessarily be the most qualified to make substantive policy decisions as they essentially must do when overseeing tax expenditures across a variety of policy areas.

63. Interview with Janet Holtzblatt, Deputy Director for Individual Taxation, Department of Treasury Office of Tax Analysis. November 10, 2003.

64. "Data Book Fiscal Year 2005" (Washington, DC: Department of the Treasury, Internal Revenue Service, 2005).

65. Interview with Janet Holtzblatt, Deputy Director for Individual Taxation, Department of Treasury Office of Tax Analysis. November 10, 2003.

66. Mary Jo Bane, Assistant Secretary for Children and Families (Health and Human Services), testified before Congress in 1993 in anticipation of the administration's proposal for welfare reforms. She stressed the importance of turning to a model that included work. She used the example of particular welfare recipients, like Letitia in Chicago who said: "I need to let my children know that it's okay to work. You have to work. I don't want to let my children see this image of me sitting on the couch—an image that I've had myself—of sitting on the couch ... and watching TV. I don't want my children to think that that's the life because that's not going to get them anywhere." House Ways and Means. *Testimony by Mary Jo Bane, Assistant Secretary for Children and Families Department of Health and Human Services on Children and Families at Risk in Deteriorating Communities*, First Session, December 7, 1993.

67. The debates surrounding the 1993 expansion of the EITC often make explicit reference to the EITC as solving many of the problems in the current welfare system. President Clinton remarked at the signing of the Budget Bill of 1993, which substantially increased the size of the EITC, on the positive influence the EITC has as opposed to welfare.

> On Thursday, I met with three families who work hard for low wages, from the states of Georgia, Kentucky and Oklahoma. Thanks to the Earned Income Tax Credit in our tax code, which reduces the tax burden on low income work-

ers, they are supporting their children instead of going on welfare. Now this is very important because 18 percent, almost one in five of American workers today actually work for wages that will not support a family of four above the poverty line. This plan has a revolutionary expansion of the Earned Income Tax Credit so that for the first time ever we can say to American workers, if you work full-time and you have children in your home, you will not live in poverty. The tax system will lift you out of poverty, not drive you into it. This is the biggest incentive for people we have ever provided to get off welfare and go to work, to reward work and family and responsibility. It is not a partisan issue, it is an American issue and it will empower all kinds of Americans to seize a better life for themselves. (William Jefferson Clinton. "Remarks by President Bill Clinton Regarding the Budget Bill." July 13, 1993.)

Again, in 1993 testimony, Bane explained that "Everyone who can, should work to support their families." She went on to say that the administration has already taken a major step toward this with the expansion of the EITC (1993).

68. Senate Finance Committee, *Testimony Bush Tax Plan: David T. Ellwood*, First Session, March 8, 2001.

69. The EITC caps the number of children at two, meaning that two or more children receive the same benefits.

70. "For Better or for Worse: Marriage and the Federal Income Tax" (Washington, DC: The Congress of the United States, Congressional Budget Office, 1997) p. xvi–xvii.

71. For example, Congressperson J. D. Hayworth (R-AZ) explains "a vote in favor of this legislation will result in tax relief for the American family." Congressman Kevin P. Brady (R-TX) states: "I think too many people in Washington are out of touch with the real world and the way families have to struggle these days...What is wrong with eliminating the marriage penalty? What is wrong with not taxing people at death?" (147 Cong. Rec. H 2204). In the Senate, Larry Craig (R-ID) commented that the Economic Growth and Tax Relief Reconciliation Act "means hardworking Americans and their families will have a little more freedom, and the Federal Government a little less control over their lives" (147 Cong. Rec. S 5770).

72. Office of Management and Budget 2003.

73. The Congress of the United States, Congressional Budget Office 1997, U.S. Senate 2001.

74. Senate Finance Committee, *U.S. Senator Charles Grassley (R-IA) Holds Hearing on Taxes*, First Session, March 8, 2001 .

75. Clinton cited the heavy cost of the measure and the disproportionate benefits given to the wealthy.

76. 147 Cong. Rec. S 5770.

77. Lori Nitschke, "Marital Status and Taxes: Irreconcilable Differences?," *CQ Weekly*, October 30, 1999.

78. U.S. Congress 2001.

79. 147 Cong. Rec. H 1302. Marriage Penalty and Tax Relief Act of 2001.

80. 147 Cong. Rec. H 1302. Marriage Penalty and Tax Relief Act of 2001.

81. 147 Cong. Rec. H 1297. Marriage Penalty and Tax Relief Act of 2001.

82. 147 Cong. Rec. H 1297. Marriage Penalty and Tax Relief Act of 2001.

83. 147 Cong. Rec. H 1302. Marriage Penalty and Tax Relief Act of 2001.

84. 147 Cong. Rec. H 1297. Marriage Penalty and Tax Relief Act of 2001.

85. 147 Cong. Rec. H 1302. Marriage Penalty and Tax Relief Act of 2001.

86. 147 Cong. Rec. H 1302. Marriage Penalty and Tax Relief Act of 2001.

87. Rea S. Hederman, "Why Congress Should Renew Its Efforts to End the Marriage Penalty," *The Heritage Foundation Backgrounder*, no. 1424 (2001).

88. Lori Nitschke, "Has the Tax Cut Crusade Lost Its Appeal," *Congressional Quarterly Weekly Report*, April 10, 1999.

89. John F. Witte, *The Politics and Development of the Federal Income Tax* (Madison: University of Wisconsin Press, 1985); W. Elliot Brownlee, "Tax Regimes, National Crisis, and State-Building in America," in *Funding the Modern American State, 1941–1995: The Rise and Fall of the Era of Easy Finance*, ed. W. Elliot Brownlee (Washington, DC: Woodrow Wilson Center Press and the Press Syndicate of the University of Cambridge, 1996).

90. "Compliance Estimates for Earned Income Tax Credit Claimed on 1999 Returns" (Washington, DC: Internal Revenue Service, 2002).

CHAPTER 6

1. Marty Strange, *Family Farming: A New Economic Vision* (Lincoln: University of Nebraska Press, 1988), 1.

2. Murray J. Edelman, *The Symbolic Uses of Politics* (Urbana: University of Illinois Press, 1985), 2.

3. Murray J. Edelman, *The Symbolic Uses of Politics* (Urbana: University of Illinois Press, 1985), 114.

4. Murray J. Edelman, *The Symbolic Uses of Politics* (Urbana: University of Illinois Press, 1985), 116.

5. Sonya Salamon, *Prairie Patrimony: Family, Farming, and Community in the Midwest* (Chapel Hill: University of North Carolina Press, 1992), 1.

6. The percent of women who operate their own farms has risen steadily in the past three decades; however, in 1997 women constituted just 9 percent of farm operators. Robert A Hoppe, "Structural and Financial Characteristics of U.S. Farms: 2001 Family Farm Report" (Washington, DC: Economic Research Service, United States Department of Agriculture, 2001). In 2006, women ran approximately 165,000 farms (USDA website: http://www.csrees.usda.gov/nea/economics/in_focus/small_business_if_women.html). For a detailed analysis of gender and agricultural life see, Sonya Salamon, *Prairie Patrimony: Family, Farming, and Community in the Midwest* (Chapel Hill: University of North Carolina Press, 1992).

7. J. S. Penn, "The Structure of Agriculture: An Overview of the Issue" (Washington, DC: United States Department of Agriculture, 1979), 2.

8. Frank R. Baumgartner and Bryan D. Jones, *Agendas and Instability in American Politics* (Chicago: University of Chicago Press, 1993), 26.

9. Gregg Easterbrook, "Making Sense of Agriculture: A Revisionist Look at Farm Policy," in *Is There a Moral Obligation to Save the Family Farm?* ed. Gary Comstock (Ames: Iowa State University Press, 1987), 3.

10. Thomas Jefferson, *Notes on the State of Virginia*, ed. William Peden (Chapel Hill: The University of North Carolina Press, 1982), 164–65.

11. Thomas Jefferson, *Notes on the State of Virginia*, ed. William Peden (Chapel Hill: The University of North Carolina Press, 1982), 165.

12. According to USDA Agricultural Economist J. S. Penn, "American agriculture is perhaps as important for what it means to people as for what it is." J. S. Penn, "The Structure of Agriculture: An Overview of the Issue" (Washington, DC: United States Department of Agriculture, 1979), 2. There are numerous discussions about the cultural importance of the family farm. See, e.g., Wendell Berry, *The Unsettling of America: Culture & Agriculture* (San Francisco: Sierra Club Book, 1977); Tom Harkin, "The Save the Family Farm Act," in *Is There a Moral Obligation to Save the Family Farm?* ed. Gary Comstock (Ames: Iowa State University Press, 1987); Lorraine Garkovich, Janet L. Bokemeier, and Barbara Foote, *Harvest of Hope: Family Farming/Farming Families* (Lexington: The University of Kentucky Press, 1995); Richard S. Kirkendall, "A History of the Family Farm," in *Is There a Moral Obligation to Save the Family Farm?* ed. Gary Comstock (Ames: Iowa State University Press, 1987).

13. PIPA/Knowledge Networks Poll: Americans on Farm Subsidies, December 19, 2003–January 5, 2004. The poll found that Americans favored subsidies to small farms in bad years only. Actual statement wording for the support of family farms reads as follows:

There is a debate about whether the US government should subsidize small farmers by giving them various forms of financial support. "Small farmers" means those who work farms that are less than 500 acres. What follows are some pairs of statements expressing some positions on this issue. Please indicate which position is closer to yours.

A. Family farming is an American way of life that should be maintained. Subsidies are the only way that small family farms can compete with large agribusiness and imports from low wage countries.

B. There are many ways of making a living that are part of the American way of life. It is unfair to subsidize farmers and not subsidize other equally American ways of making a living.

Responses: Position A (70 percent), Position B (25 percent), No answer (4 percent).

14. Zogby's Real America Poll, October 1999. Actual question wording: "(Which better describes your position?) . . . A)Large corporations [sic] farms are better for America because they provide low cost products and stable jobs. B) Small family farms are better because they are a fundamental part of our culture and are an important connection to our past." Responses: Corporate farms (16 percent), Family farms (69 percent), Neither (12 percent), Not sure (3 percent).

15. The effect of the estate tax repeal on family farms has been hotly debated. A *Washington Post* story quotes Neil Harth, an agriculture law professor at Iowa

State University, on the necessity of the estate tax repeal for farmers: "A lot of this is myth," he said. "M-Y-T-H." Glenn Kessler, "Estate Tax Repeal Bill Delivered; Democrats Assail GOP Measure as a Giveaway to the Rich" (*The Washington Post*, August 25, 2000).

16. Greenburg Quinlan Rosner Research survey of national likely voters, May 6–9, 2002. Actual question wording:

Now let me read you a couple of statements about efforts to eliminate the estate tax . . . Some people say we should eliminate the estate tax because it's nothing but a death tax that punishes those who succeed, especially small business owners and farmers. First, they spend their lives paying taxes on their hard earned money. Then, when they die, the government turns around and taxes it again. Children are often forced to sell the business or farm just to pay the taxes. We can't rob parents of the ability to provide security for their children. Other people say eliminating the estate tax represents the wrong priorities for security for their children. Other people say eliminating the estate tax represents wrong priorities for our country. Giving a new tax loophole to multi-millionaires would sacrifice our commitments to strengthen Medicare and Social Security, improve education, and fight terrorism. Instead we should reform the estate tax to protect small businesses and family farms, and not shift billions of dollars in taxes onto 99 percent of American taxpayers. Those are the right priorities. After hearing this, do you favor eliminating the estate tax or simply reforming it to protect small businesses and family farms?

Responses: Strongly favor reforming (38 percent), Somewhat favor reforming (18 percent), No change to estate tax (2 percent), Somewhat favor eliminating it (9 percent), Strongly favor eliminating it (30 percent), Don't know/Refused (3 percent).

17. NPR/Kaiser/Kennedy School of Government, February 5–March 17, 2003. Actual question wording asked of those who favor eliminating the estate tax (60 percent): "(Why do you favor eliminating the [federal] estate tax as it is now? Is this a reason or not?) . . . It might force the sale of small business and family farms."

Responses: Yes, a reason (74 percent), No, not a reason (22 percent), Don't know (4 percent).

18. Some might characterize the *New York Times* editorial board as actively hostile to farming interests by the mid-1980s. According to a 1995 editorial, "The Government has no obligation to preserve agribusiness or family farms if the consequence is to take money from poor consumers in order to pump up the bank accounts of multinational companies and often-wealthy farmers." "Mr. Clinton Bows to Farmers," *New York Times*, April 28, 1995.

19. I defined "in-depth" as entries containing ten or more references to family farms. There were 108 entries that met this criterion.

20. Because "family farms" are a subset of farms, to adequately compare in-depth family farm debates with in-depth farm debates I defined in-depth farm debates as mentioning the word "farm" no less than thirty times in a par-

ticular *Congressional Record* entry. This produced 434 *Congressional Record* entries.

21. 142 Cong. Rec. S3039.

22. Robert A. Hoppe, "Structural and Financial Characteristics of U.S. Farms: 2001 Family Farm Report" (Washington, D.C.: Economic Research Service, United States Department of Agriculture, 2001), 22.

23. Robert A. Hoppe and David E. Banker, "Structure and Finances of U.S. Farms: 2005 Family Farm Report" (United States Department of Agriculture, Economic Research Service, 2006). USDA data in this section are drawn from the aforementioned report unless otherwise noted.

24. David Brewster, "The Family Farm: A Changing Concept" (Washington, DC: United States Department of Agriculture, 1979), 77. See also David Brewster, "Changes in the Family Farm Concept" (Washington, DC: U.S. Senate, Committee on Agriculture, Nutrition, and Forestry, 1980).

25. David Brewster, "The Family Farm: A Changing Concept" (Washington, DC: United States Department of Agriculture, 1979), 78.

26. In the hundred years from 1830 to 1930, the number of persons supplied by the labor of a single farmer increased from 4 to 9.8. But in the forty years between 1930 and 1970 that number jumped from 9.8 to 47.1. "Historical Statistics of the United States: Colonial Times to 1970" (Washington: DC: United States Bureau of the Census, 1976), 498. To remain competitive and earn a living, small family farms must continually increase their productivity through the acquisition of additional land. The average farm size in 1930 was 157 acres, by 2002 it had grown to 441. "Historical Statistics of the United States: Colonial Times to 1970" (Washington: DC: United States Bureau of the Census, 1976), 457. "United States and State Data Preliminary Report: 2002 Census of Agriculture" (Washington, DC: U.S. Department of Agriculture, 2004). Suburban families looking for a quiet place to settle down, real-estate developers, and corporations that invest in farmland as part of a tax-reduction portfolio all drive up the price of land for American farmers. The direct competition for the domestic production of farm commodities is usually from other family farmers in a similar pinch to increase productivity by acquiring more land.

27. Because party platforms have limited space to air the issues important to them, I included "family farming" as well as "family farmers" as a reference to family farms. Likewise, the denominator (the total number of farm mentions) includes both "farming" and "farmers."

28. David Brewster, "The Family Farm: A Changing Concept" (Washington, DC: United States Department of Agriculture, 1979), 74.

29. Richard S. Kirkendall, "A History of the Family Farm," in *Is There a Moral Obligation to Save the Family Farm?* ed. Gary Comstock (Ames: Iowa State University Press, 1987), 89.

30. United States Senate, Committee on Agriculture and Forestry, *Agricultural Emergency Act to Increase Farm Purchasing Power*, First Session, March 17, 24, 25, 27, and 28, 1933.

31. United States Senate, Committee on Agriculture and Forestry, *Agricultural Emergency Act to Increase Farm Purchasing Power*, First Session, March 17, 24, 25, 27, and 28, 1933 .

32. Richard S. Kirkendall, "A History of the Family Farm," in *Is There a Moral Obligation to Save the Family Farm?* ed. Gary Comstock (Ames: Iowa State University Press, 1987).

33. New Deal Under Secretary of Agriculture M. L. Wilson explained three decades after the Agricultural Adjustment Act: "Everyone is a creature of his home environment, and as a child he develops in his mind stereotypes which he carries with him throughout his life. I was born in a community of corn belt farmers where the farms ranged from quarter to half-sections in size [i.e., 160 to 320 acres]. Therefore, instinctively when I am talking about farmers, I am actually thinking about the kind of farmers and farm families that live on the farms that you look down upon when you fly over the Corn Belt." Jess Gilbert, "Agrarian Intellectuals in a Democratizing State: A Collective Biography of USDA Leaders in the Intended New Deal," in *The Countryside in the Age of the Modern State: Political Histories of Rural America*, ed. Catherine McNicol Stock and Robert D. Johnston (Ithaca, NY: Cornell University Press, 2001), 221. According to European Sigmund von Frauendorfer (1929), "The family farm so predominates in the United States that everybody who uses the general term 'farmer' thinks almost automatically of the *operator or a family farm.*" As cited by David Brewster, "Historical Notes on Agriculture Structure," (Washington, DC: United States Department of Agriculture, 1979), 65.

34. Intercoder reliability on the three categories was 83 percent and when combining locale and background characteristic and distinguishing it from category (as in Figure 6.5) yields intercoder reliability of 85 percent.

35. "The New Mayor of Boston," *New York Times*, January 5, 1896.

36. "Edward W. Scripps Dies on Yacht," *New York Times*, March 14, 1926.

37. "The Nation," *New York Times*, August 20, 1944.

38. As early as 1941, the USDA published a series of bulletins on postwar plans (*Why We Must Plan for Peace; Win the War—Then the Peace; Farm Prosperity Depends on the City*). The USDA Interbureau Committee on Postwar Programs released *Agriculture When the War Ends* in October 1943, and in October 1944 the Committee on Postwar Agricultural Policy of the Association of Land-Grant Colleges and Universities released a widely circulated report titled *Postwar Agriculture Policy*. The committee's report summed up the premise of many of those concerned about long-range agriculture: "the family-type farm should remain the basis on which American agriculture is typically organized. "Postwar Agricultural Policy, Report of the Committee on Postwar Agricultural Policy of the Association of Land-Grant Colleges and Universities" (Committee on Postwar Agricultural Policy of the Association of Land-Grant Colleges and Universities, 1944), 30.

39. David Eugene Conrad, *The Forgotten Farmers: The Story of Sharecroppers in the New Deal* (Urbana: University of Illinois Press, 1965); Caleb Southworth, "Aid to Sharecroppers: How Agrarian Class Structure and Tenant-Farmer Politics Influenced Federal Relief in the South, 1933–1935," *Social Science History* 26, no. 1 (2002).

40. David Eugene Conrad, *The Forgotten Farmers: The Story of Sharecroppers in the New Deal* (Urbana: University of Illinois Press, 1965), 77.

41. R. Douglas Hurt, *American Agriculture: A Brief History* (Ames: Iowa State University Press, 1994), 303.

42. Carey McWilliams, *Factories in the Field: The Story of Migratory Farm Labor in California* (Boston: Little, Brown and Company, 1939).

43. Between 1940 and 1945, American farms saw a net migration of 6 million individuals from the farms to urban centers and military service. With the help of new technology, the average farm size increased from 171 to 195 acres, the number of tractors increased 50 percent from 1.6 million in 1940 to 2.4 million in 1945. Overall, farm productivity rose sharply. In 1940, a single farmer fed an average of 10.7 persons, but by 1945 that farmer could feed 14.6 persons. "Historical Statistics of the United States: Colonial Times to 1970" (Washington: DC: United States Bureau of the Census, 1976), 457, 469, and 498.

44. In 1948, the Senate Committee on Agriculture and Forestry released a long-range agricultural policy report. One of the "essentials" of long-range agricultural planning, according to the Senate report, was that the "owner-operated family farm, long an accepted ideal of American farm policy, needs to be continued and strengthened as the basic unit of our farm economy." The report goes on to say, "A successful farm must use the labor of the operator and his family effectively and make efficient use of capital, machinery, and modern technology. This is essential if our farms are to produce at low cost the food and fiber required by the Nation. The family farm must also provide an adequate income for the farmer's family to purchase quantities of goods and services required for a good level of living. On the other hand, the efficiency and high material well-being of the typical family farmer, and especially his development as a substantial citizen, has depended in no small measure upon his independence in operating a size of farm adapted to the use of labor-saving equipment and the agricultural information at his command." "Long-Range Agricultural Policy and Program" (Washington, DC: United States Senate Committee on Agriculture and Forestry, 1948), 29.

45 The report continues, "This adjustment of farm population, and the size of farms, to the conditions created by our technological revolution is the most fundamental long-run problem facing agriculture in the postwar period." "Postwar Economic Policy and Planning," (Washington, DC: House Special Committee on Postwar Economic Policy and Planning, 1946), 9.

46. Agriculture Adjustment Administrator, H. R. Tolley, in a 1944 speech before the Association of Land-Grant Colleges and Universities remarked: "Farmers in this country will have the most efficient farm plant in the world, the most efficient we have ever known . . . A higher level of total agriculture production than in the years before the war is almost inevitable." *Probable Trends in American Food Production After the War*, Address before the 58th Annual Convention of the Association of Land-Grant Colleges and Universities, Chicago, October 24, 1944. As cited by Murray Benedict, *Farm Policies of the United States, 1790–1950: A Study of Their Origins and Development* (New York: The Twentieth Century Fund, 1953).

47. Charles F. Brannan, then-Assistant Secretary of Agriculture, in a speech before the Catholic Tri-State Congress on September 16, 1947. "Family Farm Held Key National Cog," *New York Times*, September 17, 1947.

48. For example, Richard Kirkendall's history of the family farm explains: "American democrats, above all Thomas Jefferson, took old agrarian ideas and gave them a democratic interpretation. Here, the often expressed ideas about the benefits for the human personality of work on the land was very important. To Jefferson and others who thought like he did, such work developed the personality type needed for the success of a democratic political system. But that work must be done on family farms, and family farms must be the majority of the population." Richard S. Kirkendall, "A History of the Family Farm," in *Is There a Moral Obligation to Save the Family Farm?* ed. Gary Comstock (Ames: Iowa State University Press, 1987), 80–81.

49. Virgil W. Dean, "Farm Policy and Truman's 1948 Campaign," *The Historian* 55, no. 3 (1993): 501.

50. "Postwar Economic Policy and Planning" (Washington, DC: House Special Committee on Postwar Economic Policy and Planning, 1946).

51. Graham K. Wilson, *Special Interests and Policymaking: Agricultural Policies and Politics in Britain and the United States of America, 1956–70* (New York: John Wiley & Sons, 1977); John Mark Hansen, *Gaining Access: Congress and the Farm Lobby, 1919–1981* (Chicago: University of Chicago Press, 1991); Mancur Olson, Jr, "Space, Agriculture and Organization," *American Journal of Agricultural Economics* 67, no. 5 (1985).

52. Frank R. Baumgartner and Bryan D. Jones, *Agendas and Instability in American Politics* (Chicago: University of Chicago Press, 1993), 26.

53. The Senate had scheduled six hours of debate to discuss the FAIR conference committee report, the House debated for just one hour beginning at 11:30 p.m. Many of the House remarks are prepared statements entered into the record. The overall arguments in both the Senate and the House are quite similar.

54. Proponents promised a decisive end to invasive state-run agriculture programs, but in a compromise, Congress retained the permanent agriculture laws of 1938 and 1949, leaving the door wide open for subsidies to return at the end of seven years.

55. "Plan to Cut Farm Programs Stalls," *Congressional Quarterly Almanac* (1995): 3–47.

56. Lawmakers have never repealed the Agricultural Act of 1949, the only comprehensive permanent agriculture policy in the United States. Instead, they have reauthorized the Act every five years; the 1990 reauthorization expired at the end of 1995. If members of Congress failed to come to agreement and agriculture programs reverted to permanent law, the Agriculture Department would make loans to farmers based upon a calculation set out in the Agricultural Acts of 1938 and 1949. This means that farm loans would be based upon an early twentieth-century parity calculation—the per bushel price a farmer would need to receive in order to purchase what a bushel would have brought in 1910–14. According to *Congressional Quarterly Weekly Report*, based upon this formula, federal payments would triple to about $7.82 a bushel. "The result could propel domestic wheat prices dramatically above world price, cutting exports and forcing the Agriculture Department to buy much of the overpriced wheat. The government would face increased costs of $10 billion in the first year of wheat and feed

grain subsidies." David Hosansky, "The Perils of Permanent Law," *Congressional Quarterly Weekly Report* (1996).

57. The tone in the debate between the House and Senate because of these contrasting strategies was noticeable. In the late-night debate before voting on the conference committee recommendations, California Representative Vic Fazio, who supported the farm bill, said

You might say in their first year behind the plow, the GOP leadership used a new kind of fertilizer: partisan politics—to cultivate their favorite crop—political points. Instead of debating this legislation in a systematic fashion throughout the year, the Republicans waited until late in the year when appropriations bills, continuing resolutions, and debt ceilings held center stage. Then and only then, in a budget-driven exercise, GOP leaders decided to tie the farm bill's fate to controversial budget reconciliation legislation about which Democrats and President Clinton had expressed severe reservations. The chairman of the Agriculture Committee [Roberts] could not even muster a majority of votes within his committee and was forced to use special procedures to have the budget committee report the so-called farm bill as part of the reconciliation bill. . . . This is not the way to make national agriculture policy.

And Barney Frank (D-MA) "Well, if my colleagues do not want to debate things at 11:30, they control the House, schedule them at a reasonable hour. But to take a major piece of legislation like this and then so manipulate the schedule that they want to sneak it through without adequate debate is unworthy of the House" (142 Cong. Rec. H 3147). The sentiment in the Senate was quite different. Senator Howell Heflin (D-AL) compliments both Democrat Leahy and Republican Lugar for their work on the bill. He praises Lugar as "a good chairman. I disagreed with him on many aspects of the bill and of the overall policy but he was certainly a gentleman throughout. He made certain that everybody had an opportunity to be heard" (142 Cong. Rec. S 3039).

58. The *National Journal* reports: "Agriculture programs got reformed if they were expensive, not if they were economically intrusive. Indeed, the government's most anticompetitive farm programs got the least reform, not the most." Jonathan Rauch, "Cash Crops," *National Journal* (1996).

59. Jonathan Rauch, "Cash Crops," *National Journal* (1996): 980.

60. David Hosansky, "Farm Policy on the Brink of a New Direction," *Congressional Quarterly Weekly Report* (1996).

61. As enacted, PL 104-127 has no reference to family farms and one to family farmers in Title VII, Subtitle B "Amendments to the Consolidated Farm and Rural Development Act" in which loan guarantees for the purchase of co-operative stock are limited to family farmers (as determined by the Secretary of Agriculture).

62. For example, Senator Paul Wellstone (D-MN) remarks that the bill, "is designed to benefit large corporate agribusiness and will actually harm most family farmers. It will likely increase current trends toward economic concentration in agriculture, to the disadvantage of small and moderate-sized farm operations.

I have consistently favored long-term Federal farm policy that would promote family agriculture and revitalize our rural economy" (142 Cong. Rec. S 3039). Likewise, Ernest Hollings (D-SC) states his concern: "I am worried that this will have catastrophic effects on the small farmer in my State and that small farmers will have no choice but to harvest their fields for the last time." He goes on to equate small farms with family farms.

63. 142 Cong. Rec. S 3039.

64. 142 Cong. Rec. S 3039.

65. 142 Cong. Rec. S 3039.

66. Senator Nancy Kassebaum (R-KS) sums up why the bill deserves support: "this bill represents producer flexibility, program simplicity, and stability—all important priorities that will allow U.S. agriculture to successfully compete in the world marketplace" (142 Cong. Rec. S 3039). In the House, Representative Pat Roberts (R-KS) said: "All production incentives in the future should come from the marketplace." Representative Bill Emerson (R-MO) explained: "As we prepared for the next millennium of American agriculture, we well look to the future and see a global market that is more critical to the American producer than ever before" (142 Cong. Rec. H 3147).

67. 142 Cong. Rec. S 3039.

68. 142 Cong. Rec. S 3039.

69. Peanuts and sugar represented for many free-market conservatives the epitome of unnecessary state involvement; there is no overriding national interest for keeping these programs running as one might make the case for grains like wheat. Yet, peanut and sugar programs made it through to the final legislation—relatively unscathed—because these programs brought with them the support of many influential southern Senators and members of Congress at the same time that they did not draw money from the federal coffers (instead, they artificially raised the prices paid by consumers).

70. The Northeastern Dairy Compact would allow dairy farmers in the Northeast to artificially increase the minimum amount paid for fluid milk. Not only would northeastern dairy farms receive more than their midwestern and Californian counterparts for fluid milk (sold regionally), but surpluses (through increased production and potentially decreased consumption) would flood the national markets in the form of cheese, butter, and other manufactured dairy products.

71. 142 Cong Rec S 3039. In the House, Vermont Independent Bernie Sanders said: "All over this country, family farms have been disappearing in great numbers as a result of the failure of our current agricultural policy. In Vermont, in 1977, we had 3,300 farms. All over the country this is happening. This is an American tragedy." He goes on to say that the Dairy Compact "is an opportunity to save the family farm" (142 Cong. Rec. H 3147).

72. Feingold's fellow Wisconsin statesman, Senator Herb Kohl (D) expressed his concerns in similar language: "Our country and its Constitution are built on the concept of a unitary market without barriers. While I appreciate the efforts that have been made to water down the ill effects of the compact, I strongly believe that the long-term ramifications of this compact on a State like Wisconsin, which depends so heavily on national markets, are ominous" (142 Cong. Rec. S 3039). Similarly in the House, Representative Toby Roth (R-WI) supported the

overall bill but had problems with the Dairy Compact, "In essence, this is government-mandated protectionism for one segment of the nation's dairy industry. It goes against the rest of the bill, which moves American agriculture toward a more market-oriented system" (142 Cong. Rec. H 3147).

73. 142 Cong. Rec. S 3039.

74. "'02 Farm Bill Revives Subsidies," *Congressional Quarterly Almanac* 58 (2002): 4–3.

75. "Cash Crop," *New Republic* (1998).

76. "'02 Farm Bill Revives Subsidies," *Congressional Quarterly Almanac* 58 (2002): 4–3.

77. 142 Cong. Rec. 3039.

78. 142 Cong. Rec. 3039.

79. Jerry Hagstrom, "Growing Pains," *National Journal* (1996): 985.

80. David Orden, Don Paarlberg, and Terry Roe, *Policy Reform in American Agriculture: Analysis and Prognosis* (Chicago: The University of Chicago Press, 1999), 2, 13, 24, 38–39.

81. Adam D. Sheingate, *The Rise of the Agricultural Welfare State: Institutions and Interest Group Power in the United States, France, and Japan* (Princeton, NJ: Princeton University Press, 2000); Graham K. Wilson, *Special Interests and Policymaking: Agricultural Policies and Politics in Britain and the United States of America, 1956–70* (New York: John Wiley & Sons, 1977); Theodore J. Lowi, *The End of Liberalism: The Second Republic of the United States* (New York: Norton, 1979); Grant McConnell, *Private Power and American Democracy* (New York: Knopf, 1966).

CHAPTER 7

1. Stephen Skowronek, *Building a New American State: The Expansion of National Administrative Capacities 1877–1920* (Cambridge, MA: Cambridge University Press, 1982); Theda Skocpol, *Protecting Soldiers and Mothers* (Cambridge, MA: Belknap Press, 1992); Theda Skocpol and Kenneth Finegold, "State Capacity and Economic Intervention in the Early New Deal," *Political Science Quarterly* 97, no. 2 (1982).

2. Theda Skocpol, "The Origins of Social Policy in the United States: A Polity-Centered Analysis," in *The Dynamics of American Politics: Approaches and Interpretations*, ed. Lawrence C. Dodd and Calvin Jillson (Boulder, CO: Westview Press, 1994), 191.

3. Christopher Howard, *The Hidden Welfare State*, (Princeton, NJ: Princeton University Press, 1997).

4. Jacob S. Hacker, *The Divided Welfare State: The Battle over Public and Private Social Benefits in the United States* (Cambridge, MA: Cambridge University Press, 2002).

5. Patricia Strach and Kathleen Sullivan, "Beyond the Welfare State" (paper presented at the Annual Meeting of the Western Political Science Association, Albuquerque, NM, March 16–18, 2006); Kathleen Sullivan, *Constitutional Context: Women and Rights Discourse in Nineteenth-Century America* (Baltimore, MD: Johns Hopkins University Press, 2007).

6. Nancy F. Cott, *Public Vows: A History of Marriage and the Nation* (Cambridge, MA: Harvard University Press, 2000); Amy Murrell Taylor, *The Divided Family in Civil War America* (Chapel Hill: University of North Carolina Press, 2005).

7. Interview with Robert Rector, November 13, 2003.

8. In 1976, Jimmy Carter stressed the importance of family in his successful bid for the presidency. That same year Republicans included a plank in their platform on the American family. It began with the rather unambiguous statement: "Families must continue to be the foundation of our nation" (Republican party platform of 1976). http://www.presidency.ucsb.edu/showplatforms.php?platindex=R1976). Though prior to 1976 they had never mentioned family values, Republicans included those key words in every platform thereafter. Family has become an important part of party debate.

9. Republican party platform of 1976. http://www.presidency.ucsb.edu/showplatforms.php?platindex=R1976.

10. Republican party platform of 1976. http://www.presidency.ucsb.edu/showplatforms.php?platindex=R1976.

11. Democratic party platform of 1976. http://www.presidency.ucsb.edu/showplatforms.php?platindex=D1976.

12. Democratic party platform of 1976. http://www.presidency.ucsb.edu/showplatforms.php?platindex=D1976.

13. Deborah A. Stone, Policy Paradox: The Art of Political Decision Making, Rev. ed. (New York: Norton, 2002); Christina Wolbrecht, The Politics of Women's Rights: Parties, Positions, and Change (Princeton, NJ: Princeton University Press, 2000).

14. Nancy F. Cott, *Public Vows: A History of Marriage and the Nation* (Cambridge, MA: Harvard University Press, 2000), 155.

15. Deborah Sharp, "Elian Ruling Leaves Demonstrators Dejected Miami Kin's Options Are Running Out," *USA Today*, June 2, 2000.

16. Mary Beth Sheridan, "U.S. Immigration Restrictions Give Gay Couples Few Options," *Washington Post*, December 28, 2003.

17. Eric Connor, "Grad Tolani Looks to Future," *The Greenville News*, May 14, 2004.

18. See: http://www.fafsa.ed.gov/fotw0405/help/fftoco3k.htm, accessed June 2, 2004.

19. Interview with Joel Wanacheck, Coordinator of the Earned Income Tax Credit Outreach Campaign, at the Center for Budget and Policy Priorities, November 17, 2003.

20. Christine Scott, "The Earned Income Tax Credit (EITC): Policy and Legislative Issues" (Washington, D.C.: Congressional Research Service, 2003), 6.

21. Christine Scott, "The Earned Income Tax Credit (EITC): Policy and Legislative Issues" (Washington, D.C.: Congressional Research Service, 2003), 6.

22. Janet Holtzblatt and Robert Rebelein, "Measuring the Effect of the EITC on Marriage Penalties and Bonuses," *National Tax Journal* 53, no. 4 (2000): 59.

23. The following quotes are from Chuck Hassebrook, "Lower Estate Taxes Will Hurt Small Farmers," *New York Times*, July 15, 1997.

Bibliography

"Adopted Children and Stepchildren: 2000." Washington, DC: U.S. Census Bureau, 2003.

"Adoption Bill Gains." *New York Times*, November 20, 1975, 32.

Aldous, Joan, and Wilfred Dumon. "Family Policy in the 1980s: Controversy and Consensus." *Journal of Marriage and the Family* 52 (1990): 1136–51.

Aldrich, Daniel P. "Controversial Project Siting: State Policy Instruments and Flexibility." *Comparative Politics* 38, no. 1 (2005): 103–23.

Alex-Assensoh, Yvette M. *Neighborhoods, Family, and Political Behavior in Urban America*. New York: Garland, 1998.

"Alien-Infants-Adoption." Washington, DC: U.S. Senate, Committee on the Judiciary, 1975.

"Amending the Immigration and Nationality Act, and for Other Purposes." Washington, DC: U.S. House of Representatives, Committee on the Judiciary, 1965.

"Annual Statistical Supplement to the Social Security Bulletin, 2005." 1–10. Washington, DC: Social Security Administration, 2006.

Appleby, Joyce. "Republicanism in Old and New Contexts." *William and Mary Quarterly* 43 (1986): 20–34.

Aristotle. *Politics*. New York: Oxford University Press, 1995.

"Armed Forces' Tax Guide." Washington, DC: Department of the Treasury, Internal Revenue Service, 2005.

Astleithner, Florentina, and Alexander Hamedinger. "The Analysis of Sustainability Indicators as Socially Constructed Policy Instruments: Benefits and Challenges of 'Interactive Research.'" *Local Environment* 8, no. 6 (2003): 627–40.

Baker, Paula. "The Domestication of Politics: Women and American Political Society, 1780–1920." *The American Historical Review* 89, no. 3 (1984): 620–47.

Balla, Steven J., and John R. Wright. "Interest Groups, Advisory Committees, and Congressional Control of the Bureaucracy." *American Journal of Political Science* 45, no. 4 (2001): 799–812.

Banning, Lance. "Jeffersonian Ideology Revisited: Liberal and Classical Ideas in the New American Republic." *William and Mary Quarterly* 43 (1986): 3–19.

Bansal, Sangeeta, and Shubhashis Gangopadhyay. "Tax/Subsidy Policies in the Presence of Environmentally Aware Consumers." *Journal of Environmental Economics and Management* 45, no. 2 (2003): 333–56.

Barker, David C., and James D. Tinnick III. "Competing Visions of Parental Roles and Ideological Constraint." *The American Political Science Review* 100, no. 2 (2006): 249–63.

Baumgartner, Frank R., and Bryan D. Jones. *Agendas and Instability in American Politics.* Chicago: University of Chicago Press, 1993.

Baumgartner, Frank R., and Beth L. Leach. "Interest Niches and Policy Bandwagons: Patterns of Interest Group Involvement in National Politics." *The Journal of Politics* 63, no. 4 (2001): 1191–213.

Beck, Paul Allen, and M. Kent Jennings. "Family Traditions, Political Periods, and the Development of Partisan Orientations." *The Journal of Politics* 53, no. 3 (1991).

Becker, Gary S. *A Treatise on the Family.* Cambridge, MA: Harvard University Press, 1981.

Benedict, Murray. *Farm Policies of the United States, 1790–1950: A Study of Their Origins and Development.* New York: The Twentieth Century Fund, 1953.

Berkowitz, Edward, and Kim Mcquaid. "Businessman and Bureaucrat: The Evolution of the American Social Welfare System, 1900–1940." *Journal of Economic History* 38 (1978): 120–42.

Berry, Wendell. *The Unsettling of America: Culture & Agriculture.* San Francisco: Sierra Club Book, 1977.

Bianchi, Suzanne M., and Lynne M. Casper. "American Families." *Population Bulletin* 55, no. 4 (2000).

Bittker, Boris I. "Federal Income Taxation and the Family." *Stanford Law Review* 27 (1975): 1389–1463.

Boadway, Robin. "Redistributing Smarter: Self–Selection, Targeting, and Non-Conventional Policy Intruments." *Canadian Public Policy* 24, no. 3 (1998): 363–70.

Braybrooke, David, and Charles Lindblom. *A Strategy of Decision: Policy Evaluation as a Social Process.* New York: Free Press of Glencoe, 1963.

Brewster, David. "Changes in the Family Farm Concept." 18–23. Washington, DC: U.S. Senate, Committee on Agriculture, Nutrition, and Forestry, 1980.

———. "The Family Farm: A Changing Concept." 74–79. Washington, DC: United States Department of Agriculture, 1979.

———. "Historical Notes on Agriculture Structure." 65–73. Washington, DC: United States Department of Agriculture, 1979.

Brown, Michael K. *Race, Money, and the American Welfare State.* Ithaca, NY: Cornell University Press, 1999.

———. "State Capacity and Political Choice: Interpreting the Failure of the Third New Deal." *Studies in American Political Development* 9 (1995): 187–212.

Browne, William P. *Cultivating Congress: Constituents, Issues, and Interests in Agricultural Policymaking.* Lawrence: University Press of Kansas, 1995.

Brownlee, W. Elliot. *Federal Taxation in America: A Short History.* Cambridge, MA: Cambridge University Press, 1996.

———. "Tax Regimes, National Crisis, and State-Building in America." In *Funding the Modern American State, 1941–1995: The Rise and Fall of the Era of Easy Finance,* ed. W. Elliot Brownlee, 37–106. Washington, DC: Woodrow Wilson Center Press and the Press Syndicate of the University of Cambridge, 1996.

"Budget Options." 207. Washington, DC: Congressional Budget Office, 2003.

Burns, Nancy, Kay Lehman Schlozman, and Sidney Verba. "The Public Consequences of Private Inequality: Family Life and Citizen Participation." *American Political Science Review* 91, no. 2 (1997): 373–89.

Burns, Nancy, Kay Lehman Schlozman, and Sidney Verba. *The Private Roots of Public Action: Gender, Equality, and Political Participation.* Cambridge, MA: Harvard University Press, 2001.

Burnstein, Paul, R. Marie Bricher, and Rachel L. Einwohner. "Policy Alternatives and Political Change: Work, Family, and Gender on the Congressional Agenda, 1945–1990." *American Sociological Review* 60, no. 1 (1995): 37–83.

Campbell, Bruce. "A Theoretical Approach to Peer Influence in Adolescent Socialization." *American Journal of Political Science* 24 (1980): 324–44.

Campbell, Heather. "Prices, Devices, People or Rules: The Relative Effectiveness of Policy Instruments in Water Conservation." *Review of Policy Research* 21, no. 5 (2004): 637–62.

Carpenter, Daniel P. *The Forging of Bureaucratic Autonomy.* Princeton, NJ: Princeton University Press, 2001.

Carter, Susan B., ed. *Labor Force.* Ed. Susan B. Carter. Vol. II, *Historical Statistics of the United States: Earliest Times to the Present.* Cambridge, MA: Cambridge University Press, 2006.

Carter, Susan B., Scott Sigmund Gartner, Michael R. Haines, Alan L. Olmstead, Ricard Sutch, and Gavin Wright, ed. *Historical Statistics of the United States: Earliest Times to the Present.* Cambridge, MA: Cambridge University Press, 2006.

"Cash Crop." *The New Republic* (1998): 7.

Casper, Jonathan. "The Supreme Court and National Policy Making." *American Political Science Review* 70 (1976): 50–63.

Clark, James W. "Family Structure and Political Socialization Among Urban Black Children." *American Journal of Political Science* 17, no. 2 (1973).

"Compliance Estimates for Earned Income Tax Credit Claimed on 1999 Returns." Washington, DC: Internal Revenue Service, 2002.

Connoll, R. W. "Political Socialization in the American Family: The Evidence Re-Examined." *Public Opinion Quarterly* 36, no. 3 (1972): 323–33.

Connor, Eric. "Grad Tolani Looks to Future." *The Greenville News,* May 14, 2004, 13D.

Conrad, David Eugene. *The Forgotten Farmers: The Story of Sharecroppers in the New Deal.* Urbana: University of Illinois Press, 1965.

Cott, Nancy F. *Public Vows: A History of Marriage and the Nation.* Cambridge, MA: Harvard University Press, 2000.

"Counting Couples: Improving Marriage, Remarriage, and Cohabitation Data in the Federal Statistical System." Bethesda, MD: The Data Collection Committee of the Federal Interagency Forum on Child and Family Statistics, 2001.

Cox, Gary W., and Matthew D. McCubbins. "Bonding, Structure, and the Stability of Political Parties: Party Government in the House." In *Positive Theories of Congressional Institutions*, ed. Kenneth A. Shepsle and Barry R. Weingast, 101–18. Ann Arbor: University of Michigan Press, 1995.

———. *Legislative Leviathan: Party Government in the House*. Berkeley: University of California Press, 1993.

Dahl, Robert. "Decision-Making in a Democracy: The Supreme Court as a National Policy-Maker." *The Journal of Public Law* 6 (1957): 279–95.

———. *Who Governs? Democracy and Power in an American City*. New Haven, CT: Yale University Press, 1961.

"Data Book Fiscal Year 2005." Washington, DC: Department of the Treasury, Internal Revenue Service, 2005.

Dean, Virgil W. "Farm Policy and Truman's 1948 Campaign." *The Historian* 55, no. 3 (1993): 501–16.

Devine, Donald John. *The Political Culture of the United States: The Influence of Member Values on Regime Maintenance*. Boston: Little, Brown, 1972.

Dewbre, Joe, and Cameron Short. "Alternative Policy Instruments for Agriculture Support: Consequences for Trade, Farm Income, and Competitiveness." *Canadian Journal of Agricultural Economics* 50, no. 4 (2002): 443–65.

Diamond, Irene. *Families, Politics, and Public Policy: A Feminist Dialogue on Women and the State*. New York: Longman, 1983.

Diaz, Kevin. "Singles 'Being Dismissed' in Tax Debate." *Star Tribune*, May 4, 2001.

"Digest of Education Statistics Tables and Figures." Washington DC: Department of Education, National Center for Education Statistics, 2005.

Doern, G. Bruce, and V. Seymour Wilson. *Issues in Canadian Public Policy*. Toronto: Macmillan, 1974.

"Earned Income Credit." Washington, DC: Department of the Treasury, Internal Revenue Service, 2005.

Easterbrook, Gregg. "Making Sense of Agriculture: A Revisionist Look at Farm Policy." In *Is There a Moral Obligation to Save the Family Farm?*, ed. Gary Comstock, 3–30. Ames: Iowa State University Press, 1987.

Edelman, Murray J. "Political Language and Political Reality." *PS* Winter (1985): 10–19.

———. *The Symbolic Uses of Politics*. Urbana: University of Illinois Press, 1964.

———. *The Symbolic Uses of Politics*. Urbana: University of Illinois Press, 1985.

"Edward W. Scripps Dies on Yacht." *The New York Times*, March 14, 1926, 3.

Edwards, Rebecca. *Angels in the Machinery: Gender in American Party Politics from the Civil War to the Progressive Era*. New York: Oxford University Press, 1997.

Elder, Charles D., and Roger W. Cobb. *The Political Uses of Symbols*. New York: Longman, 1983.

Epstein, Lee, Jack Knight, and Andrew Martin. "The Supreme Court as a *Strategic* National Policymaker." *Emory Law Journal* 50 (2001): 583–612.

"Estimates of Federal Tax Expenditures for Fiscal Years 2001–2005." Washington, DC: Joint Committee on Taxation, 2001.

"Estimates of Federal Tax Expenditures for Fiscal Years 2006–2010." Washington, DC: Joint Committee on Taxation, 2005.

"Family Farm Held Key National Cog." *New York Times*, September 17, 1947.

Fineman, Martha. *The Neutered Mother, the Sexual Family, and Other Twentieth Century Tragedies*. New York: Routledge, 1995.

Fischer, Carolyn, Ian W. H. Parry, and William A. Pizer. "Instrument Choice for Environmental Protection when Technological Innovation Is Endogenous." *Journal of Environmental Economics and Management* 45, no. 3 (2003): 523–46.

Folbre, Nancy. *The Invisible Heart: Economics and Family Values*. New York: The New Press, 2001.

"For Better or for Worse: Marriage and the Federal Income Tax." Washington, DC: The Congress of the United States, Congressional Budget Office, 1997.

"Ford News Conference." *Congressional Quarterly Weekly Report* 33, no. 15 (1975): 754–55.

Fraser, Nancy, and Linda Gordon. "Decoding 'Dependency': Inscriptions of Power in a Keyword of the US Welfare State." In *Reconstructing Political Theory: Feminist Perspectives*, edited by Mary Lyndon Shanley and Uma Narayan, 25–47. University Park: Pennsylvania State University Press, 1995.

Garkovich, Lorraine, Janet L. Bokemeier, and Barbara Foote. *Harvest of Hope: Family Farming/Farming Families*. Lexington: The University of Kentucky Press, 1995.

Giaimo, Susan, and Philip Manow. "Adapting the Welfare State." *Comparative Political Science* 32, no. 8 (1999): 967–1001.

Gielen, Dolf J., and Yuichi Moriguchi. "Materials Policy Design." *Environmental Economics and Policy Studies* 5, no. 1 (2002): 17–38.

Gilbert, Jess. "Agrarian Intellectuals in a Democratizing State: A Collective Biography of USDA Leaders in the Intended New Deal." In *The Countryside in the Age of the Modern State: Political Histories of Rural America*, ed. Catherine McNicol Stock and Robert D. Johnston, 213–39. Ithaca, NY: Cornell University Press, 2001.

Gilligan, Carol. *In a Different Voice: Psychological Theory and Women's Development*. Cambridge, MA: Harvard University Press, 1982.

Gimpel, James G., and James R. Edwards Jr.. *The Congressional Politics of Immigration Reform*. Boston: Allyn and Bacon, 1999.

Glaser, William A. "The Family and Voting Turnout." *Public Opinion Quarterly* 23, no. 4 (1959–1960): 563–70.

Goldsmith, Stephen, and William D. Eggers. *Governing by Network: The New Shape of the Public Sector*. Washington, DC: Brookings Institution Press, 2004.

Goldstein, Kenneth M. *Interest Groups, Lobbying, and Participation in America*. Cambridge, MA: Cambridge University Press, 1999.

Gottschalk, Marie. *The Shadow Welfare State: Labor, Business, and the Politics of Health Care in the United States*. Ithaca, NY: Cornell University Press, 2000.

Graetz, Michael J., and Deborah H Schenk. *Federal Income Taxation: Principles and Practices*. Third ed. Westbury, NY: The Foundation Press, 1995.

"Granting an Alien Child Adopted by American Unmarried United States Citizen the Same Immigration Status as an Alien Child Adopted by a United States Citizen and His Spouse." Washington, DC: U.S. House of Representatives, Committee on the Judiciary, 1975.

Hacker, Jacob S. *The Divided Welfare State: The Battle over Public and Private Social Benefits in the United States*. Cambridge, MA: Cambridge University Press, 2002.

———. "Privatizing Risk without Privatizing the Welfare State: The Hidden Politics of Social Policy Retrenchment in the United States." *American Political Science Review* 98, no. 2 (2004): 243–60.

Hagstrom, Jerry. "Growing Pains." *National Journal* (1996): 982–85.

Hall, Richard L, and Frank W. Wayman. "Buying Time: Moneyed Interests and the Mobilization of Bias in Congressional Committees." *The American Political Science Review* 84, no. 3 (1990): 797–820.

Halpern, Charlotte. "Institutional Change Through Innovation: The URBAN Community Initiative in Berlin, 1994–1999." *Environment and Planning C: Government and Policy* 23 (2005): 697–713.

Hansen, John Mark. *Gaining Access: Congress and the Farm Lobby, 1919–1981*. Chicago: University of Chicago Press, 1991.

Harkin, Tom. "The Save the Family Farm Act." In *Is There a Moral Obligation to Save the Family Farm?*, ed. Gary Comstock, 388–97. Ames: Iowa State University Press, 1987.

Hartz, Louis. *The Liberal Tradition in America: An Interpretation of Political Thought Since the Revolution*. New York: Harcourt, Brace, 1955.

Hassebrook, Chuck. "Lower Estate Taxes Will Hurt Small Farmers." *New York Times*, July 15, 1997, A19.

Heady, Bruce W. "Trade Unions and National Wage Policies." *Journal of Politics* 32 (1970): 407–39.

Hederman, Rea S. "Why Congress Should Renew Its Efforts to End the Marriage Penalty." *The Heritage Foundation Backgrounder*, no. 1424 (2001).

"Historical Statistics of the United States: Colonial Times to 1970." Washington: DC: United States Bureau of the Census, 1976.

Hoffman, Saul D., and Laurence S. Seidman. *Helping Working Families: The Earned Income Tax Credit*. Kalamazoo, MI: W. E. Upjohn Institute for Employment Research, 2003.

Holtzblatt, Janet, and Robert Rebelein. "Measuring the Effect of the EITC on Marriage Penalties and Bonuses." *National Tax Journal* 53, no. 4 (2000): 1107–33.

Hood, Christopher. *The Tools of Government*. London: MacMillan, 1984.

Hoppe, Robert A. "Structural and Financial Characteristics of U.S. Farms: 2001 Family Farm Report." Washington, DC: Economic Research Service, United States Department of Agriculture, 2001.

Hoppe, Robert A., and David E. Banker. "Structure and Finances of U.S. Farms:

2005 Family Farm Report." United States Department of Agriculture, Economic Research Service, 2006.

Hosansky, David. "Farm Policy on the Brink of a New Direction." *Congressional Quarterly Weekly Report* (1996): 786–88.

———. "The Perils of Permanent Law." *Congressional Quarterly Weekly Report* (1996): 297.

Howard, Christopher. *The Hidden Welfare State*. Princeton, NJ: Princeton University Press, 1997.

———. "Is the American Welfare State Unusually Small?" *PS: Political Science and Politics* 36, no. 3 (2003): 411–15.

Howlett, Michael. "Policy Instruments, Policy Styles, and Policy Implementation: National Approaches to Theories of Instrument Choice." *Policy Studies Journal* 19, no. 2 (1991): 1–21.

Howlett, Michael, and M. Ramesh. *Studying Public Policy: Policy Cycles and Policy Subsystems*. New York: Oxford University Press, 1995.

"Humanitarian Aid." *Congressional Quarterly Weekly Report* 33, no. 15 (1975): 754.

Huntington, Samuel P. *American Politics: The Promise of Disharmony*. Cambridge, MA: Belknap Press, 1981.

Hurt, R. Douglas. *American Agriculture: A Brief History*. Ames: Iowa State University Press, 1994.

"Immigration Expansion." *CQ Almanac* 44 (1988): 112–14.

Jarvis, Lovell S. "The Rise and Decline of Rent-Seeking Activity in the Brazilian Coffee Sector: Lessons from the Imposition and Removal of Coffee Export Quotas." *World Development* 33, no. 11 (2005): 1881–903.

Jefferson, Thomas. *Notes on the State of Virginia*. Ed. William Peden. Chapel Hill: The University of North Carolina Press, 1982.

Jennings, M. Kent, and Richard G. Niemi. *Generations and Politics: A Panel Study of Young Adults and their Parents*. Princeton, NJ: Princeton University Press, 1981.

Josephson, Jyl J. *Gender, Families, and State: Child Support Policies in the United States*. Lanham, MA: Rowman & Littlefield Publishers, Inc., 1997.

Kautto, Petrus, and Jukka Simila. "Recently Introduced Policy Instruments and Intervention Theories." *Evaluation* 11, no. 1 (2005): 55–68.

Kerber, Linda K. *No Constitutional Right to be Ladies: Women and the Obligations of Citizenship*. New York: Hill and Wang, 1998.

———. "The Republican Mother: Women and the Enlightenment—An American Perspective." *American Quarterly* 28, no. 2 (1976): 187–205.

Kessler, Glenn. "Estate Tax Repeal Bill Delivered; Democrats Assail GOP Measure as a Giveaway to the Rich." *Washington Post*, August 25, A4.

Kessler–Harris, Alice. "Designing Women and Old Fools: The Construction of the Social Security Amendments of 1939." In *U.S. History as Women's History*, ed. Linda K. Kerber, Alice Kessler–Harris and Kathryn Kish Sklar, 87–106. Chapel Hill: University of North Carolina Press, 1995.

Kingdon, John. *Agendas, Alternatives, and Public Policies*. Boston: Little, Brown, 1984.

Kirkendall, Richard S. "A History of the Family Farm." In *Is There a Moral Ob-*

ligation to Save the Family Farm, ed. Gary Comstock, 79–111. Ames: Iowa State University Press, 1987.

Kloppenberg, James T. "The Virtues of Liberalism: Christianity, Republicanism, and Ethics in Early American Political Discourse." *Journal of American History* 74 (1987): 9–33.

Kraditor, Aileen S. *The Ideas of the Woman Suffrage Movement, 1890–1920.* New York: Columbia University Press, 1965.

Krause, Harry D. *Family Law in a Nutshell.* St. Paul, MN: West Publishing, 1977.

Krehbiel, Keith. *Pivotal Politics: A Theory of U.S. Lawmaking.* Chicago: University of Chicago Press, 1998.

Krikorian, Mark. *Prepared Testimony on Proposals for Reform of Legal Immigration Policy.* Subcommittee on Immigration and Claims, Committee on the Judiciary. May 17, 1995.

Landes, Joan B. "Introduction." In *Feminism: The Public and the Private*, edited by Joan B. Landes. New York: Oxford University Press, 1998.

Lapinski, John S., Pia Peltola, Greg Shaw, and Alan Yang. "Trends: Immigrants and Immigration." *Public Opinion Quarterly* 61, no. 2 (1997): 356–83.

Lee, Kenneth K. *Huddled Masses, Muddled Laws.* Westport, CT: Praeger, 1998.

Legomsky, Stephen H. *Immigration Law and Policy.* New York: The Foundation Press, 1992.

Lieberman, Robert C. "Ideas, Institutions, and Political Order: Explaining Political Change." *American Political Science Review* 96, no. 4 (2002): 697–712.

Light, Paul C. *The True Size of Government.* Washington, DC: The Brookings Institution, 1999.

Lindblom, Charles. "The Science of Muddling Through." *Public Administration Review* 19, no. 2 (1959): 79–88.

———. "Still Muddling, Not Yet Through." *Public Administration Review* 39, no. 6 (1979): 517–26.

Lindblom, Charles, and Robert Dahl. *Politics, Economics and Welfare: Planning and Politico-Economic Systems Resolved into Basic Social Processes.* New York: Harper, 1957.

Linder, Stephen H., and B. Guy Peters. "Instruments of Government: Perceptions and Contexts." *Journal of Public Policy* 9, no. 1 (1989): 35–58.

Lipset, Seymour Martin. *The First New Nation: The United States in Historical and Comparative Perspective.* New York: Basic Books, 1963.

Locke, John. "The Second Treatise of Government." In *Two Treatises of Government*, ed. Mark Goldie. London: Everyman, 1690/1993.

Londregan, John, and James M. Snyder Jr.. "Comparing Committee and Floor Preferences." In *Postive Theories of Congressional Institutions*, ed. Kenneth A. Shepsle and Barry R. Weingast, 139–72. Ann Arbor: University of Michigan Press, 1995.

"Long-Range Agricultural Policy and Program." Washington, DC: United States Senate Committee on Agriculture and Forestry, 1948.

Lopez, Ian Haney. *White by Law: The Legal Construction of Race.* New York: New York University Press, 1997.

Lowi, Theodore J. "Decision Making vs. Policy Making: Toward an Antidote for Technocracy." *Public Administration Review* 30, no. 3 (1970): 314–26.

———. *The End of Liberalism: The Second Republic of the United States*. New York: Norton, 1979.

———. "Four Systems of Policy, Politics, and Choice." *Public Administration Review* 32, no. 4 (1972): 298–311.

Mackett, Roger L., Lindsey Lucas, James Paskins, and James Turbin. "A Methodology for Evaluating Walking Buses as an Instrument of Urban Transport Policy." *Transport Policy* 10, no. 3 (2003): 179–87.

Majone, Giandomenico. *Evidence, Argument, and Persuasion in the Policy Process*. New Haven: Yale University Press, 1989.

"Mandatory Joint Returns." *New York Times*, March 26, 1942, 22.

Manna, Paul. *School's In: Federalism and the National Education Agenda*. Washington, DC: Georgetown University Press, 2006.

Mayer, Kenneth. *With the Stroke of a Pen: Executive Orders and Presidential Power*. Princeton: Princeton University Press, 2002.

McConnell, Grant. *Private Power and American Democracy*. New York: Knopf, 1966.

McWilliams, Carey. *Factories in the Field: The Story of Migratory Farm Labor in California*. Boston: Little, Brown and Company, 1939.

Mead, Lawrence M. *The New Politics of Poverty: The Nonworking Poor in America*. New York: BasicBooks, 1992.

Meissner, Doris. *Prepared Statement on Legal Immigration Reform*, Subcommittee on Immigration, Committee of the Judiciary, September 13, 1995.

Merelman, Richard M. "The Family and Political Socialization: Toward a Theory of Exchange." *The Journal of Politics* 42, no. 2 (1980): 461–86.

Mettler, Suzanne. *Soldiers to Citizens: The GI Bill and the Making of the Greatest Generation*. New York: Oxford University Press, 2005.

Minow, Martha, and Mary Lyndon Shanley. "Revisioning the Family: Relational Rights and Responsibilities." In *Reconstructing Political Theory: Feminist Perspectives*, ed. Mary Lyndon Shanley and Uma Narayan, 84–108. University Park: The Pennsylvania State University Press, 1997.

Morris, John D. "'Community Property' is Big Tax Bill Item." *New York Times*, February 1, 1948, E7.

———. "Inequities in Tax Cited by Treasury." *New York Times*, June 19, 1947, A4.

"Mr. Clinton Bows to Farmers." *New York Times*, April 28, 1995, A32.

"The Nation." *New York Times*, August 20, 1944, E2.

"The New Mayor of Boston." *New York Times*, January 5, 1896, 17.

Niemi, Richard G. *How Family Members Perceive Each Other: Political and Social Attitudes in Two Generations*. New Haven, CT: Yale University Press, 1974.

Nitschke, Lori. "Has the Tax Cut Crusade Lost Its Appeal." *CQ Weekly Report*, April 10, 1999, 826–32.

———. "Marital Status and Taxes: Irreconcilable Differences?" *CQ Weekly Report*, October 30, 1999, 2581–85.

Noddings, Nel. *Caring: A Feminine Approach to Ethics and Moral Education.* Berkeley: University of California Press, 1984.

Nuschler, Dawn. "Social Security Reform." Washington, DC: Congressional Research Service, 2005.

"'02 Farm Bill Revives Subsidies." *Congressional Quarterly Almanac* 58 (2002): 4–3 to 4–12.

Oliver, Thomas R., Philip R. Lee, and Helene L. Lipton. "A Political History of Medicare and Prescription Drug Coverage." *The Milbank Quarterly* 82, no. 2 (2004).

Olson, Mancur, Jr. *The Logic of Collective Action: Public Goods and the Theory of Groups.* Cambridge, MA: Harvard University Press, 1965.

———. "Space, Agriculture and Organization." *American Journal of Agricultural Economics* 67, no. 5 (1985): 928–37.

Ooms, Theodora. "Families and Government: Implementing a Family Perspective in Public Policy." *Social Thought* 16, no. 2 (1990): 61–78.

Orden, David, Don Paarlberg, and Terry Roe. *Policy Reform in American Agriculture: Analysis and Prognosis.* Chicago: The University of Chicago Press, 1999.

Orren, Karen, and Stephen Skowronek. *The Search for American Political Development,* 2004.

Pateman, Carole. *The Sexual Contract.* Stanford, CA: Stanford University Press, 1988.

Paul, Randolph E. *Taxation in the United States.* Boston: Little, Brown and Company, 1954.

Pear, Robert. "Clinton Embraces a Proposal to Cut Immigration by a Third." *New York Times,* B10.

Penn, J. S. "The Structure of Agriculture: An Overview of the Issue." 2–23. Washington, DC: United States Department of Agriculture, 1979.

Peters, B. Guy. *American Public Policy: Promise and Performance.* Chappaqua, NY: Chatham House/Steven Rivers, 1999.

Pierson, Paul. *Dismantling the Welfare State? Reagan, Thatcher and the Politics of Retrenchment.* Cambridge, MA: Cambridge University Press, 1994.

———. *Politics in Time: History, Institutions, and Social Analysis.* Princeton, NJ: Princeton University Press, 2004.

"Plan to Cut Farm Programs Stalls." *Congressional Quarterly Almanac* (1995): 3–47 to 3–56.

Plutzer, Eric, and Michael McBurnett. "Family Life and American Politics: The 'Marriage Gap' Reconsidered." *Public Opinion Quarterly* 55, no. 1 (1991): 113-27.

Pollock v. Farmer's Loan & Trust Co., 158 US 601 (1895).

Polsby, Nelson. *Political Innovation in America: The Politics of Policy Innovation.* New Haven, CT: Yale University Press, 1984.

Poole, Keith T., and Howard Rosenthal. *Congress: A Political–Economic History of Roll Call Voting.* New York: Oxford University Press, 1997.

"Postwar Agricultural Policy, Report of the Committee on Postwar Agricultural Policy of the Association of Land-Grant Colleges and Universities." Committee on Postwar Agricultural Policy of the Association of Land-Grant Colleges and Universities, 1944.

"Postwar Economic Policy and Planning." Washington, DC: House Special Committee on Postwar Economic Policy and Planning, 1946.

Prince v. Massachusetts, 158 321 (1944).

Quadagno, Jill. *The Color of Welfare: How Racism Undermined the War on Poverty*. New York: Oxford University Press, 1994.

Quirk, Paul J., and Bruce Nesmith. "Divided Government and Policy Making: Negotiating the Laws." In *The Presidency and the Political System*, ed. Michael Nelson, 531–54. Washington, DC: CQ Press, 1995.

Rauch, Jonathan. "Cash Crops." *National Journal* (1996): 978–81.

Renshon, Stanley Allen. "Personality and Family Dynamics in the Political Socialization Process." *American Journal of Political Science* 19, no. 1 (1975): 63–80.

Requate, Till. "Dynamic Incentives by Environmental Policy Instruments—A Survey." *Ecological Economics* 54 (2005): 175–95.

Rimlinger, Gaston V. *Welfare Policy and Industrialization in Europe, America, Russia*. New York: Wiley, 1971.

Rogers, Elizabeth Selden. "Letter to the Editor: Against Joint Returns." *New York Times*, January 31, 1934, 16.

Rohde, David W. "Parties and Committees in the House: Member Motivations, Issues, and Institutional Arrangements." In *Positive Theories of Congressional Institutions*, ed. Kenneth A. Shepsle and Barry R. Weingast, 119–38. Ann Arbor: University of Michigan, 1995.

Rosenberg, Gerald N. "The Road Taken: Robert A. Dahl's *Decision-Making in a Democracy: The Supreme Court as a National Policy-Maker*." *Emory Law Journal* 50 (2001): 613–30.

Rubin, Alissa J. "Tax Issues Divide Parties, Chambers." *Congressional Quarterly Weekly Report* 55, no. 29 (1997): 1682.

Ryan, Mary P. "Gender and Public Access: Women's Politics in Nineteenth-Century America." In *Feminism: The Public and the Private*, edited by Joan B. Landes. New York: Oxford University Press, 1998.

Sabatier, Paul A., and Hank C. Jenkins-Smith. "The Advocacy Framework: An Assessment." In *Theories of the Policy Process*, ed. Paul A. Sabatier, 117–66. Boulder, CO: Westview Press, 1999.

Sairinen, Rauno. "The Politics of Regulatory Reform: 'New' Environmental Policy Instruments in Finland." *Environmental Politics* 12, no. 1 (2003): 73–93.

Salamon, Lester M. "The New Governance and the Tools of Public Action: An Introduction." In *The Tools of Government: A Guide to New Governance*, ed. Lester M. Salamon, 1–47. New York: Oxford University Press, 2002.

———. "Rethinking Public Management: Third-Party Government and the Changing Forms of Government Action." *Public Policy* 29, no. 3 (1981): 255–75.

Salamon, Sonya. *Prairie Patrimony: Family, Farming, and Community in the Midwest*. Chapel Hill: University of North Carolina Press, 1992.

Sapiro, Virginia. "Private Costs of Public Commitment or Public Costs of Private Commitments? Family Roles versus Political Ambition." *American Journal of Political Science* 26, no. 2 (1982).

Saxton, Jim. "Tax Expenditures: A Review and Analysis." Washington, DC: Joint Economic Committee, 1999.

Schattschneider, E.E. *Politics, Pressures and the Tariff: A Study of Free Private Enterprise in Pressure Politics, as Shown in the 1929–1930 Revision of the Tariff.* New York: Prentice Hall, 1935.

——. *The Semi-Sovereign People.* New York: Holt, Rinehart, Winston, 1960.

Schlozman, Kay Lehman, and John T. Tierney. *Organized Interests and American Democracy.* New York: Harper and Row, 1986.

Schneider, Anne, and Helen Ingram. "Behavioral Assumptions of Policy Tools." *Journal of Politics* 52, no. 2 (1990): 510–29.

Schneider, Anne Larson, and Helen Ingram. *Policy Design for Democracy.* Lawrence, Kansas: University Press of Kansas, 1997.

Schneider, Mark, and Paul Eric Teske. "Toward a Theory of the Political Entrepreneur: Evidence from Local Government." *The American Political Science Review* 86, no. 3 (1995): 737–47.

Schneider, Mark, Paul Eric Teske, and Michael Mintrom. *Public Entrepreneurs: Agents for Change in American Government.* Princeton, NJ: Princeton University Press, 1995.

Scott, Christine. "The Earned Income Tax Credit (EITC): Policy and Legislative Issues." Washington, DC: Congressional Research Service, 2003.

Segal, Jeffrey, and Harold J. Spaeth. *The Supreme Court and the Attitudinal Model Revisited.* Cambridge,MA: Cambridge University Press, 2002.

Senate Finance Committee. *Testimony Bush Tax Plan: David T. Ellwood*, First Session, March 8, 2001.

Senate Finance Committee. *U.S. Senator Charles Grassley (R-IA) Holds Hearing on Taxes*, First Session, March 8, 2001.

"Senate Votes to Revise Allocations." *Congressional Quarterly Almanac* 45 (1989).

Sharp, Deborah. "Elian Ruling Leaves Demonstrators Dejected Miami Kin's Options Are Running Out." *USA Today*, June 2, 2000, 4A.

Sheingate, Adam D. "Political Entrepreneurship, Institutional Change, and American Political Development." *Studies in American Political Development* 17 (2003): 185–203.

——. *The Rise of the Agricultural Welfare State: Institutions and Interest Group Power in the United States, France, and Japan.* Princeton: Princeton University Press, 2000.

Sheridan, Mary Beth. "U.S. Immigration Restrictions Give Gay Couples Few Options." *The Washington Post*, December 28, 2003, C01.

Simon, Herbert A. *Administrative Behavior.* New York: MacMillian Co., 1947.

Skocpol, Theda. "The Origins of Social Policy in the United States: A Polity-Centered Analysis." In *The Dynamics of American Politics: Approaches and Interpretations*, edited by Lawrence C. Dodd and Calvin Jillson, 182–206. Boulder, CO: Westview Press, 1994.

——. *Protecting Soldiers and Mothers.* Cambridge, MA: Belknap Press, 1992.

Skocpol, Theda, and Kenneth Finegold. "State Capacity and Economic Intervention in the Early New Deal." *Political Science Quarterly* 97, no. 2 (1982): 255–78.

Skocpol, Theda, and Gretchen Ritter. "Gender and the Origins of Modern Social Policies in Britain and the United States." In *Social Policy in the United States*, ed. Theda Skocpol. Princeton: Princeton University Press, 1995.

Skowronek, Stephen. *Building a New American State: The Expansion of National Administrative Capacities 1877–1920*. Cambridge, England: Cambridge University Press, 1982.

Smith, Rogers. "Beyond Tocqueville, Myrdal, and Hartz: The Multiple Traditions in America." *American Political Science Review* 87, no. 3 (1993): 549–66.

———. *Civic Ideals: Conflicting Visions of Citizenship in U.S. History*. New Haven, CT: Yale University Press, 1997.

Soss, Joe. "Lessons of Welfare: Policy Design, Political Learning, and Political Action." *The American Political Science Review* 93, no. 2 (1999): 363–80.

Southworth, Caleb. "Aid to Sharecroppers: How Agrarian Class Structure and Tenant-Farmer Politics Influenced Federal Relief in the South, 1933–1935." *Social Science History* 26, no. 1 (2002).

"Special Immigrant Visas." *Congressional Quarterly Almanac* 30 (1972): 758.

"Staff Memo: Tax Revision 1937, Project No. 3." Washington, DC: Treasury Department, Division of Tax Research, 1936.

"Statistical Abstract of the United States: 2002." Washington, DC: U.S. Census Bureau, 2002.

"Statistical Abstract of the United States: 2006." Washington, DC: U.S. Census Bureau, 2005.

"Statistics of Income." Washington, DC: Department of Treasury, Internal Revenue Service, 2005–2006.

Stevens, Jacqueline. *Reproducing the State*. Princeton, NJ: Princeton University Press, 1999.

Stolley, Kathy S. "Statistics on Adoption in the United States." *The Future of Children* 3, no. 1 (1993): 26–42.

Stone, Deborah A. "Causal Stories and the Formation of Policy Agendas." *Political Science Quarterly* 104 (1989): 281–300.

———. *Policy Paradox: The Art of Political Decision Making*. Rev. ed. New York: Norton, 2002.

Strach, Patricia, and Kathleen Sullivan. "Beyond the Welfare State." Paper presented at the Annual Meeting of the Western Political Science Association, Albuquerque, NM, March 16–18, 2006.

Strange, Marty. *Family Farming: A New Economic Vision*. Lincoln: University of Nebraska Press, 1988.

"Study of the Overall State of the Federal Tax System and Recommendations for Simplification, Pursuant to Section 8022 (3)(B) of the Internal Revenue Code of 1986—Volume II: Recommendations of the Staff of the Joint Committee on Taxation to Simplify the Federal Tax System." 23–148. Washington, DC: Joint Committee on Taxation, 2001.

Subcommittee on Immigration and Claims, Committee on the Judiciary. *Prepared Testimony on Proposals for Reform of Legal Immigration Policy*, May 17, 1995.

Subcommittee on Immigration, Committee on the Judiciary. *Prepared Statement on Family Reunification Provisions Within the Proposed Simpson Bill*, September 13, 1995.

Subcommittee on Immigration, Senate Judiciary Committee. *U.S. Senator Sam Brownbeck (R-KS) Holds Hearing on Immigration Policy*, April 4, 2001.

Sullivan, Kathleen. *Constitutional Context: Women and Rights Discourse in Nineteenth-Century America*. Baltimore, MD: Johns Hopkins University Press, 2007.

Surrey, Stanley S. *Pathways to Tax Reform: The Concept of Tax Expenditures.* Cambridge, MA: Harvard University Press, 1973.

"Tax Benefits for Education." Washington, DC: Department of Treasury, Internal Revenue Service, 2006.

"Tax Rules for Children and Dependents." Washington, DC: Department of the Treasury, Internal Revenue Service, 2005.

Taylor, Amy Murrell. *The Divided Family in Civil War America*. Chapel Hill: University of North Carolina Press, 2005.

Thomas, Gwynn. "Ties that Bind and Break: The Uses of Family in the Political Struggles of Chile, 1970–1990." Dissertation, University of Wisconsin, 2005.

Thornton, Arland. "Changing Attitudes toward Family Issues in the United States." *Journal of Marriage and the Family* 51, no. 4 (1989): 873–93.

———. "Four Decades of Trends in Attitudes Toward Family Issues in the United States: The 1960s Through the 1990s." *Journal of Marriage and the Family* 63, no. 4 (2001): 1009-37.

Tichenor, Daniel. *The Politics of Immigration Control in America*. Princeton, NJ: Princeton University Press, 2002.

Tronto, Joan C. "Women and Caring: What Can Feminists Learn about Morality from Caring?" In *Gender/Body/Knowledge: Feminist Reconstructions of Being and Knowing*, ed. Alison M. Jaggar and Susan Bordo. 172-87. New Brunswick: Rutgers University Press, 1989.

"2004 Green Book: Background Material and Data on the Programs within the Jurisdiction of the Committee on Ways and Means." Washington, DC: U.S. House of Representatives, Committee on Ways and Means, 2004.

"2005 Social Security/SSI Fact Sheet." Washington, DC: Social Security Administration, 2005.

United States Congress. House of Representatives Subcomittee on Immigration and Claims, Senate Subcomittee on Immigration, *Testimony on Immigration Report*, June 28, 1995.

United States House of Representatives, Committee on Ways and Means. *Testimony by Mary Jo Bane, Assistant Secretary for Children and Families Department of Health and Human Services on Children and Families at Risk in Deterioating Communities*, First Session, December 7, 1993.

United States Senate, Committee on Agriculture and Forestry. *Agricultural Emergency Act to Increase Farm Purchasing Power*, First Session, March 17, 24, 25, 27, and 28, 1933.

United States Senate, Committee on Veteran's Affairs. *Hearing on Benefits for Survivors: Is America Fulfilling Lincoln's Charge to Care for the Families of Those Killed in the Line of Duty*, February 3, 2005.

"U.S. Government Civilian Employees Stationed Abroad." Washington, DC: Department of the Treasury, Internal Revenue Service, 2005.

"United States and State Data Preliminary Report: 2002 Census of Agriculture." Washington, DC: U.S. Department of Agriculture, 2004.

Vatn, Arild. "Rationality, Institutions, and Environmental Policy." *Ecological Economics* 55 (2005): 203–17.

Vedung, Evert. "Policy Instruments: Typologies and Theories." In *Carrots, Sticks, and Sermons: Policy Instruments and Their Evaluation*, ed. Marie Louise Memelmans-Videc, Ray C. Rist, and Evert Vedung, 21–58. New Brunswick: Transaction Publishers, 1998.

"Visa Bulletin." Washington, DC: United States State Department, 2006.

Weaver, R. Kent. "The Politics of Blame Avoidance." *Journal of Public Policy* 6, no. 4 (1986): 371–98.

Wilensky, Harold L. *Industrial Society and the Supply and Organization of Social Welfare Service in the United States*. New York: Russell Sage Foundation, 1958.

——. *The Western State and Equality: Structural and Ideological Roots of Public Expenditures*. Berkeley: University of California Press, 1975.

Wilson, Graham K. *Special Interests and Policymaking: Agricultural Policies and Politics in Britain and the United States of America, 1956–70*. New York: John Wiley & Sons, 1977.

Wilson, James Q. *The Moral Sense*. New York: The Free Press, 1993.

Wisensale, Steven K. *Family Leave Policy: The Political Economy of Work and Family in America*. Armonk, NY: M. E. Sharpe, 2001.

Witte, John F. *The Politics and Development of the Federal Income Tax*. Madison: University of Wisconsin Press, 1985.

Wolbrecht, Christina. *The Politics of Women's Rights: Parties, Positions, and Change*. Princeton, NJ: Princeton University Press, 2000.

Wood, Gordon. *The Creation of the American Republic, 1776–1787*. Chapel Hill: University of North Carolina Press, 1969.

Yamin, Priscilla. "Nuptial Nation: Marriage and the Politics of Civic Membership in the US." Dissertation, New School for Social Research, 2005.

"Yearbook of Immigration Statistics: 2005." Washington, DC: Department of Homeland Security, 2006.

Yu, Chilik, and Laurence J. Jr. O'Toole. "Policy Instruments for Reducing Toxic Releases." *Evaluation Review* 22, no. 5 (1998): 571–90.

Index